MANAGING
MONEY

A Center Director's Guidebook

Exchange Press, Inc.

PO Box 3249 • Redmond, WA 98073-3249
(800) 221-2864 • www.ChildCareExchange.com

Managing Money

"The Best of Exchange"

This is a Best of Exchange Collection of Articles originally published in *Exchange, The Early Leaders' Magazine Since 1978.* The issues in which these articles originally appeared are noted in the Table of Contents on the following pages.

Every attempt has been made to update information on authors and other contributors to these articles. We apologize for any biographical information that is not current.

Exchange is a bimonthly management magazine for directors and owners of early childhood programs. For more information about *Exchange* and other *Exchange* publications for directors and teachers, contact:

Exchange Press, Inc.
PO Box 3249
Redmond, WA 98073-3249
(800) 221-2864
www.ChildCareExchange.com

ISBN 978-0-942702-43-9

Printed in the United States of America

Managing Money
A Center Director's Guidebook

Table of Contents

Managing Money

Basic Tools

*"Financial management tools,
all based on a sound
budgeting process,
enable the director
to keep a finger on the pulse
of the organization's financial health."*

Managing Money As If Your Center Depended Upon It

by Roger Neugebauer

Directors of child care centers must be as effective at managing money as they are at caring for children. This lesson, had it not been learned too late, would have saved a local nursery school. This school provided a wonderful environment for children — the staff were creative and nurturing, and the parents loved the experiences their children were having. However, the school was closed shortly after the original director left. Her replacement was an outstanding curriculum planner, but she was totally unable to come to grips with managing money. After a few minor financial crises, the school was forced to close its doors.

Unfortunately, this scenario is not rare. Many child care centers and nursery schools are plagued by faulty money management.

If child care centers were highly profitable or generously funded, the consequences of ineffective money management would not be severe. Most centers, however, operate painfully close to the red ink on a daily basis.

The waste of a few dollars here and the loss of some expected income there

can cause a center to delay or even cancel a pay day. If income and expenses are not carefully planned and controlled, a center can go out of business in a remarkably short period of time.

In helping centers with financial difficulties, I have noticed that a few problems tend to pop up time and again. I have described below the five most common money management pitfalls as well as some proposed remedies.

1. The Programmed-to-Fail Budget

A director draws up a budget for which projected income equals projected expenses. However, the budget will inevitably fail because faulty assumptions were made in projecting both income and expenses.

The most common mistake here is to project income by multiplying weekly fees by the number of spaces in the center by the number of weeks the program is open. This does project a center's maximum potential income if every space is filled for every week. But this will never happen! Inevitably, a few children will leave the school in the middle of the year, and a lag of a week or more will occur before they are replaced; or a child will leave with two months remaining in the school year, and the space won't be filled; or a family will move out of town and neglect to pay their past due fees; or the welfare department will refuse to provide reimbursement for several snow days. A center that fails to account for shortfalls such as these in planning its budget will find that it never quite has enough money to pay all of its bills.

For a new center, it is difficult to predict what the shortfall in income will be. It might be risky to expect more than 60% of potential income in the first year.

For an older center, the shortfall can probably be reasonably estimated based on previous years' experiences. This can be done by calculating the maximum potential income the center could have received in the past 12 months and dividing this amount into the amount of income the center actually received for the 12 months. For example, if a center had a maximum potential income of $50,000 for last year, but only received $45,000, this means it only received 90% of its potential income ($45,000 ÷ $50,000 = .90 or 90%). For the coming year, this center should set its budget no higher than 90% of its potential income.

Centers often under project expenses by failing to include certain line items altogether. Most frequently neglected are expenses for staff training, leave time, salary increases, fuel cost increases, and major appliance repairs. Certain of these expenses (such as fuel and repairs) cannot be ignored — money must be found to pay for them. Others (such as training and salary increases) can be ignored, and frequently are, but only at the cost of severely undermining staff morale and program quality.

2. Penny Wise and Dollar Foolish Cost Cutting

A center short of funds responds by vigorously cracking down on expenditures for supplies. Napkins are cut in half, drawing is done on recycled computer paper, and free materials are scrounged everywhere.

Such a response is typical, and typically it is ineffective. Even if the average center cut its supply costs in half (which would begin to have a noticeable impact on curriculum quality), the net effect would be to only reduce the center's overall costs by about 1%.

This does not mean that centers shouldn't try to save money on supplies. Certainly all centers have an obligation to parents to keep costs as low as possible. The danger, however, is that the director and teachers will work so hard on scrounging materials and other similar activities that they will begin to think they are doing all they can to solve their money problem. In other words, they will be distracted from effectively addressing the problem.

To put cost cutting efforts into perspective, it is helpful to analyze the savings potential of each budget item (such as in the example in Exhibit A). First, the annual amount allocated for each line item in the budget should be listed. Then, the percent that each line item would have to be cut in order to save $1,000 per year should be calculated. This is done by dividing $1,000 by the amount of each line item. For example, in Exhibit A, the line item teachers' salaries would have to be cut by 2.9% ($1,000 ÷ $34,500) to save $1,000.

A quick review of the resulting figures will identify those areas where significant cuts can be made without having a dramatic negative impact on the program. For example, the Hippy Dippy Child Care Center would have to cut the social services line item by 50%, the training line item by 40%, or the health line item by 67% to save $1,000. Obviously, cuts of this magnitude would dramatically alter these aspects of the program. On the other hand, there are four line items — teachers' salaries, administrative salaries, nutrition, and occupancy — which would be reduced by less than 7% if $1,000 were cut from them. These are clearly areas where Hippy Dippy Child Care staff should concentrate cost savings efforts in order to have the least adverse impact on the program.

By going through this process, a program will quickly be able to identify three or four areas where attention should be focused in cutting costs. Unfortunately, it will not provide directions on how to make the actual cuts. No charts or formulas can relieve the pain from these decisions.

3. The Fruitless Fundraiser

A center pours considerable time and energy into a fundraising project which generates only limited funds. For example, a local nursery school sponsors a fair every year. One year the school netted $725 after expenses. To earn this amount, parents and staff donated over $100 in cash and 500 hours in labor. If, instead, each parent had donated only $7, the center would have raised as much money with no effort.

Before engaging in any fundraising project, a center should perform a cost-benefit analysis. First, estimate the maximum amount of money the project could yield after expenses. Then, estimate the number of staff and volunteer hours required to carry out the project. Finally, divide the dollars by the hours. If the result is less than $10 per hour, the project is probably not worth the effort. From $10-25 per hour, it is of marginal value. Above $25 per hour, it is clearly worthwhile. Really successful fundraisers have been known to yield over $100 per hour.

4. Checkbook Balance Money Management

A center's director controls income and expenses solely by observing the checkbook balance. If the checkbook balance is high, the director freely spends money. If the balance is low, the director spends money cautiously and works hard to cut costs. If the balance is in the red, the director launches a fund-raising project.

Such a casual day-to-day form of money management could have disastrous consequences for the average child care center. A center could be deeply in debt but still have a positive checkbook balance because several major purchases were made on credit to be paid 30 days later. It could be forced to raise fees in the middle of the year because no funds were set aside in the fall to cover high heating costs in the winter, or it could simply run short of money at the end of every month and not know why or what to do about it.

To effectively keep a handle on a center's financial status, a director must know much more than how much money is in the checking account. She must know how much money has been expended on each budget item, how much income has

Exhibit A
Hippy Dippy Child Care — Cost Savings Analysis

Budget Item	Annual Budget Amount	Percent of Reduction to Save $1,000
Teachers' Salaries	$34,500	3%
Administrative Salaries	20,000	5
Program Supplies/Equipment	3,000	33
Office Supplies/Equipment	2,000	50
Nutrition	15,500	7
Occupancy	15,000	7
Health	1,500	67
Transportation	4,000	25
Training	2,500	40
Social Services	2,000	50
Miscellaneous	1,000	100

been received, whether these expense and income amounts are in line with what was budgeted, and whether sufficient funds are available for upcoming major expenses. This information can all be obtained by preparing a *monthly status report.*

The monthly status report can be relatively easy to prepare and interpret, yet it provides invaluable information. The report format has all of the income and expense line items from the budget listed vertically on the left hand side, followed by three columns of figures. In the first column, headed *Actual Activity to Date,* is recorded the total of all income or expenses incurred for each budget item as of the last day of the month being reviewed (the closing date). For example, in the report in Exhibit B, $15,000 in parent fees had been received and $20,810 in staff salaries had been expended as of June 30. These figures should be readily available from the center's accounting records. (To simplify the prepara-

tion of status reports, one account or group of accounts in these records should be set up for each budget item.)

In the second column, headed *Projected Activity to Date,* is recorded the cumulative amount the center had planned in the budget to have received or expended as of the closing date. Hippy Dippy Child Care had projected receiving $14,500 in parent fees and expending $20,600 in staff salaries as of June 30. These projections are derived from the budget. The easiest way to do this is to divide each budget item by 12 to arrive at a monthly figure. This figure is then multiplied by the number of the months that have passed in the budget year. In the example, the *Projected* figure for rent is $2,550, or $425 per month times 6 months.

For certain budget items, projections cannot be made so easily. For centers in the north, utility expenses are seldom the same every month as heating costs soar in the winter. Similarly, parent fees and staff salaries may dip in the summer months when enrollments decline. For variable items such as these, it may be necessary to project income or expenses month by month, based on previous years' experiences.

In the third column, headed *Percent of Target Achieved*, is recorded the percent of the projected amount that the center actually received or expended for each budget item. As of June 30, Hippy Dippy Child Care had received only 89% of its projected Title XX income and had spent 101% of its projected salary expenses. The percentage figure is computed by dividing the *Actual* amount by the *Projected* amount (for example, $11,760 ÷ $13,250 = 89%).

There are a number of points to check in reviewing the monthly status report. First, of course, one should check the bottom line — the *Balance* (calculated by subtracting *Total Expenses* from *Total Income*). In the example, there is a positive balance of $200 as of June 30. This is bad news since the projected balance was $2,000.

This means that not enough money has been set aside to cover future expenses. Once a problem is found, the next step is to trace the cause by reviewing the *Percent* column. The objective here is to find income items that are significantly below 100% of the projected amounts and expense items that are significantly above 100%. In the example, Title XX income (89%) and fundraising income (10%) are both far too low and substitute expenses (120%) are running far too high.

Exhibit B
Hippy Dippy Child Care Monthly Status Report
As of June 30

Income	Actual Activity to Date	Projected Activity to Date	Percent of Target Achieved
Parent Fees	$15,000	$14,500	103%
Title XX	11,760	13,250	89
Food Program	5,550	5,700	97
United Way	5,250	5,250	100
Fundraising	40	400	10
Total Income	$37,600	$39,100	96%
Expenses			
Salaries	$20,810	$20,600	101%
Substitutes	1,680	1,400	120
Fringe	3,260	3,200	102
Legal	600	800	75
Training	150	300	50
Rent	2,550	2,550	100
Utilities	300	350	86
Food	5,700	5,600	102
Supplies	1,200	1,150	104
Insurance	250	250	100
Loan	900	900	100
Total Expenses	$37,400	$37,100	101%
Balance	+ $ 200	+ $ 2,000	10%

With this report the director has discovered that even though there is money in the checkbook, there is a serious problem developing. She also knows that to correct it she must focus her attention on the problems with Title XX, fundraising, and substitutes. In addition, she can see that small surpluses are accumulating in certain expense items (legal and audit, training, and utilities) which could be shifted over to partially offset the substitute deficit.

5. The False Sense of Security

A center's board of directors requires that every expenditure be approved by the board and that every check be signed by two designated individuals. The board has adopted these requirements in order to safeguard the center's funds.

Controls such as these may seem to be foolproof. In practice, they are often foolhardy. To be effective, the two signature procedure requires that both individuals signing any check review background documentation to be satisfied that the expenditure is appropriate. More often than not, the second person signing the checks automatically signs them, assuming that the first person has already checked them out.

The two signature procedure can also be inefficient. If both signers are not located in the center, much time can be wasted chasing after the second person. In cases where potential signers are unavailable, major payments or a payroll can be delayed. Some centers circumvent this problem by having one party sign a number of blank checks in advance. This, of course, undermines the safeguarding aspect of the system.

In a non profit center, having all expenditures approved by the board can also be counterproductive. It drains valuable board time and energy away from crucial policymaking and evaluative functions. Instead of developing a sliding fee scale policy, the board debates what brand of construc-

tion paper to purchase. Just as importantly in retaining decisionmaking of this detail, the board can undermine the staff commitment and leadership. The message conveyed to the director and teachers is that they are not trusted and that their function is simply to carry out orders from above.

The biggest danger of both of these safeguards is that they provide a false sense of security. They give the appearance of security without providing it in reality.

To provide effective security, a number of approaches can be implemented:

• All money coming into the center should be documented with duplicate copies of prenumbered receipts.

• All expenditures should be made with prenumbered checks and a file maintained with backup invoices, receipts, or explanations for each check.

• The check writing function should be separated from the bookkeeping and checkbook balancing functions.

• In a larger center in which responsibility for purchasing is delegated by an

owner, executive director, parent agency, or board of directors, two signatures should be required on all large purchases with the limit clearly established by the delegator. (Some public and private funding organizations may, of course, require two signatures on all checks.) In addition, two signatures should be required on all withdrawals from savings accounts.

• Someone in a position of authority should regularly review monthly status reports to seek explanations for any expense items that are exceeding budgeted amounts or income items that are lagging behind projections.

References and Resources

Gross, Malvern J., Jr., et al. (1995). *Financial and Accounting Guide for Not-for-Profit Organizations* (Fifth Edition). New York: John Wiley and Sons, Inc.

Morgan, Gwen. (1982). *Managing the Day Care Dollars: A Financial Handbook.* Cambridge, MA: Steam Press. Distributed by Gryphon House, PO Box 207, Beltsville, MD 20704-0207.

Budgeting for Quality *and* Survival in the 21st Century

by R. Ann Whitehead

A *great deal has changed since I began my first child care center over 25 years ago, ranging from the dramatic increase in the cost of doing business to the level of intense competition many of us now experience. Running a child care program has always been a delicate balance between what we would ideally like to do and what we can actually afford based upon our financial resources. But, now more than ever before, it isn't enough to be committed to quality programs for children, we must be able to harness and utilize our financial resources wisely so that our programs can continue to survive even during difficult and uncertain times.*

It is essential for directors and/or owners to create realistic goals that reflect the actual tuition income and the financial resources available. In order to maintain control of our finances, we must develop a well thought-out budget every year, and continuously monitor and revise it as we go. It is the only way to ensure we have the resources to not only maintain our priorities but to guarantee stability in our organizations. It can no longer be something we hope to get around to, budgeting must be one of our top priorities.

According to the experts, the three most important components of running a successful business or organization are the finances (our budgets and financial decisions), the operations (our programs), and sales or income (our enrollment). These three components are like a three legged-stool; any one of the legs breaks down and the entire thing topples over.

Unfortunately, the financial component is the one we are most likely to put off, because we are the least familiar with this area. Many of us are in this field because we care about children and not necessarily because we are astute business people.

Establishing Your Priorities

I routinely meet with our directors and other administrative staff each month to define our priorities and then to plan how to pay for and implement them. Once a clear set of priorities are agreed upon, it's easier to recognize what options we have and what kinds of compromises we can make.

The quality of our programs is tied to the following variable expenses, which typically fluxuate with our gross tuition:

- Offering competitive wages and benefits to attract and keep good teachers.

- Providing healthy food (not just convenient snack foods) for children.

- Having well-equipped classrooms and playrounds for a wide range of developmental activities which meet our curriculum goals.

■ Maintaining our facilities so they are aesthetically pleasing as well as safe for children and staff.

■ Providing training programs for our staff, including both in-house and outside workshops.

Establishing Your Tuition Rate

Establishing your tuition rate is the beginning of that special balancing act. It is essential to plan your tuition rates based on what it actually costs to run your program. This may sound obvious, but *many child care providers feel guilty about charging enough to pay for their true costs!*

If we don't share those costs with parents, we must cut other expenses which directly affect the children and the quality of our programs. If you offer quality programs that clearly demonstrate how they benefit children, you can usually charge enough to meet the cost of the program and still remain competitive.

The Budget Process

Establishing Your Projected Monthly Enrollment and Gross Income

Your own school's history is the best indicator for anticipating the following year's enrollment. If you are beginning a new program, check with other child care center owners and/or directors in your area about their experiences. Do not use arbitrary numbers that may not reflect the reality of your particular community.

Whatever criteria you use, it is always wise to be conservative. If you've had two great years and one marginal year, you might average the three to come up with your projected monthly tuition income. Personally, I never project a *great* year by assuming each of my schools will have peak enrollment. Instead, I prefer to be pleasantly surprised at the end of the year.

Using the Concept of Equivalent Children

We use the concept of *equivalent children* (EC) to project our tuition each month. Equivalent children is your average tuition rate divided by your actual or projected monthly gross tuition. For instance, if our tuition rate is $600 per month and I expect about $27,000 in monthly tuition, I divide the tuition income ($27,000) by the monthly tuition rate ($600), indicating approximately 45 *equivalent children*.

Budgeting Your Variable and Fixed Expenses

As I'm sure you are aware, your variable expenses are those that fluctuate, usually reflecting the changes in your gross income, such as staff wages and benefits, and materials/supplies. Fixed expenses such as lease or debt payments, utilities, and property taxes are those that remain more or less constant whether or not your enrollment goes up or down.

Variable Expenses

The variable expenses are the most important aspect of our budget, and they therefore require the most monitoring. Since many of these expenses should fluctuate with the number of

children enrolled, they can be directly tied to a percentage of your gross income. Good examples are your payroll, materials/supplies, and food which ideally reflect the number of children in your program.

Since these percentages are somewhat discretionary, they should reflect your program priorities and your personal goals. If you find that you spend everything your center has earned by the end of each month, you may never create financial stability for your organization. On the other hand, to ensure quality it is necessary to spend enough to meet the needs of the children and your curriculum goals.

Tracking Actual Costs

So, after all the discussion, how do you decide what percentages to use for these various expenses? It's always important to be realistic about your current costs and your organization's goals.

Payroll costs in any program can vary widely depending upon the age groups a center serves. Infant programs have significantly higher teacher-child ratios which result in higher payroll costs, while a school-age program may have a lower payroll than a class of three- and four-year olds. Since our programs include broad age ranges, I prefer to use the average payroll of the entire program to determine my projected payroll costs.

Budgeting Your Fixed Expenses

After you have negotiated your loans, leases, and janitorial contracts, etc., it's easy to forget about your fixed expenses. However, these and other fixed expenses have a significant impact on your bottom line and should be monitored periodically along with the variable expenses.

Creating the Budget

Each new year I create projections for each month for each of my schools. I use the final year-end financial statement my bookkeeper gives me as the basis for my projections. Keeping in mind all the expected changes for both our variable and fixed expenses, such as any increases in our employee benefits and, of course, workmen's compensation, I try to anticipate the income and the expenses for each month. Our tuition usually steadily increases from January through May and begins to drop in June and continues somewhat downward during the summer, so my budgets reflect these fluctuations.

Your budget should also have columns for your projected expenses versus the actual amounts that were spent. Once the worksheet has been created with the proper formulas, it takes a relatively short time to put numbers into the computer at the end of each month. Of course, anytime you make significant changes in your expenses, you need to revise your projections.

Monitoring Your Actual Financial Statements

Accurate and Timely Financial Statements

In a labor-intensive field such as ours, where the income margins can be relatively low, it is essential to know

what your income and expenses are each month (once a quarter is definitely not enough!). Around the tenth of the month, you should have a financial statement showing both your actual variable and fixed expenses for the prior month (have your accountant or office clerk do it or do it yourself). In addition, the statement should show the percentage of the gross income for each of the expenses.

Comparing and Tracking Your Variable Expenses

The variable expenses are the most important aspect of your budget and require the most attention. These are the expenses that can make or break a child care center. All your key people must understand the necessity of your budget and be aware when spending is way beyond your projected percentages.

By comparing your actual expenses with your budget, you can decide whether you need to take steps to change a troubling trend. If your payroll was significantly higher than expected, was it due to a temporary cause, such as having the flu run through your staff, or does it reflect lower enrollment than you anticipated? If this indicates a problem with low enrollment, you may have to find creative ways to lower your payroll or create a new marketing plan. It is important to recognize that any significant deviation from your budget requires your attention. Analyzing this information is absolutely essential to controlling your costs and maintaining the stability of your organization.

Tracking Your Fixed Expenses

We often have more control over our fixed expenses than we realize. It is

important to consider whether loans could be refinanced for better terms or whether to pay down extra principal if you have extra cash available. One of our schools is in a leased space, and when its enrollment plummeted, I renegotiated for lower lease payments to ensure we could continue at that site.

Many of us have experienced higher insurance rates because of September 11, along with an increase in workman's compensation. It is wise to consider getting alternate bids for these items from time to time.

Monthly Income After Expenses

You should also know precisely what you have in the bank at the end of each month. Do you have enough left over to pay your quarterly income taxes and to set aside something for future expenditures? For my peace of mind, I budget both for the future as well as the present. Whenever possible, I set aside a percentage of our income after expenses for future capital improvements, such as vans, new furnaces, and unexpected contingencies. Typically, I set aside money for contingencies beginning in the fall through spring knowing that our cash flow decreases in summer months. Keeping an eye on your cash flow can also help you to create your future plans.

Comparing This Month's Actual Income and Expense With Your Budget Projections

Each month, as I plug the actual expense amounts into my projections, I can clearly see whether my budget is working. If my projections are off significantly, I will change my projections for the month or even the rest of the year. This is particularly true with the monthly gross tuition which seems to be the most difficult for me to predict, so I expect to adjust it throughout the year.

Evaluating the Item Categories

Also, if you find that certain categories in your financial statements are confusing or don't meet your purposes, it's a good idea to change the category names or add new ones.

I found that our category called "materials/supplies" was often much higher than my budgeted percentage. I discovered that my financial person was also including materials/supplies purchased with fundraiser money into this line item. This significantly distorted the percentages for which our directors were accountable. We created a new category called "special materials/supplies" which includes only items purchased with fundraiser money. Now I have a much more accurate picture of the directors' spending for their routine materials/supplies.

Conclusion

In spite of the fact that you will spend several hours each January creating new income and expense projections, in the long run it will save you valuable time and energy throughout the year. When financial challenges arise, you will have the information to make appropriate decisions quickly. By tracking and monitoring your expenses each month, it will be possible for you to ward off small problems before they become large, out-of-control problems.

You do not have to have an MBA to run a financially viable child care center, but it is necessary to have the tools to monitor your finances and to be able to make appropriate business decisions. Each time I visit a classroom and observe our teachers supporting happy children in a wide range of meaningful and fun activities, I am reminded how important our organization is to these children, their families, the teachers, and our communities. I come away with a renewed commitment to keeping our organization on a sound financial basis for today and for the future.

References

Caplan, S. (2000). *Streetwise Finance & Accounting: How to Keep Your Books and Manage Your Finances without an MBA, a CPA or a Ph.D.* Holbrook, MA: Adams Media Corporation.

Lonier, T. (1999). *Smart Strategies for Growing Your Business.* New York: John Wiley & Son.

Bruce, A., & Langdon, K. (2000). *Strategic Thinking.* New York: Dorling Kindersley.

R. Ann Whitehead is the president and founder of The Child Day Schools, LLC consisting of five child care centers and a private elementary school in the San Francisco East Bay area.

Ms. Whitehead opened her first child care center in 1976 in Lafayette and opened a second facility in San Ramon in 1983. Her most recent project has been to establish the Hidden Canyon Elementary in San Ramon, which utilizes a modified integrated curriculum approach. In order to expand into neighboring communities, Ms. Whitehead has had to carefully budget her programs and create financial strategies to maintain an expanding educational organization.

Looking At Revenue In A Different Way: Playing the Slots!

by Bob Siegel

As directors of early childhood programs we are all expected to be responsible for our center's financial performance. Even when we believe or are told that we have no fiscal responsibility, we actually do, even if it's simply in terms of keeping our customers satisfied so the center can stay full. Too often, a child care director ends up in that unenviable role of middle manager when it comes to being in charge of the budget. This means that you end up with lots of responsibility, not too much actual authority, and few resources to truly handle the job. We now have the fiscal dilemma.

Ah, how to go about defeating the monster of the *fiscal dilemma*? Initially, when a director first learns there are budget problems or that she needs to "meet her budget this year," her first thought is to stop spending money. Too often our initial answer to everything is to find the same items cheaper. Finding puzzles at 12% less isn't the answer, yet it's our first instinct. Note that in most centers, our classroom supply allocation runs only about 1-3% of the total budget, yet it's the first place we go.

The next place we turn is toward personnel costs, often comprising 60-90% of the budget, and clearly needing attention. But it's here that we run into the age old question of quality vs. affordability.

Personnel expenses certainly do need attention, but let's focus this discussion on the revenue side of the budget and what we CAN DO about it. Why is it that income is the last place we turn to when encountered by financial challenges? In truth, your center's income is the place where you as a director probably have the most influence, yet we don't typically see it that way. Almost all of us "leave money on the table" every year through operating decisions that we do have control over.

Over the years I have provided management training for child care directors on fiscal performance. One of the first questions I ask is, "What is your business commodity?" and then, "Give me a verb for what we do with it." This generally perplexes a group of directors who want to answer, "We educate children." In that case, is our commodity children? No, they do not belong to us. Educating children is one of the (many) services offered in our business, but it's not our business commodity. Could it be that "we serve families"? Sounds like a dinner offering . . . but no. Again, the families are not our property to trade upon. In fact, each family is, in reality, the customer. Let me suggest that, financially speaking, we are in the business of *leasing slots*, which is not the generally acceptable way that we typically think about what it is we do.

Given the challenges of operating a fiscally sound child care business, I recommend we begin to change the way we think about what we do — at least in financial terms. Look up at the state license on the wall and see where it states your legal capacity, telling you how many children can be enrolled at the same time. That number, in effect, has defined the maximum number of slots you can lease at any one time. Why call it leasing? The reality is that we don't sell them. A parent makes a decision to enroll her child for a specified amount of time, which in effect means she has leased one of our slots. The more slots we can lease for the greatest number of weeks per year, the better.

Now that you've learned about the concept of **leasing slots**, let me introduce the most fiscally important phrase into your professional lexicon, **Potential Slot Income** (PSI).

What is it? Potential Slot Income is a way of measuring how well we achieve success in our business of *leasing slots*. It is also the key for looking at learning about the consequences of our program operations decisions. Here's the formula to figure out what your center's PSI is:

# of slots × **fee charged** × **unit of time fee is based on**

Determining your PSI will tell you what is the most amount of money you can take in, based on the number of slots you have. Although there are sometimes small ways of increasing that potential, you should regard this number as a hard limit. Your budget should never reflect an expectation that your slot income in a given year will be more than this calculated PSI.

All of this additionally assumes a demand for your services; i.e., there are kids of all ages on your wait list. If there is not an overwhelming demand, you have other problems; however the need for proper enrollment protocols still hold true. This brings us to important concept number three, **Recommended Enrollment Protocols.**

Most commonly, centers get themselves into financial difficulties well before they open their doors. This happens in the way that we configure our groups and classrooms. I offer the following **Recommended Enrollment Protocols prior to opening your center.**

Set up your group sizes to be exact multiples of the adult:child ratios you want to run. Setting these maximum group sizes and ratios is one of your first business decisions and is certainly influenced, and at times is also minimally mandated by external sources (e.g., licensing regs). Ultimately though, it is management that makes the final determination as to the adult:child ratios that will be in place for the program. Some examples of

this would be a *two-year-olds classroom* with a group size of 14 children, operating at a 7:1 ratio; *a toddler classroom* with a group size of 12 operating at a 4:1 ratio; or a *preschool classroom* with a group size of 18 operating at a 9:1 ratio.

Overlap the age group range. For example, instead of having one classroom for 12-24 months and another room for 24-36 months, set your age range at 10-26 months and the next for 21-39 months. This allows greater flexibility to "move kids up" when you actually have room for them. Educationally, this protocol also allows movement of children when it is more developmentally appropriate rather than on their date of birth. You may also want to set up mixed-age classrooms for this purpose, for example, two preschool classrooms of children three through five years of age instead of having both a three-year-old room and a four-year-old room.

Think of your slots as containing 1.00 F.T.E. (full-time equivalency) each. Try and avoid enrolling too many part-time children; you usually end up with

Some examples are:

A. 100 slots	× $125	× 52 weeks	= PSI of $650,000
for a typical child care for 3-5 year olds, with weekly fees			
B. 60 slots	× $400	× 9 months	= PSI of $216,000
for a typical part-time preschool, charging a monthly tuition			
C. 80 slots	× $21.50	× 253 days	= PSI of $435,600
for a different center, charging a daily based fee			

or multiple formulas when you have different rates…

D. 8 infant slots	× $160	× 52 weeks	= $ 66,560
24 toddler slots	× $140	× 52 weeks	= $174,720
38 preschool slots	× $120	× 52 weeks	= $237,120
	TOTAL CENTER PSI		= $478,400

slots not filled at all times during the week, and the center experiences a loss of potential slot income. When you do enroll part-time children, charge a premium of at least 10-20% for part-time enrollees; e.g., if your weekly fee is $150.00, then a three-day enrollee (or a .60 FTE enrollment) will be charged $90.00 plus $10.00 premium for a fee of $100.00 (a .67 FTE revenue rate).

Hopefully it goes without saying these days, but you charge for the enrolled day, not based on attendance. The fee is paid regardless of whether the child attends or not; we still incur all costs and the slot was "leased for that day."

Once your center is open, I offer the following **Recommended Enrollment Protocols for operating the center.** When your classroom is at the first ratio maximum (such as seven enrolled children in a classroom of 14 with a 7:1 ratio), do not enroll just one child; hold that enrollment until you can enroll several more children. This avoids having to hire another teacher for "just one kid" budget-wise. There are generally two or three main periods of the year for enrollment, with the exception of infants who enroll at all times of the year. These are beginning of the school year, start of summer, and sometimes right after the New Year's holiday. If considering enrolling that eighth or ninth toddler into this classroom, review where you are in the year and what your past patterns of enrollment have been. In this case, I would probably enroll an extra child or two in this room in early September, but not in mid-February.

When you are in a situation with people wanting your services, do not take and hold an enrollment for months in the future if you feel you

could fill that slot earlier. You can offer to hold a slot if the parents pay that tuition to hold it; sometimes half-tuition is enough and more reasonable. Know your waiting list movement and find out what other centers in your community do.

Upon enrollment, collect from each family the tuition for the child's first week of child care as well as the last two weeks. This security deposit assures that you are paid for the final weeks of a child's enrollment even if he/she leaves in a hurry, by obligating the parents to inform you of the child's last two weeks of care. This process also turns out to be a great PR move, in that a family always leaves liking you because their last two weeks feel like they've been free. NOTE: It can be a hardship for some families to come up with that much cash. In that case, set up a plan for them to pay an additional $25-35 per week until the necessary reserve has been built up, usually 6-8 weeks.

Assure that children at the top of your waiting list are "pre-processed" and have their enrollment paperwork completed. This allows you to move a child into the slot without any lag time.

Understand and compute how much potential slot income you are losing out on as a result of enrolling children at a discounted rate. A discounted rate in this case means any protocol that allows a child to be enrolled under conditions where the center receives less than the full potential income for that slot! Although we rarely use the terminology "discount," the intention of our enrollment decisions may not be to discount, but the effect often is. Please note that as you read down this

list of possible discounts that I am not advocating that centers never offer discounts, but rather that we do not offer more than we can afford. Historically, child care has offered the following discounts:

■ A **sibling discount**, almost always for 10% less for the older (i.e., the cheaper) child

■ A **discount for staff member's children**, most generally falls between 20-33% discount, but I've seen it for 5% up to a 100% discount . . . that's free if you're actually doing the math . . .

. . . and now for the discounts that are called something else . . .

■ A discount in the manner of being allowed **vacation time** where no fees are paid. In some communities, it's typical practice in the marketplace for centers to offer one or two weeks off where the parents can stipulate that it's a vacation week and no fees are paid. If you do offer this vacation time, your protocol should stipulate that it be arranged for in advance. This allows the possibility of shifting staff since it often occurs during winter vacation or the end of summer when attendance is low. This becomes a discount by reducing your potential income for that slot. When you compute PSI, the formula of slot capacity X rate, then is multiplied by either 51, or even 50 instead of by 52 (weeks). This in effect gives a family over a 4% discount. A more extreme version of this is when we enroll a child for only a portion of the year, often a 9 month school year or less. What we've done in effect here is allow a child to occupy a slot for only a 70-75% rate throughout the year where we could have filled that slot with a 100% payer.

■ **Sliding fee scales and scholarships for need** are another common practice in our industry — or at least are commonly used terms. In reality, however, these are truly only scholarships or a sliding fee scale when there is a separate pot of money, not from your operating budget, available for use to replace the lost slot income. If there are no other dollars entering your budget to make up for the lesser amount you've chosen to charge that family, then it's not a scholarship, it's just a discount. In our example, when we allow a family to come on half-tuition for two months, we have in effect voluntarily given them a $540.00 discount.

■ **Children who are enrolled on contract with an outside payer** at a lesser rate than your published and budgeted rate. The most common example is children on a **subsidized program rate for low-income families**. In many states, this (CCDBG) rate is comparably lower than centers' regular rates. When you enroll these children, you again are agreeing to a discounted rate. For example, your regular fee for preschoolers is $120.00 per week, but the state rate calls for a total of $19.00 per day or only $95.00 per week for that contracted child. This is not limited to just low-income subsidies. Other discounts for outside payers also

include discounts for other organizations who fund you or for partners, discounts to attract employees of a nearby corporate employer, or even children who are wards of the state.

In addition to these discounting practices, there are other common ways that we rob ourselves of some of that potential slot income that we work so hard for. The primary example is uncollected tuition. I have a simple solution: that regular fees are paid before the child receives service. If they have not been paid, the child does not get in. Do this for two or three weeks and the word will get out. It will also be most appreciated by the remainder of your parents who make the effort to always pay on time.

Most child care organizations measure enrollment success by quoting their percent of capacity enrolled. We'll report to our supervisors "the center is enrolled at 92% capacity . . . we have only 4 open slots." While simply viewing that percentage is a decent guide to how we are doing, it's now essential to go beyond that and compare our efforts to how well it is possible to do. As a beginning, figure your PSI for the last fiscal year, then look at actual slot income. Where do you stand? How much better can you do with different enrollment protocols? Here are some guidelines to assess performance, assuming that you have demand for your services.

Measure percentage of PSI to actual slot income	
Under 80%	Needs work
81 to 90%	Good
91 to 95%	Very good
Over 95%	Outstanding

Please allow me to reiterate that I am NOT recommending that you never offer appropriate or necessary discounts. Just know that some practices our industry has historically engaged in result in huge losses of potential slot income. In some cases, these are the centers that are desperately in need of increased revenue.

It might shock you to discover that your own decisions around enrollment protocols have allowed dollars to be left on the table — leaving us back where we started. Here is your opportunity to change the way you do business and have the income to address some of the issues of quality as well.

Bob Siegel is in his 32nd year in the child care business. Currently, he is the national director of the Easter Seals Child Development Center Network and president of his own training and consulting company, Partners in Professional Development. In addition to his current position, Bob has worked as a preschool teacher, long-time child care director, graduate school teacher, children's museum director, and ECE management consultant and trainer.

Cost-Benefit Analysis: Tools for Decision Making

by Gary Bess

If you are like most child care center directors, you have a healthy respect for your center's bottom line. At minimum, you want to be assured that **inflows**, revenues that you derive from fees, grants, contracts, and other income-generating activities, is equal to your **outflows**, your expenses that enable you to remain in the **black**. But, there may be a time that your **inflows** do not exceed your **outflows**, and you find yourself involuntarily dipping into savings, drawing on your line of credit, or cutting costs that may affect program quality.

Even if your agency is not spewing *red ink*, you are still wise to continuously assess the *cost-effectiveness* of your programs. As an administrator, you have likely made decisions based on your intuitive criteria of cost-efficiency, choosing among alternative approaches that are least costly, and yet provide high quality child care services. Have you, however, put pen to paper to consider the specific costs associated with each alternative approach? Probably, your answer is "no."

What is Cost-Benefit Analysis?

One way to assess cost-effectiveness is cost-benefit analysis, an administrative tool for choosing among several alternative approaches to determine the most economical way to manage a program or service. It provides the "best results for any given resource outlay," thus helping you to determine your program's minimum resource requirements (Levin, 1983).

Said another way, cost-benefit analysis enables you to maximize your efficiency, while achieving your program's intended

outcomes. It is also a way of justifying your approach to your board of directors and external stakeholders such as grantors or elected officials, who, like you, have an appreciation for each dollar saved or spent. This article will provide an overview of cost-benefit analysis and how it is used in child care administrative decision making. Perhaps the best way to understand how it can be used is with an example:

ABC Child Care Center was experiencing declining enrollment, the result of layoffs by the primary manufacturing business in town. Parents were withdrawing their children to care for them at home until the economy improved and they would be rehired. The center director's first reaction to declining enrollment was to cut costs by reducing her staff. Though sometimes this is an inevitable response, reductions in staff are more than a proportional adjustment in worker to child ratios. Reductions in quality, effectiveness, and morale can also occur.

With fewer staff, responsibility for secondary activities such as food preparation and cleaning will fall on the remaining workers. Parents who favored one of the laid off workers may withdraw their children, or remaining staff members, fearing that the ax may next fall on them, will find employment elsewhere. Thus, a downward spiraling occurs, affecting program quality and efficiency as other valued employees depart.

Fortunately, there are alternatives to this scenario that a prudent director may wish to consider. An analysis of the differences in each approach can help to illustrate the best course of action for the ABC Child Care Center.

How Do You Analyze Costs and Benefits?

The cost-benefit approach considers alternatives based on anticipated expenses and their effect on a particular set of financial outcomes (Lewis, et al., 2001). Only approaches that target the same outcomes (e.g., an increase in enrollment or stabilization at current enrollment levels) can be assessed together. Also required is a common measure of effectiveness that can be applied to each intervention. For example, the number of child care slots to be retained would need to be established as the outcome for each of the three approaches.

With our focus on adjusting to the loss of income associated with a sudden decline in enrollment, the director would need to consider alternative interventions that address the common measure of enrollment stabilization at the current level. For example, three possible solutions she could consider are: (a) reduce her child care staff proportional to current enrollment ratios; (b) reduce all workers by 20% (one day a week); or (c) increase fees to help defray fixed operational expenses. Let's look at each of these approaches, assuming hypothetically that we wish to, at minimum, stabilize our decline until the economy improves, which would require a budget reduction of $60,000.

Scenario A would require the laying off of two full-time workers, valued at $30,000 each, for a 12-month savings of $60,000. In Scenario B, a workforce reduction of 20% would yield a near similar $55,000 savings or benefit for the same period, and in Scenario C, the center would net an additional $15,000 a year in increased fees from the remaining families by increasing tuition. Each of these three approaches has corresponding assumptions about costs and benefits as the matrix in Table 1 demonstrates.

The first column in Table 1 lists your alternative *approaches* based on the discussion above. The *cost* column represents the loss of annual revenues associated with a declining enrollment.

It could also represent anticipated expenses, if the analysis were to focus on different questions such as which alternative way of delivering lunchtime meals should your agency choose, or which alternative methods of promoting your services (e.g., low introductory fees, ads in local newspapers, or billboard advertising) is most cost effective.

The *benefits* column shows the anticipated changes in financial terms. In this example, the benefit is the cost savings that is equal to the reduction in staff. In other scenarios, however, benefits can be a calculation of new revenues to be received or of estimates of later-life societal cost-savings (Lewis, et al., 2001) that result from your program's intervention (e.g., early identification of children with special needs or parenting education and support). The requirement is to translate anticipated benefits into financial terms, and to be consistent in your calculations across differing approaches.

The column titled *c/b* refers to the ratio of costs to benefits. This is a common measure of cost-effectiveness analysis (Yates, 1996). We ideally want to achieve a statistic that represents either a balance between costs and benefits (e.g., break even), or where benefits exceed costs (<1). The lower the ratio, the stronger the benefit, while numbers greater than one (1) suggest higher costs compared against benefits.

Table 1 — Hypothetical Costs and Benefits				
Approach	Cost	Benefits	C/B	Net Benefit
Reduce staff proportional to enrollment	$60,000	$60,000	1	$0
Workforce reduction of 20 percent	$60,000	$55,000	1.09	–$ 5,000
Increase in fees	$60,000	$15,000	4	–$45,000

The final column — *net benefits* — shows the financial savings in expenses as a difference between costs and benefits. This represents the anticipated net savings or expenditures associated with each project.

Though there are political as well as financial risks associated with all three approaches, the *risk* of reducing staff proportional to enrollment, no matter how personally troublesome, is clearly the most cost-effective approach based on this analysis. But wait! Does this convey the full picture? There may be another interpretation and course of action when you also consider *additional factors*.

For example, the remaining four staff members may view your decision to lay off staff as "writing on the wall" concerning the longevity of their own employment, and one or two may quietly decide to seek work elsewhere. You know from experience that it will cost you upwards to $7,500 an employee for recruitment, hiring, and training before a new employee is operating at full potential. With workforce reductions you, too, fear that an employee

may leave; but, based on your experience and knowledge, only one is likely to leave.

You also know that among the staff to be let go is a newer and well-liked employee — someone, parents have commented to you, is one reason why they have chosen your center over others. If you lay this person off, as you feel bound by the policy of "last hired is the first fired," upward to two parents may also leave, which is valued at $12,000 ($6,000 a year in tuition for each). You additionally believe that by avoiding full layoffs, you will be in a better position to build enrollment and that within the next 12 months, you will be able to increase your enrollment by three children. Being down two staff positions will make it more difficult to increase your census.

The third approach of increasing fees is also not without risk. Some parents may decide to place their child with another agency if fees are increased. We assume in our scenario that two parents will withdraw from our program if fees are hiked.

These additional factored costs must also be considered into each decision as Table 2 demonstrates. In this approach, we see that a workforce reduction of 20% represents the better choice. If the scenario is correct, we actually show a cost-benefit ratio of less than 1, meaning that benefits clearly outweigh costs.

Let's take a look at a second example: Due to increasing costs, XYZ Child Care Center is considering an alternative to its present system of providing lunchtime meals prepared by its staff to 60 children each day. At a staff meeting it was suggested the agency consider hiring an outside company to cater lunches or that beginning with the next program year, parents be required to prepare meals for their child's lunch.

Like before, the question is which of these three alternatives is most cost-effective? Should XYZ Child Care Center (a) continue to provide meals prepared by its staff; (b) arrange for catering by contract; or (c) require parents to send a lunch for their child? Staff discussion concerning each approach identified several hidden

Table 2 — Hypothetical Costs and Benefits, Including Intangible Costs

Approach	Direct Cost	Additional Factored Costs	Total Costs	Benefits	C/B	Net Benefit
Reduce staff proportional to enrollment		$15,000*				
		$12,000**				
	$60,000	$27,000	$87,000	$60,000	1.45	-$27,000
Workforce reduction of 20%		-$18,000**				
		$ 7,500*				
	$60,000	-$10,500	$49,500	$60,000	.9	$7,500
Increase in fees	$60,000	$12,000**	$72,000	$15,000	4.8	-$57,000

*Retraining of employees at $7,500 each.
**Addition or loss of child care slots at $6,000 each.

Table 3 — Summary Matrix of Lunchtime Alternatives

Approach	Food	Staffing	Consumables	Drinks	Total
Continue Current Lunchtime Meal Program	$15,145	$13,520	$1,560	$780	$31,005
Engage Catering Company	$21,060	$13,520	$0	$780	$35,360
Requirement that Parents Send Meals	$15,145	$13,520	$0	$780	$29,445

costs and benefits. A 12 month review of agency expenditures for food showed that the agency spent $15,925 ($1.25 per child each day) in direct expenses for lunch, including food stuffs, fruit drinks and milk, and paper products. It additionally incurred approximately four hours each day in staff time devoted to meal preparation and cleanup. This was estimated to cost $13,520, or an additional 86 cents each day based on a census of 60 children.

On top of these expenses, there were periodic costs associated with pot, pan, and kitchen utensil replacements, and consumable supplies such as dish washing liquid, paper towels, and gas to shop for food and supplies. This was estimated at an additional $1,560 each year, or 10 cents per child each day. It became clear that the cost of lunchtime meals was $1.98 per child each day when the full costs were considered.

Two catering companies were called to see what they would charge to deliver meals each day. Based on comparable menus proposed by the two com-

panies, it was found that the price per day for each child would be $1.35, which would be inclusive of food and paper products, but would not include drinks, which you knew from your research cost your agency an average of five cents per child each day or $780 each year.

Considering your third alternative — having parents send lunches for their child — you reasoned that you could not rebate to parents the $5,070 in staff time devoted to food preparation as these are fixed staff costs that you would want to retain. But you could adjust fees to account for your annual food expenses of $15,925, minus the five cents per child each day in drinks. The net amount to be adjusted would be $15,145 in annual revenues, or $252.41 a year for each child (84 cents each day).

A summary matrix of the three alternative costs is presented in Table 3. You may be surprised that in the *food* column for the third alternative — the requirement that parents bring lunchtime meals — includes an expense equal to the first approach of continu-

ing the current lunchtime meal arrangement. This is because forfeiture of income, the $15,145 that parents will not be paying for child care, represents an *expense* in the sense that the agency has willfully incurred this reduction, which is equal to the direct cost of food and related products.

In Table 4, we examine the cost-benefit of each approach based on the summary of *direct costs* drawn from Table 3, and our known *benefit* of $31,005, which is the current total expense of having our staff prepare lunchtime meals. We see from this analysis that the third approach of requiring parents to send their child's meal is the most cost-effective approach based on a *c/b* ratio of .95. Supporters of this approach would also likely argue that the four hours each day in staff expenses that is no longer needed for food preparation, could be reassigned to child care duties.

Discussion

You have seen that cost-benefit analysis can be a helpful tool for assessing difficult and complex problems. Its

Table 4 — Hypothetical Costs and Benefit Analysis

Approach	Direct Cost	Benefits	C/B	Net Benefit
Continue Current Lunchtime Meal Program	$31,005	$31,005	1	$0
Engage Catering Company	$35,360	$31,005	1.15	—$4,335
Require That Parents Bring Meals	$29,445	$31,005	.95	$1,560

rational approach can help quantify and explain to stakeholders and others why you made the decision that you did. It also helps you to define and select the conditions on which to base your alternative choices. There also is a firm bottom line in cost-benefit analysis that we try not to cross: benefits must be at least equal to costs (Levin, 1985).

One difficulty in using this approach, however, is that benefits must be equated in financial terms. We must be able to determine a monetary equivalency in areas where it is sometimes difficult to do so. How do we equate a cost to parenting education or early identification of children with special needs? Well, there are ways to do so, but some may disagree with your assumptions. We can look at public costs associated with child abuse and neglect or serving children with special needs, and suggest that with early interventions, these expenses are sometimes reduced.

It is also important to be clear about your audience when performing a cost-benefit analysis. Are they board members, elected officials, donors, or parents? Again, some may disagree with your assumptions or the values that you place on certain functions. And, even when you are clear as to your audience, you must realize, too, that other audiences may read your report and review your decision. As Levin states: "The importance of determining which audiences one is addressing and for what purposes is that these data guide the level and nature of the presentation and the types of information and analysis that should be forthcoming" (1985, p. 39).

At a time when terms like *logic models* and *evidence-based practice* seem to be directed at raising the bar on administration standards, cost-benefit analysis should be in your toolbox so that when questions are raised — "Is there a less costly way to do this?" or "Is there another better way?" — we

know how to respond to these questions.

References

Levin, H. M. (1993). *Cost-Effectiveness: A Primer*. Beverly Hills: Sage Publications.

Yates, B. T. (1989). *Analyzing Costs, Procedures, Processes, and Outcomes in Human Services*. Thousand Oaks, CA: Sage Publications.

Lewis, J. A., Lewis, M. D., Packard, T., & Souflee, Jr., F. (2001). *Management of Human Services Programs*. Belmont, CA: Brooks/Cole.

Gary Bess, Ph.D., is a management consultant for nonprofit health and human services organizations, and teaches part-time in the School of Social Work, California State University, Chico.

Fourteen Steps to More Effective Cash Flow Management

by Roger Neugebauer

As anyone who has been in the early childhood business for more than a few days knows, managing cash flow is an incredibly important skill for a center director. Even a center with an annual budget showing a healthy surplus may experience brief periods where funds in the checkbook are insufficient to pay all the bills.

To discover how successful directors manage cash flow in tight times, we surveyed members of the *Exchange Panel of 300*. Summarized below are their tips for planning ahead, suggestions on what to do in the midst of a cash flow crisis, and tempting solutions to avoid.

Prepare Today

The most important steps you can take to deal with a cash flow crisis are those you take before the crisis occurs:

■ **Always budget conservatively**. A common mistake of rookie directors is to develop an annual budget based on full enrollment. Even the very best centers find it impossible to maintain enrollment at 100% as there are inevitable lags between one family leaving and another enrolling. More often centers operate at between 80% and 85% capacity. To avoid creating unnecessary cash flow surprises, make sure that you budget income with considerable conservatism and expenses with considerable pessimism. Any surprises you experience in this mode should be pleasant ones.

■ **Build credibility with your creditors**. One of the simplest, yet most effective cash flow management steps you can take is to pay your bills on time. If you build high credibility with your creditors when times are good, you are more likely to win their support when times are not so good.

■ **Establish a line of credit**. If you are in the midst of a financial crisis, no bank is likely to rush to your rescue. Remember that a bank's practice is loaning money to people who don't need it. So the best time to arrange for a line of credit you may need to get you through a difficult patch is when your center is doing well. Go to the bank when your center's financials are strong and arrange a line of credit sufficient to carry you through two or three difficult months. Then pretend you don't have it, so you don't get complacent in your money management.

■ **Set up a rainy day fund**. An alternative, or maybe a supplement, to a line of credit is a reserve fund that you establish when the center has a surplus. When you have money in the bank, it's awfully tempting to go out and buy that new playground structure or to finally repaint the center. However, before you make these decisions you should seriously consider salting some of these funds away into a fund to provide some cushion during hard times.

■ **Develop the habit of analyzing cash flow**. Every director should develop the discipline of analyzing cash flow year round, not just when times are tight. For at least 12 months ahead, project when income and expenses will occur. This will enable you to foresee times when expenses will exceed income, and to start taking action in advance. Some directors do these projections on a monthly basis, whereas others do them week by week (which is most important during periods of crisis). Again, as with budgeting, you should be pretty conservative in making these projections. For example, don't assume that all parents will pay their fees on time, and never assume a public agency will process invoices on time.

Work Hard to Survive

Once a cash flow crisis has set in, it's time to change tactics:

■ **Maintain confidence in your program**. Even though you as director may be under tremendous stress, you can't afford to spread your anxiety to teachers and parents. If parents think that your program is in trouble, they may start looking for other options, which will only exacerbate your problems. Likewise, if staff are worried about the survival of the center, they too may start jumping ship, or at least lose some of their motivation.

This doesn't mean, of course, that you should pretend that everything is rosy. When times are tight, staff and parents will inevitably pick up on the signs of stress. If they sense that times are a bit tight and you are acting like nothing is wrong, rumors may start to build out of proportion to reality. Rather, you should let parents and staff know that the center is experiencing a "cash flow crisis" while expressing confidence that this is only a temporary condition. Be honest, but confident.

■ **Manage cash flowing in**. The bottom line is that there are really only two surefire ways to survive a cash flow crisis — speeding up the flow of cash coming in, and slowing down the flow of cash going out. In the first instance, the most important way to speed the inflow of cash is to be vigilant about fee collections — making sure that invoices are processed on a timely basis, rewarding parents for paying fees early, penalizing parents for paying fees late (as long as you don't ignore usury laws, of course), and paying close attention to parents who are starting to get behind in their fees. Other less likely solutions are to move up in time scheduled fundraisers or special money making projects.

■ **Manage cash flowing out**. This is where your good bill paying behavior will pay off. If you have established a dependable payment history with vendors, they will be likely to work with you and stretch their payment terms a few weeks when you are in trouble. However, vendors don't like surprises. You will get more cooperation from a vendor you owe money if you come to them before the payment is due and ask for some extra time, than if you wait for them to call you after the payment is overdue.

In addition, you should look for major purchases you can defer in order to improve cash flow. For example, if you are planning to purchase a new computer for your office in February, but through doing careful cash flow analysis see that the month of March is going to be a tight one, put off this purchase until May, thereby lessening the hill you need to climb in March.

■ **Carefully monitor staff schedules**. Since anywhere from 70% to 80% of a center's expenditures go for staff salaries, attention to this line item is paramount. You are trying to balance three factors — you want to maintain the quality of your services, you want to avoid over expenditures on staffing, and you want to maintain staff morale. If you cut staff hours across the board, you will impact quality. If you have staff coming and going on an hourly basis based on daily fluctuations in attendance, you may damage staff morale. Yet, if you do nothing, you may not be able to pay your bills.

Your best bet is to explain the challenge to staff and work with them to develop as lean a schedule as possible based on attendance patterns. If you end up having a few staff members who are paying a higher price for this — working split shifts or changing their hours from week to week — make sure you show your recognition of their sacrifices and try to assure them that this is a short term situation.

■ **Focus on solutions with a future**. During major cash flow crises, there is a temptation to reach out for quick one-shot solutions — organizing a fundraising, seeking grants, seeking donations from current and former parents. These solutions will demand a lot of energy and time to pull off, with no guarantee of success. Rather than investing your resources into such one-shot solutions, you should consider new ventures that can fit into the long range plans of the organization. For example, it may be a better use of everyone's time to launch a new after-school component than to organize a pancake breakfast; to create a new one-Friday-a-month "parents' night out" service, than to hold a center-wide yard sale.

Avoid Common Mistakes

Panel of 300 members shared some cash flow management mistakes as well. Here are a few paths not to follow:

■ **Don't delay taking action**. When an organization starts sliding into a rough patch, it's always tempting to deny what is happening and hope the crisis will pass. However, the longer a director delays in taking action, the steeper the hill will be to climb. If a director foresees a cash flow shortage looming a month away, this provides four weeks of income and expenses that can be manipulated to ease the crisis. If you wait until the crisis is upon you, your options are significantly reduced.

■ **Don't defer payroll**. Given that staff salaries constitute the bulk of your expenditures, it's tempting to take the easy way out when funds are short and to delay a payroll for a week or two. However, the risks to destroying staff morale are too great. Having a payroll delayed sends a chilling message to staff that should be avoided at all costs. Delay payroll only as a last resort.

■ **Don't defer payroll taxes**. An even more dangerous temptation is to get into the habit of delaying the deposit of payroll taxes. Too many centers have ended up paying severe tax penalties when they got caught playing this game.

■ **Don't borrow from your future**. Another temptation to avoid is to dip into funds that are designated for future activities. For example, if you collect advances from families for your summer camp, it may be tempting to use these advances to cover a cash flow gap. The problem is that come summer camp you won't have these funds to cover your expenses. If you do find it necessary to dip into funds for future events, make sure that your cash flow recovery plan includes provisions for replenishing these funds.

■ **Don't delude yourself**. Part of your analysis of a cash flow crisis is to decide if it truly is a "temporary cash flow crisis" or something more serious. When a center seems to go from one cash flow crisis to another, this may be an indication that there is a fundamental problem with the financial structure of the center. Possibly your fee is simply set too low, maybe your enrollment is steadily declining, maybe your expenses are out of control. So while you are struggling through a difficult cash flow period, take a step back and analyze whether this is a temporary challenge or a more basic financial issue.

Panel of 300 Contributors

The following *Panel of 300* members contributed to this article:

Carolyn Barnes, Gateway Christian Preschool, Pensacola, FL; Mary Lou Beaver, Dover Children's Centers, Dover, NH; Judy Chosy, Smoky Row Children's Centers, Powell, OH; Kathy Cronemiller, Child Care Inc., Midwest City, OK; Marie Darstein, The Sunshine House, Rock Hill, SC; Betty DePina, Mountain Area Child and Family, Asheville, NC; Marsha Enquist, Chicago, IL; Melissa Hoover, Seven Bends Student Centers, Woodstock, VA; Sarah Horn, Allegheny Child Care Academy, Pittsburgh, PA; Amy Huppe, Wee Play School, Manchester, NH; Dr. Raina Jain, Witty Kids, Mumbai, India; Barbara Lynn, Community Preschool, Jacksonville, FL; Suzanne Martin, Kids Life Academy, Cordova, TN; Jacqueline Nirode, Grand Care LLC, Franklin, WI; Jennifer Nizer, John Hopkins Bayview Medical Center Child Development Center, Baltimore, MD; Julia Rand, Kids-Play, Uniontown, OH; Debbie Ritter, Small World Montessori Academy, Jensen Beach, FL; Kathy Sarginson, ABCs of Children's Care, Foxboro, Ontario, Canada; Sherri Senter, National Pediatric Support Services, Irvine, CA; Deborah Sheely, Tabitha Intergenerational Center, Lincoln, NE; Elizabeth Shephard, Ready-Set-Grow, Inc., Auburn, MI; Pam Tuszynski, First Presbyterian Church Preschool, Hollywood, CA; Linda Zager, Bloomington Developmental Learning Center, Bloomington, IN.

Child Care Administration Software

by Michael Kalinowski

Specialized child care administrative software packages may offer the right combination of breadth, convenience, and ease of operation to enhance your center management. For 14 years, *Exchange* has been providing guidance on the selection and use of such products. This year, we take a broad look at recent questions from the field.

Is this a good or bad time to purchase center management software?

I think this is one of the best times ever for such a purchase for three reasons. First, things are more stable, with fewer center management software companies entering and departing the market. Since a potential buyer wants to have confidence that the company will remain in business to provide service and upgrades, stability is a critical variable in this industry. Second, many companies have recently made substantial improvements to their product lines, and have had a year or two to debug these updates, leading to substantially better software. In general, brand new customers are getting up to speed quickly, and

customers migrating from DOS to Windows-based products are moving forward reasonably well. Third, Y2K has come and gone and the effects were much fewer than feared.

What does center management software offer that is unique?

Such software may offer a better fit because it is specifically designed for center management tasks, and therefore more appropriate than an integrated business product (Microsoft® Office) for those tasks. Such software may be better supported in the sense that customer service understands not only the product's technical features but also has a general sense of the field and the typical tasks and frustrations directors face each day. Finally, such software may be both more comprehensive and integrated than generic business software. The ability to generate lists of children and parents once, and then to be able to use and resort the same list for every function needed, without having to reenter names, is a very powerful feature, and one that is

very challenging for non-center-specific software.

What are the three biggest things to consider in selecting such a software product?

Need, need, and need. This really can't be overemphasized. It is essential to ask exactly what it is that the product is expected to help you accomplish. For example, if creating billing invoices and tracking tuition payments are all that is really necessary, there are several business products available. However, if you need variable attendance management with a time clock card reader; or the ability to reconfigure the database as families divorce, remarry, and/or have additional children; or the ability to create specialized monthly financial reports as a condition of funding by different agencies (or to develop child care food program report records), then your needs become more specialized and the list of appropriate products may get considerably smaller.

What is the most essential long-term feature to consider?

Flexibility. A consistent finding of surveys of center directors' use of center management software is their desire for products that can be customized. In some ways, this is a little ironic because a program that is very flexible can seem initially overwhelming to mildly computer-anxious directors. It is natural to desire simplicity in starting out, in order to gain confidence quickly. However, over a longer time interval, the ability to adapt a program to meet one's needs is often the primary variable in determining whether the product remains an indispensable daily tool or becomes less and less functional over time.

What are some indicators of flexibility in such products?

Can the user add fields to the screen (examples might include a new state immunization requirement or the addition of beeper or cell phone numbers)? Can the user sort and select everyone with one similar criterion (for example, all parents in one area code) and change that field for the entire group? How few clicks does it take to get from one screen to a separate but linked component? Can one create variable reports (can you easily adapt pre-designed reports to meet your unique needs and requirements)?

Is there anything else a director should be cautioned about?

Directors should not automatically believe everything they are told. A company that may be terrific at reaching potential customers does not necessarily have the best, or perhaps the most appropriate, product for a particular director. A useful strategy here is to ask a vendor to prove, by physically demonstrating, the feature in which you are interested. I advise special caution with companies that market their product primarily by denigrating those of their competitors. It is more effective to show what one company's product can do than to simply say that others are not good.

How is technology likely to change over the next three years?

Computers are likely to get smaller (some the size of a phone book), faster (chip speed will continue to increase), and cheaper (at the high end but not at the low end of the market). Internet connection speed will become more important than computer processing speed. High-speed cable access via DSL (digital subscriber line) and cable modem will skyrocket. Some companies will partner with others in a burgeoning web presence that will lead to more shakeout. Better center management software companies are likely to create more useful and somewhat more interactive web sites to facilitate customer service issues, moving beyond sites designed primarily to introduce products.

How will this affect a director?

In many ways it won't. For example, while the speed of PCs will continue to increase, additional speed in a center management context may not really mean all that much. In two to three years, a 500 megahertz PC should still run 95% of what has become available in the meantime.

What are some of the things not likely to change over the next three years?

Putting software on web servers and charging people to access them is likely to become one alternative to delivering flexible products, but overcoming technological and security problems to accomplish this probably won't be totally resolved in the short term. The current Microsoft court problems may mean somewhat fewer product innovations over the next few years as the implications from this case are sorted out.

What might the future look like?

Here's one potential office image from Mark Smith, manager of appliance platforms at H-P labs, as quoted in a recent article in *Time* magazine:

You'll walk into the building like you own the place. . . . When you arrive at work, you could simply stroll through a secure, smart door and listen as your desktop virtual assistant reads aloud your schedule for the day. The temperature and lighting will adjust automatically to your preferences. . . . And forget about typing: sophisticated voice recognition will let you tell your PC what to do [although all that yakking could just as easily make you hoarse].
(Eisenberg, May 22, 2000, p. 48)

I know exactly what I want my PC to say to me: *You are a fabulous director and everyone really appreciates all you are doing for families. Relax. Today will be a good day. No crises are in the forecast!*

Dr. Michael Kalinowski is associate professor of family studies at the University of New Hampshire, and former director of the UNH Child Study and Development Center. Involved in the study of technology for the past 15 years, he continues to analyze software for administrators and children.

Financial Evaluation Tools

*"An effective director is a cynic,
always asking questions,
never relaxing when things
seem to be going well,
ever alert to signs of trouble."*

Financial Management Assessment Guide

by Roger Neugebauer

*T*he soundness of a center's financial management system is determined by the extent to which it meets these criteria:

Security — *The system should provide safeguards against accidental or fraudulent loss of assets as well as insure that all financial obligations are met.*

Efficiency — *The system should minimize time spent on paperwork and procedures.*

Effectiveness — *The system should provide accurate information to decisionmakers on a timely basis.*

The following questions are designed to be used as guides, by both non profit and for profit centers, for assessing whether the major components of a center's financial management system meet these criteria.

Establishing the Budget

____ Does your center annually develop a formal budget which balances projected income and expenditures?

____ Does your center annually establish program goals and strive to allocate sufficient funds in the budget for achieving these goals?

____ Are income projections in the budget realistic — i.e., are estimates of fundraising, grants, and in-kind income achievable; and are losses of potential income due to typical under-enrollments taken into account?

____ Have all potential sources of income been explored, such as parent fees, employer contributions, United Way, public subsidies, tax credits?

____ Are expense projections in the budget realistic — i.e., are likely price increases for supplies and services factored in, and is provision made for unexpected costs such as repairs and replacements of equipment?

____ Does the budget provide for staff development, staff benefits, payroll taxes, leave time, salary increases, evaluation, and future planning?

____ Are funds set aside each year for long-range capital improvements?

Receiving and Spending Money

____ Are all monies received documented with duplicate copies of prenumbered receipts?

Managing Money

____ Are all monies received promptly deposited into the center's bank account?

____ Have procedures been estalished for avoiding overdue payments and for collecting those that do occur?

____ Are all disbursements made by prenumbered checks and supported by valid invoices, receipts, or other documentation?

____ Do procedures for signing checks and withdrawing funds from savings accounts incorporate safeguards to avoid the improper expenditure of funds?

____ Can signed checks always be obtained on time so as not to delay purchases or paydays?

____ Is the petty cash system secure — i.e., is money kept in a safe place, is documentation maintained for all purchases, and are periodic checks made to verify the balance in the fund?

Recordkeeping and Monitoring

____ Has your accounting system been designed to meet the specific information needs of the center — i.e., can financial data needed for decisionmaking and reporting be readily obtained?

____ Is data on income and expenses recorded in such a form that it can be applied directly in preparing tax reports, grant claim vouchers, monitoring reports, and annual budgets?

____ Whenever possible, is bookkeeping and checkbook reconciliation performed by someone other than the person(s) who receive money, write checks, and handle petty cash?

____ Are records maintained of the center's assets and liabilities, such as major equipment and appliances, savings accounts, insurance policies, outstanding loans, and tax liabilities?

____ Does the center maintain a written schedule of reports and tax payments due to public and private agencies, and is this schedule adhered to?

____ Are checking account balances reconciled monthly?

____ Is a trial balance prepared monthly?

____ Is a cash flow report periodically prepared and analyzed?

____ Is a financial status report comparing current income and expenditures against the projected budget prepared and analyzed on a monthly basis?

____ When financial problems or opportunities are identified in cash flow and financial status reports, are these situations reacted to quickly?

Credits

Assistance in preparing this guide was provided by:

• Annice Probst from the Preschool Association of the West Side in New York City;

• Marlene Scavo, director of child support services at Fort Lewis, Washington; and

• Carl Staley and David Delman of United Day Care Services in Greensboro, North Carolina.

Number Crunching: Monitoring Your True Enrollment

by L. Steven Sternberg

Anyone who has directed an early childhood program for at least a week recognizes that strong enrollment is vital to the success of a center. A small change in a center's enrollment can make the difference between financial stability and disaster.

But keeping tabs on your enrollment is not always a simple procedure. If your center enrolls some children part time and some full time, a simple head count of enrolled children will not give you a meaningful enrollment number.

To monitor enrollment accurately, you need to be able to add up all the hours of service your center is providing and convert this total into units of full-time care. You need to be able to calculate your full-time equivalent (FTE) enrollment.

This article will lead you through a three step process for calculating and analyzing FTEs.

Step 1: Set Basic Assumptions

Before you even start crunching numbers, you need to define what your center considers *full-time enrollment* and *total capacity*. These numbers will be used as the baseline for all the calculations that follow.

There is no commonly held definition of full-time care (it's really not just a math but also a political problem) — how much time must a child spend in a program to be called full time? Politics are far beyond the scope of this paper; I'll stick to the math.

The number you select will depend upon the nature of the program you offer as well as the needs of the population you serve. If you operate a preschool offering a four-hour morning and a four-hour afternoon session, your full time enrollment would be 8 hours a day. If you serve working parents, and your center is open from early in the morning to well into the evening, you could define full time as 9, 10, 11, or 12 hours a day.

Defining your center's total capacity is also a political statement of sorts. One definition of capacity is *licensed capacity*; you may choose to use this as your maximum potential enrollment. However, many centers are not comfortable providing care for as many children as the licensed capacity allows and set a limit below this number. In any case, you need to determine a number that represents your definition of total capacity.

Step 2: Calculating FTEs

To calculate your FTE enrollment, you first need to total the number of hours of enrolled care your center is providing on a weekly basis. (Note: While I have chosen to do the calculations in this article on a weekly basis, you can, of course, calculate FTEs on a daily, monthly, or annual basis.) Let's take the examples of ABC Kids' Place and XYZ Child Care, both of which:

- define full-time care as 10 hours per day;

- define total capacity as 60 children; and

- serve 50 children.

The weekly hours of care provided by both centers are detailed in the following table.

By adding all the enrolled hours of care in these two centers, we find that ABC Kids' Place provides a total of 1,550 hours a week and XYZ Child Care provides 1,950. To determine the FTEs for these centers, we use the following formula:

Child FTE = Total Enrolled Child Hours/Definition of Full Time

Plugging in the numbers, we find that ABC has a weekly FTE enrollment of 31:

1,550 hours/50 hours per week = 31 FTE

And XYZ has a weekly FTE enrollment of 39:

1,950 hours/50 hours per week = 39 FTE

Enrollment at ABC Kids' Place

Full time, five days a week	= 20 children	=	1,000 hours per week
Full time, three days a week	= 10 children	=	300 hours per week
Half time, three days a week	= 10 children	=	150 hours per week
Half time, two days a week	= 10 children	=	100 hours per week
	50 children		1,550 hours per week

Enrollment at XYZ Child Care

Full time, five days a week	= 30 children	=	1,500 hours per week
Full time, three days a week	= 10 children	=	300 hours per week
Half time, three days a week	= 10 children	=	150 hours per week
	50 children		1,950 hours per week

This means that even though ABC has enrolled 50 children, it is only delivering the equivalent of full-time care for 31 children. XYZ also has enrolled 50 children, and is delivering the equivalent of full-time care for 39 children. XYZ Child Care is providing 26% more weekly enrolled care than ABC Kids' Place.

Note on school-age care: If your program serves school-age children as well as preschool children, you should consider school-age children as part-time enrollees for purposes of calculating FTEs.

Add the total number of hours that school-age children are enrolled in your program to the total enrolled hours for all children before dividing by your definition of full-time care per week.

If your program serves *only* school-age children, you may want to define full-time care as the maximum length of time a school-age child can attend your program. Thus *full time* may mean 15 to 25 hours a week in your program.

This will give you a more meaningful number for internal monitoring. However, you must be aware that in comparing your FTEs to those of a garden variety of preschool programs you will not be comparing the same number of hours of enrolled care.

Step 3: Putting Your FTE to Work

FTE is the key that unlocks a wealth of evaluative data. It provides an accurate gauge for monitoring and analyzing the performance of your center. By calculating and recording FTEs every week, you can spot enrollment trends that may not be obvious by looking strictly at the number of enrolled children.

For example, let's assume that ABC Kids' Place adds ten children to its half-time, two days a week program and loses five full-time, five days a week children. This would mean that the number of children enrolled would increase to 55. However, when you calculate the new FTE, you would find that the center has actually lost ground in that its FTE is now 28.

Another way of analyzing enrollment trends is to track the center's occupancy rate on a weekly basis. Use the following formula to calculate your occupancy rate:

Occupancy Rate = FTE/Total Capacity

Running the original numbers for ABC Kids' Place, we find that it had a 52% occupancy rate:

$$31/60 = 52\%$$

After the enrollment changes, its occupancy rate dipped to 47%:

$$28/60 = 47\%$$

FTE can also provide you with a standard basis for comparing your center's enrollment with that of other centers. Commonly used points of comparison, children enrolled and licensed capacity, have little comparative value. As we have seen in the comparison between ABC and XYZ, the number of children enrolled is not an accurate indicator of hours of service provided. Likewise, licensed capacity tells you little more than the size of the building, not how much it is being used.

By using FTEs as your yardstick, you have a reliable measure of your center's performance. Your FTE should be as familiar to you as the balance in your checkbook.

*Steve Sternberg was the director of the University of Michigan Children's Centers for 11 years. This article is a result of his work on the published **Child Care Decision Support System**, a software modeling program for child care professionals.*

The True Cost of Quality in Early Care and Education Programs

by Billie Young

What's the gap between the price that families pay for child care and the "true cost" of quality care?

Is there agreement among child care providers about elements of quality and what they cost?

If providers understood their budgets better and were clear about the funding they would need to reach the "true cost" of quality, would they be empowered to advocate more successfully for increased funding?

Supposing parents understood the gap between the price they pay and the true cost — would they be willing to pay more?

These questions were the catalyst for the True Cost of Quality project launched in the spring of 2001 by the City of Seattle's Northwest Finance Circle. The mission of the Northwest Finance Circle, a community collaboration, was to improve and expand the financing of early childhood and after-school programs by creating a new system of financing and by testing out innovative financing strategies.

Over two years, we sponsored True Cost of Quality (TCOQ) budgeting classes for over 50 child care center directors and 16 family child care homes. The TCOQ project had two goals:

■ to get a better understanding of the gap between the current price of care and the cost of high quality child care, and

■ to help providers gain budget skills and become more powerful advocates for funding reform.

Believing the answers to our questions would be very different for family child care homes and child care centers, we developed TCOQ budgeting courses tailored to each group. This article will focus on our work with child care center directors.

Defining "True Cost"

Job number 1 was defining "true cost." We brought together a group of skilled child care center directors to seek agreement on the elements and definition of "true cost," and to create a spreadsheet template.

The budget masters group was followed by three TCOQ classes, reaching over 50 child care center directors, who each prepared three budgets: current, true cost of quality, and ideal. TCOQ classes were seven weeks long, from 6:30 to 9 p.m., with dinner provided and stipends for directors who completed all three budgets. We analyzed their budgets to better understand the gaps between current costs, prices charged to families, and the true cost of quality. Finally, we created and disseminated a toolkit that included a definition of TCOQ standards and Excel spreadsheets that directors could use to construct their own budgets.

Reaching Agreement on Standards

Our first hurdle was distinguishing between **current**, **true cost**, and **ideal** (or full cost) budgets. We had to help directors see the difference between the **price** they charge and the **actual cost** of care. Getting to **true cost** meant taking a giant leap — from their current costs to what it would take to provide high quality child care *every day.*

A **true cost** budget was defined as the expense required to meet national accreditation standards (NAEYC and NASA[1]) on a consistent basis. Example costs included: classrooms consistently in ratio, reduced staff turnover, wages and benefits commensurate with those paid to others working in similar jobs, adequate facilities and equipment, funds for family support, professional development, office assistance, and release time for teachers to plan. True Cost budgets included both ongoing costs to maintain the standards and one-time only costs needed to bring programs up to standard, such as facility modifications, playground construction, disability access modifications, and purchase of equipment such as computers.

In addition to accreditation, master budgeters agreed to the **Model Work Standards** created by the Center for the Child Care Workforce as the guideline for staff benefits and working conditions.

The debate over *true cost* intensified when it came time to set goals for wages. How much is "too much?" We finally agreed to use the wage scale established for staff in state college child care centers, because they were developed as part of a Washington State Higher Education Commission comparable worth study in the late 1980s. *True Cost* course instructor Julie Bisson found that in every class, students vigorously debated about what people thought was "reaching too high" for wages and benefits. They weren't sure it was feasible or even acceptable to use the state wage scale — even though it was mandated for state employees by the commission.

In the words of master budgeter Jennifer Hess, director of Blazing Trails, "It was a struggle to think beyond 'bare bones' and to get past our pride in doing so well with so little. We make *something* out of *not enough* every day. It felt like a *true cost* budget was asking for too much." We realized that we needed to ask directors to develop **ideal** budgets in order to put the **true cost** budget in perspective.

Ideal budgets exemplified those expenses required to provide the best possible program — if there were no financial constraints. Ideal budgets could include anything directors dreamed of, as long as it could be tied to standards of quality.

Examples of students' ideal costs included on-site nurses and therapists; outreach workers; coverage for teachers to do advocacy; an on-site sick room; art and music studios; grantwriters; and an emergency fund for families.

Bisson noted that students had trouble reaching for the possibilities — and even ideal budgets were modest in their dreams.

Directors Gained Valuable Lessons from True Cost Budgeting

Jodi Nishioka, TCOQ project coordinator noted that students universally rated the class as valuable. "Many of the students had never prepared a budget, much less used Excel spreadsheets. Our most successful class was located in a computer lab, and we were able to help students learn how to use Excel during class."

Even though directors know that creating and monitoring budgets is a critical part of their jobs, it's hard to find the time to spend on a task that is perceived as hard and not a lot of fun. Diana Bender, one of the TCOQ project coordinators said, "It's like taking cod liver oil. You know it's good for you, but it's not a lot of fun to think about taking it — you kind of want to put off taking it as long as you can."

Fortunately, there were enough "ah has" to keep directors moving through the process of creating not one, but three budgets. One director's big "ah ha" moment was realizing that everything she cared about in early childhood was connected to financing; another's was realizing she was the lowest paid director in the room. She took the director salary survey students compiled in class to her board and got a raise! Other directors got peer support to build in modest annual increases in parent fees instead of fighting for big ones every few years.

On average, child care centers currently spend about 77% of their revenues on personnel, 1% on foregone revenue, 6% on occupancy, 6% on administration, and 10% on other costs. Reaching the true cost of quality would require increases of about 106%, with the biggest gap in wages. Average teacher wages in 2002 were about $9.94 an hour, while the true cost standard was $17.98.

Parents Can't Afford It, So We Can't Charge It

True Cost instructors Julie Bisson and Juanita Bejaraños mediated the ever-present debate amongst directors: If we set our standards "too high" will we price ourselves out of the market? What will happen to parents who can't afford the cost of true quality? We have to charge what it costs or we'll never be able to break the link and achieve quality for children. Bisson and Bejaraños brainstormed with directors on using their new budgets to motivate parents and boards of directors or owners to reach for quality-based budgets.

The debate about charging the true cost is overlaid with the realities of classism and racism. Programs in higher income neighborhoods could get closer to the true cost of quality, while those serving low-wage families who were often families of color, felt stuck.

Jennifer Hess, director of Blazing Trails said, "On the one hand, to reach quality we must pay good people well, and on the other, we have no program if we charge more than parents can pay. So we can't pay our staff worthy wages, and parents can't pay the *already* unaffordable fees."

Like many directors, Michael Brown of the NIA Center, faces tough realities. "I got a handle on our operating costs and what we'd really need to reach quality, but at the same time it was overwhelming. Programs with high numbers of children who are subsidized by the state are at the whim of government rates. You can't raise your rates enough to reach the *True Cost* levels and you hit a wall between your reality and your dream."

Jennifer and Michael are eloquent on the subject of true cost budgeting and the reality of closing the gap between price and the true cost of quality. We will never close the gap without systemic change in the way the United States finances child care. Creating that change demands persistent advocacy from parents and child care advocates, armed with the knowledge about the true cost of quality and united in a vision of quality for children and families.

Tips for successful TCOQ projects

■ Design separate courses for centers and family child care.

■ Try to pry students out of the minimalist "box" in which child care providers dwell.

■ Make time to debate definitions of **true** and **ideal** costs, and to reach agreement on shared standards.

■ Afterschool requires two spreadsheets — for school year and summer — because revenue and staffing structures are unique.

■ Access to a computer lab helps. Plan time to teach even experienced students to use spreadsheets. We found that about a third of the students didn't know how to read a budget and had never created one.

■ Students may have math anxiety or "budget phobia." It takes a skilled instructor to demystify budgeting, help students talk about resistance and make it fun.

■ Offer dinner, stipends for directors to complete all three budgets, and one-on-one mentoring for inexperienced directors.

■ Spend time coaching directors to use budgets to advocate for change. Consider a buddy system for presentations to boards of directors and using a TCOQ invoice for parents that clearly identifies the gap between the **price** they are paying and the **true cost of quality**.

■ Plan in plenty of time for directors for networking and learning from each other.

— *Jodi Nishioka and Diana Bender, TCOQ coordinators*

Resources for True Cost Budgeting:

■ *Budgeting the True Cost of Quality Toolkit* by Julie Bisson. Available on the web at: www.ci.seattle.wa.us/ humanservices/fys/ TrueCostQualityCare/

■ *Managing Money: A Center Director's Guidebook* by Roger and Bonnie Neugebauer, published by Exchange Press, www.childcareexchange.com

■ *Model Work Standards*, *the Center for the Child Care Workforce*, www.ccw.org

End Notes

[1] NAEYC is the National Association for the Education of Young Children (www.naeyc.org); NASA is the National AfterSchool Association (www.nasa.org).

Billie Young, M.S.W., is Director of Early Learning and Family Support Programs for the City of Seattle and one of the founders of the Northwest Finance Circle. She is co-author with Jodi Nishioka of Child Care is Not Child's Play: an Economic Analysis of the Child Care Industry in Washington State (September 2004).

Five Fundamentals of Financial Health

by Mary R. Brower and Theresa M. Sull

When child care centers are in poor financial health, the quality of care for children can decline, affecting their future success as students and, eventually, as employees. Research demonstrates that by the time children are in second grade, those who attended high quality child care centers have better academic and social skills than children from low quality centers. In addition, the benefits of high quality child care affect children from all socioeconomic backgrounds, including families with both high and low income.

In our list of *Building Blocks in a Foundation of Financial Health* we name at least 40 indicators of good financial management for child care programs, but five stand out as *fundamental* to a program's financial health (see sidebar on page 44). To illustrate these fundamentals, we've used stories that are compilations of experiences in real programs, but none of the following profiles represent actual, individual, child care centers.

Enrollment is at Capacity, With a Waiting List in Place

Child care centers operate on a tight budget. High quality care is labor-intensive, and requires well-equipped, well-maintained, and spacious facilities. The income adequate to support quality, whether obtained from private-pay families or from public subsidy, is dependent on enrollment. When centers don't consider seasonal fluctuations in enrollment, and don't maintain an active waiting list, enrollment may slip below the program's budgeted capacity, resulting in loss of income.

One center with an enrollment capacity of 35 children, did not maintain a waiting list, instead relying on unsolicited phone calls. For example, the County Department of Social Services (DSS) counted on this center to accept children whenever they called the director. And the center staff were proud that they always had a slot. But when the economic climate of the state suffered, counties experienced funding shortfalls that were passed on to social service agencies.

In August, when four year olds typically move on to public kindergartens, there was no subsidy funding to pick up new families, so enrollment in the center dropped to 18. With its long history of relying on DSS for referrals, this center was unprepared to maintain enrollment with private-pay families. Within two months, the center was experiencing a cash flow crisis. The director continued to make payroll — just barely — but taxes and bills went unpaid, and soon they had growing debt.

Advertise! Keep your program in the public eye, even when enrollment is at capacity.

Tuition is Based on the Full Cost of Care

Even when programs maintain adequate enrollment, they may be selling themselves short by neglecting to base tuition rates as closely as possible on the full cost of care. For years, one popular center used a sliding fee scale to help low-income families who could not afford the full cost of care. This center also maintained about 75 percent publicly subsidized enrollment, again trying to meet the needs of low-income families in their community. In addition, the private pay rate was set below market rate, which meant that payment from the county for subsidized children was lower than the center's private pay rate.

Although this program had budgeted funds for some scholarships, administrators failed to recognize and record the cost of default scholarships created by the difference between market rates and their private pay rates, not budgeting this difference as a real expense. What's more, the center did nothing to raise additional funds to close the gap between budgeted revenue and the full cost of care. As a consequence, this lack of financial planning resulted in teachers' underwriting these scholarships with their low salaries and lack of benefits.

Because this poor financial management continued for years, this program eventually found itself with delinquent obligations — to the Internal Revenue Service for payroll taxes, to the caterers for children's meals, and to local vendors — to the tune of over $65,000. Operating in a survival mode, the director sought grant funding for new initiatives that, without adequate planning and a new board-approved budget, cost more than they brought in. Taking on new initiatives, such as Early Head Start and a school-age program, did not improve the financial health of the

center because the initiatives were based on projected enrollments that did not materialize. The new programs were not marketed adequately. And children who *were* enrolled — only 25 percent of budgeted capacity — were all subsidized by the county at market rates that did not reach full cost of care.

Compute the full cost of care for each classroom! Compare that cost to tuition charged private-pay families and to market rates paid by agencies that subsidize families.

Family Fees are Paid on Time

It's essential that programs establish a written policy regarding *what* family fees are due, *when* they are due, and what *penalties* will be imposed when fees are late. Because the staff of child care centers are often made up of dedicated individuals who want to serve children and families, they sometimes take excuses for late fees.

In one program, collecting family fees was an on-going problem. The director and staff were very sympathetic to families with cash flow problems and did not operate under the written policies that parents had signed. Neither the board of directors, nor the bookkeeper, was aware that many parent fees were delinquent. In fact, *several teachers* with children enrolled in the center were among the parents who had not paid their fees. When discovered, the uncollected fees for the prior 12 months totaled in excess of $30,000. By this time, families who owed a lot of fees, some even thousands of dollars, could not come up with the funds, and took their children out of the program, default-

ing on payment. This put the center on a financial slippery slope from which it could never recover. After 25 years of serving their community, the program went out of business.

Collect family fees on time and apply penalties when necessary!

Program's Bills and Taxes are Paid on Time

Good cash management can mean the difference between paying your bills on time and paying them late, incurring finance charges, interest, and penalties. Paying bills late can mean putting your child care program's credit worthiness in jeopardy.

Understanding the cycle of how and when cash flows into your business is the key to managing how and when it flows out. In managing the program's disbursements, administrators should prepare and use a *cash flow budget*. This financial management tool can point out cash shortages due to a drop in enrollment, a delay in food program or subsidy reimbursements, or slow collection of parent fees.

Payroll is usually at the top of any administrator's list of obligations to be paid. And the taxes withheld from payroll should be next in importance. Missing a tax payment deadline can carry heavy financial penalties. In one program, the director expected positive cash flow based on the annual budget, but by the beginning of the second quarter, the center was in trouble. The program was feeling the effects of under-enrollment, a decreased number of new referrals, and a delay in reimbursements due to a state budget shortfall.

This center did not use a cash flow budget and it failed to react to these changes in the financial climate. Soon the center found its debt increasing each month. The only way the program could continue was by not paying some bills, including taxes. But by choosing to leave taxes unpaid, the program quickly began to owe government fines and interest. Before long, the administrator was contacted by the IRS who had placed a lien on the property held by the center and garnished their subsidy reimbursement. Poor financial management by this administrator and a lack of oversight by the board of directors led this center deeper into debt and put at risk their ability to continue to deliver services.

Always pay taxes! And negotiate credit terms with vendors based on the program's cash flow. Negotiations with vendors can provide additional time to pay bills without jeopardizing the center's credit rating.

A Cash Reserve to Cover Operating Expenses

One component of every sound budget plan is including some savings for contingencies. A cash reserve can carry a child care program through the inevitable fluctuations in income. A cash reserve may also be needed for unexpected expenses, like new playground surfacing, another child-sized sink, or repair to a weather-damaged roof.

Experts recommend having enough cash to cover three months of the center's expenses. But administrators can begin to build this reserve slowly. Including in their annual budget as little as $100 savings per month can

---

> ### Five Fundamentals for a Foundation of Financial Health for Child Care Programs
>
> 1. Enrollment of program is at capacity, with a waiting list in place.
>
> 2. Tuition is based on the full cost of care.
>
> 3. Family fees are paid on time.
>
> 4. Program's bills and taxes are paid on time.
>
> 5. A cash reserve can cover operating expenses for three months.

---

start a center down the road to financial health. It's worth noting that none of the troubled centers mentioned in this article had a cash reserve.

The ribbon running through these five fundamentals is *planning*. Financial planning is not a once-a-year exercise, but an on-going effort. Administrators and boards of directors must work together to meet new circumstances and make adjustments when necessary for continued financial health of a child care program. Only by maintaining financial health can a child care center insure the high quality care that children deserve.

Suggested Reading

Brower, M. R., & Sull, T. M. (November/December 2001). "Is Your Center in Good Financial Health?: Six Symptoms and Some Prescriptions." *Exchange, 142*, 32-34.

Cherry, C., Harkness, B., & Kuzma, K. (2000). *Child Care Center Management Guide* (3rd ed.; revised by B. Harness and D. Bates). Torrance, CA: Fearon Teacher Aids.

Neugebauer, R., & Neugebauer, B. (2006). *Managing Money: A Center Director's Guidebook*. Redmond, WA: Exchange Press.

Mary R. Brower has been providing financial services to child care centers for more than 15 years. After 11 years as the accounting director with a non-profit agency that served the child care community, she is currently working with child care programs providing financial management consulting and direct financial services.

Theresa M. Sull, Ph.D, is an author, presenter, and early childhood educator. During her 25-year career, she has taught young children both with and without special needs, consulted to their families, taught college students and teachers, published articles, and coordinated public school, university, and non-profit programs.

Mary and Theresa operated a non-profit agency, Child Care Business & Education Resources. Theresa can be reached at tsull@nc.rr.com.

Surviving Tight Times

by Roger Neugebauer

> **"D**addy said tight times is why we all eat Mr. Bulk instead of cereals in little boxes."

In the children's book *Tight Times* Barbara Shook Hazen portrays a little boy learning what financial crises are all about. Anyone who works in a child care center probably needs no such introduction. As in nearly all small businesses, financial ups and downs are a seemingly inevitable part of the organizational life cycle. Leading one's center through tight times is an unwritten yet central aspect of all center owners' and directors' job descriptions.

However, if your center is now facing a financial crisis, you know that it will take more than serving Mr. Bulk instead of cereals in little boxes to pull through. It will require an array of aggressive actions as well as a large measure of tenacity. The following are some of the strategies recommended by small business experts to help for profit and non profit centers survive tight times.

Find Out What's Wrong

Neighborhood Child Care Center was broke. Director Jones, assuring everyone that this was just a temporary shortfall, whipped up enthusiasm for a major fundraising effort to pay off all the center's debts. Much to everyone's surprise, three months later Director Jones was again rounding up support for another fundraiser to help the center over another temporary crisis.

The reason that Director Jones' solutions failed is that she never grasped what the real problem was. If she had taken the time to analyze the situation, she would have found that the center's enrollment had been gradually, yet steadily, declining over the past six months. To solve the problem, Director Jones needed to focus her energy on building enrollments, not on organizing one-shot fundraisers.

For profit center operators can experience a similar blindness to reality. I once observed, for example, a center owner who kept borrowing more and more money to get by "temporary cash flow crises." Unfortunately, he ignored the fact that over the years his expenses had crept up and up, while he had not raised parent fees significantly. In other words, his cash flow problems were not the result of temporary setbacks, but rather the fact that his budget was fatally flawed.

One of my favorite Monty Python skits is the "Changemakers." In this skit a banker explains their popular new program of providing customers with $1.05 in change for $1. When asked how the bank could possibly make money on this arrangement, he replied, "Oh, that's simple — volume."

When your center is running on empty, it is critical to find out why. You need to know if you are spending $1.05 for every $1 you take in.

You can't solve a problem until you know what's causing it. You should be able to get to the heart of the matter by finding answers to the following questions:

Are your income and expenses in line?

Often, as in the case of Neighborhood Child Care Center, directors' valiant efforts to keep their centers in the black only serve to mask a fundamental problem. This underlying problem frequently has to do with the bottom line. Sometimes centers keep encountering financial crises because their costs of doing business have inflated to the point where their fees (whether they are paid by parents or a public agency) are no longer high enough to cover expenses.

When tight times arrive, one of the first things a director should do is to perform a breakeven analysis. The purpose of this analysis is to determine your breakeven point — the fee level above which your center is making money and below which it is losing money.

If your fees are set well above your current breakeven point, you know that you need to look elsewhere for the cause of your financial problems. If your fees are set close to, or below, the breakeven point, this is undoubtedly a major cause (but sometimes not the only cause) of your problems.

Large organizations will need to perform separate breakeven analyses for each distinct cost center. For example, if your organization has a separate fee scale for its infant, preschool, and after-school components, each component should be analyzed as a separate cost center. If your organization provides care in more than one location,

you may want to analyze each site as a separate cost center.

Following this approach you may find, for example, that your preschool and after-school components are operating above their breakeven points; but, your infant component is so far below breakeven that it is dragging the whole operation under. Or, you may find that you are making money in certain locations, but losing it in others.

Is your enrollment declining?

Go back and check your enrollment records for the past few months. Is your enrollment increasing, holding steady, or declining? How does it compare to the same time last year?

If your enrollment is declining, you need to know why. There are three likely culprits, each requiring different actions on your part.

■ **Customer satisfaction may be eroding**. This can happen to any center, but it is a particularly common affliction in centers that have enjoyed extended periods of success. Month after month of long waiting lists and positive press coverage can lull any staff into taking parent satisfaction for granted. In the success mode it is easy to relax and fail to attend to all the details that make a difference in the program; to fall into a rut and become less creative and spontaneous; to stop taking the time to really communicate with parents.

Call up a random selection of your parents and talk to them informally about their attitudes about the program and where it is headed.

Spend some time observing staff-child interactions in the classrooms and staff-parent interactions at drop-off and pick-up times. Talk to staff members to see if they have noticed any changes in the program.

If you find that your quality is slipping, you must act immediately to turn things around. Make restoring customer confidence your top priority. Give program improvement high profile in staff meetings, written communications, and in frequent personal tours of the classrooms. Keep in touch with parents to see if the results are being noticed.

■ **Competition may be heating up**. Five years ago you may have been the only show in town. But today, there may be a number of centers that are chipping away at your customer base.

Conduct exit interviews when parents withdraw their children from your center. Do follow-up calls to parents who made initial inquiries about your center but did not enroll their children. Find out why parents are electing to place their children in centers other than your own.

Once you determine what your competitors' advantages are, you need to decide how to respond. For example, if you are losing customers because the other centers' prices are lower, you may choose to lower your prices as well. However, in doing so you may dilute your quality to the point where you drive away your firmest supporters. An alternative might be to raise your prices and gear your program more specifically towards families that are willing and able to pay for high quality.

■ **Your market may be changing**. Demographic shifts may be occurring in your community that are impacting the demand for your services. Maybe the neighborhoods around your center are aging, so there just aren't as many preschool children as there used to be. Maybe your neighborhoods are being overrun by Yuppies who are looking for a glitzier program than you provide. Maybe household incomes aren't keeping pace with inflation, and families can't afford you anymore. Maybe your traditional funding bases, such as the United Way or the Junior League, no longer see child care as a priority.

If your market is changing dramatically, you may be fighting an uphill battle. Temporary infusions of cash may keep the program afloat for a few months, but at some point you will need to face some tough decisions. It may be necessary to change your location, to substantially reduce your operations, or maybe even to call it quits.

Are your receivables mounting?

Caring is what running a center is all about. Sometimes, however, a director can become so concerned about caring for people that she avoids pressing them when they get behind in paying their fees.

Take a look at your accounts receivable report. Has the bottom line been building up from month to month? Is your laxity in collecting overdue fees starting to undermine the financial stability of the center? If there is a problem developing in the receivables area, you need to respond quickly and firmly.

The longer you delay in responding, the more you will end up writing off as bad debts.

Monitor Cash Flow Diligently

Once you have discovered the source of the problem, you need to determine how serious it is. The best way to do this is by preparing a cash flow analysis. Such an analysis enables you to predict when your center won't have enough cash in the bank to pay its bills and how big the deficit will be.

Routinely, cash flow projections should be made on a monthly basis. However, when tight times arrive, it is advisable to monitor cash flowing in and out of your center on a weekly basis. This will enable you to pinpoint most accurately the weeks where money will be the tightest as well as those weeks where you may have a little breathing room. This information is extremely helpful because it gives you a clear picture of the extent of the problem.

As you proceed through a rocky period, you will find that the weekly cash flow projections are also an invaluable tool for working on solutions. By keeping the projections up-to-date, you can closely monitor your progress, or lack thereof, in dealing with the problem. You can test out various proposed solutions to see their impact. For example, you could hypothesize, "What if we raised fees in the infant room by $2 per week?," plug the new income projections into your cash flow, and see how that impacts the bottom line week by week.

Trim the Fat

When your financial ink turns red, your first thought is often, "Where can we cut back?" This is, in theory, the reasonable thing to do. But, in practice, it may not do the trick. After you exempt those expenditures you are contractually bound to, those you can't cut without a corresponding reduction in income, and those that would detract noticeably from program quality or staff morale, you often are left with little fat to trim.

Nonetheless, in tight times you do need to analyze the savings potential in each line item in the budget to see if there are some real opportunities to absorb some of the red ink. The most effective way to do this is to list the monthly allocation for each line item and then to calculate the percent each line item would have to be cut in order to save $100 (divide 100 by the amount of each line item). A quick review of the resulting figures will identify those areas where significant cuts can be made without a dramatic negative impact on the program.

Slow Outflow of Cash

If cutting costs doesn't seem to be the answer, deferring costs is another approach that can help an ailing cash flow. If planned major expenditures (such as resurfacing the playground) can be delayed for weeks or months, this can often help more than making painful budget cuts.

At the outset of a crunch period, you should also consider meeting with your major creditors to see if they would be willing to extend your credit. If you owe a sizable amount to a bank, for example, you should explain your financial dilemma and request a restructuring of the note. While bankers will grunt and groan and make all sorts of *our-hands-are-tied* statements, basically they will do what they have to do to get their money back. If they drive you out of business by holding you to the original payment schedule, they stand to be the losers. (See the box "How to Keep the Wolves from the Door" for more thoughts on how to deal with people trying to collect money from you.)

Speed the Inflow of Cash

Looking now at the other end of the cash flow equation, red ink can also be combated by speeding up the rate at which money owed to you is collected. There are a number of steps you can take in this regard:

■ **Invoice promptly.** You can't expect people to pay you on time if you are tardy in billing them.

■ **Reward early payers.** Announce a discount for paying within the first few days of a billing cycle, or an even larger discount for paying in advance.

■ **Punish late payers.** Announce penalties (in line with state regulations on interest charges) for late payments, and enforce them religiously.

■ **Stay on top of overdue fees.** Don't let late payers get very far behind without letting them know you are on their case. Directors have found that if families get more than three months behind in their payments they are much more likely to drop-out than to pay up. By getting in touch with families falling behind early and working out short term, spread out,

repayment plans, you are much more likely both to retain them as your customers and to eventually receive payment in full.

■ **Expedite other income.** If you have been awarded a grant by a local business or United Way, see if you can receive the money early, or secure a temporary loan from a bank in anticipation of this income. See if you can get the state to pay you monies they owe you early or on time (we had to throw this one in for laughs). If you have an annual fundraiser, check into scheduling it earlier this year.

Explore New Income Sources

Pumping new currency into your center's money veins can also be invigorating. When a cash flow crisis is on the horizon, you could call a meeting of key people within your organization who have a stake in its success, as well as resourceful people from outside who care about your organization. Use this as an occasion to brainstorm all kinds of ways your center could generate new money. The possibilities come in all shapes and sizes:

■ **Raising fees** — for everyone, for new enrollees only, or for certain cost centers.

■ **Boosting enrollment** — turning around declining enrollments or over-enrolling to maintain nearly full capacity.

■ **Expanding the program** — adding an after-school component, adding two more children to each current classroom, opening a new center.

■ **One-shot activities** — dinners, fairs, house tours, raffles, auctions, cookbook sales, and jog-a-thons.

■ **One-shot appeals** — annual membership drives, jog-a-thons, direct mail solicitation campaigns, corporate appeals, one-on-one appeals.

■ **Annual events** — taking a one-shot activity or appeal and repeating it every year.

■ **Ongoing activities** — parenting seminars, convention child care, weekend activity classes, computer classes, family kitchens, thrift shops.

■ **Grants-in-aid** — foundation grants, United Way funding, public funding, local grants.

■ **Loans** — from banks, the SBA, local business people, Aunt Emma.

■ **Investments** — forming a partnership, securing outside investors, selling shares.

Once you have a long list of possibilities, evaluate each one in terms of the following criteria:

■ **How soon will it generate income?** If you are going to be $3,000 in the red in three weeks, and the idea under review won't kick in for two months, keep looking.

■ **Is it cost effective?** Estimate how much income the idea would generate, how much it would cost to carry it out, and divide the balance by the number of person-hours required to carry it out. This computation will tell you how much profit you will generate for every hour of effort. Successful fundraisers generate anywhere from

$25 to $200 per hour. If a project will produce less than $10 per hour of effort, think twice before giving the go-ahead.

■ **Do we possess appropriate resources?** In their popular book, *In Search of Excellence*, Thomas J. Peters and Robert H. Waterman, Jr. observe that one of the traits of successful businesses is that they stick to their knitting, they know what they are good at and don't go far afield in developing new products or services. In evaluating new income generating thrusts for a child care center, you need to question whether this is an activity that builds on your current strengths (where you have people — paid or volunteer — with appropriate skills, space, and materials that are appropriate, and an established reputation in the area) or one which would require your organization to start from scratch.

■ **What is the likelihood of success?** During a financial crisis, the time of the director and other key center people needs to be focused exclusively on high impact activities. Time wasted on nonproductive or marginally productive activities could spell the difference between surviving and failing. Putting together a prospectus to attract investors can take weeks and weeks of top management time, as can putting together a grant proposal for a foundation. Yet in both cases the likelihood of success is extremely low. Before committing that kind of time to an activity, you need to do some preliminary research which assures you that you are not diverting much needed energy into a dead end project.

■ **What are the side-effects of the idea?** If we raise our fees, will we lose half our customers? If we start another center, will we have to pull too many of our best teachers away from our existing center? If we attract an investor, will we have to turn over too much control to a third party? If we get a United Way grant, will we be bogged down in their red tape? If we get a loan from Aunt Emma, will we feel guilty until we pay her back?

After weighing all these issues, you should be able to identify several hot ticket income generators. You can now throw these into the hopper with all your other potential cash flow solutions — ideas for speeding up income, deferring expenses, and cutting expenses. From among all of these possibilities you will need to construct a combination of actions that will pull you out of debt.

Hang In There

Tight times can cause more than a financial strain. Eventually they cause excruciating emotional and physical strain for the leaders of the organization.

Al Masini has observed that nothing raises the energy reservoir like success and nothing depletes it like failure. Working hard on a venture that is taking off is exhilarating, but slaving away on a venture mired in red ink is enervating.

Worrying about money for weeks on end is mentally and socially taxing. After awhile you eat, sleep, and drink cash flow. All you can think or talk about is whether you can meet the payroll on Friday. You end up being a not very fun person to be around.

Having creditors insult you, swear at you, and threaten you gets to be a drag. Friendships turn sour as you fall behind on financial obligations. As Orson Welles remarked, "When you're down and out, something always turns up — and it's usually the noses of your friends."

What often determines whether an organization survives a financial crisis is the tenacity of the persons at the top — their ability to endure all the strain and work effectively toward a solution. Actress Helen Hayes once commented that talent and ability are not enough: "Nothing is any good without endurance."

Not only must the leaders of the center hang in there, but they also must maintain a positive public attitude. Although your inner self may be crying out for pity, you can't afford to cry on the shoulders of your customers or your staff. If parents get the message that your center is on the rocks, they will start looking for a more stable child care arrangement. Staff, likewise, may start abandoning a ship that they believe is sinking. This is not to say you should deceive parents and staff into thinking everything is rosy. If you don't say anything, rumors of all sorts will start flying as soon as the first signs of red ink appear. When you are about to experience an extended dry spell you should inform staff and parents in a businesslike manner that cash flow difficulties will call for some careful budgeting over the coming weeks. But assure them that the long term projections are positive, so that any inconvenience will be temporary.

Then, when good times arrive, throw a party.

Don't Let It Happen Again

After you mount a prodigious effort and pull through a financial crisis, it is easy to succumb to traumatic amnesia — you forget about how bad things were. You are so relieved to have survived that you let your guard down and relax too long. And before you know it, the grocer is calling to find out when he can expect payment on his overdue invoice. To avoid this cycle:

■ Do keep your finger on the financial pulse of the organization.

■ Don't let up on closely monitoring the cash flow.

■ Do periodically check your break-even points to make sure you are not involuntarily becoming a charitable institution.

■ Do develop an annual budget and monitor your performance monthly.

■ Don't confuse growth with profits. Remember, just because your organization is getting bigger, it is not necessarily doing better on the bottom line.

■ Don't live it up too soon. After your checkbook shows a positive balance, don't rush out and make all the purchases you put off.

■ Do work to reestablish a solid credit rating. Pay your bills promptly. Supply your banker and funders with monthly balance sheets and income statements. Apply for an adequate line of credit after an

How to Keep the Wolves From the Door

How do you keep your creditors satisfied when times are tight? Here are some pointers:

■ **Goodwill is money in the bank**. Anyone with a thick enough skin can stave off creditors indefinitely. However, while a totally hard-nosed approach may help you survive a crisis, what price will you pay? If you alienate everyone you buy services and supplies from during tight times, they may refuse to do business with you when the good times arrive. Even when the creditors are pressing hard, you should strive to salvage some degree of goodwill by treating them in a respectful, business-like manner.

■ **Creditors don't like surprises**. When you know you are going to have a problem meeting a financial obligation, call the creditor in advance to let him know you've got a problem. This demonstrates that you take your obligations seriously and gives him time to adjust his cash flow projections. A creditor will be much less conciliatory if he has to call you after your account becomes delinquent.

■ **Honesty is still the best policy**. Popular myth has it that you keep creditors at bay through a series of deceptions — "Haven't we already paid that? I'll have to check our records." Such transparent ruses tend to aggravate creditors and motivate them to become more aggressive in their actions against you. Honestly explain that your center is experiencing a severe, yet temporary, cash flow problem and that you will pay what you owe as quickly as you can.

■ **Promise only what you can deliver**. Creditors will want you to commit to a repayment schedule. Unless you are really certain about improving prospects in the near future, avoid making specific commitments. If you fail to meet a new due date, you are going to double a creditor's frustration.

■ **Less is more**. Try to make small partial payments periodically to all creditors, rather than paying in full the ones that scream the loudest. Even a trickle of cash will let creditors know your center is still in business and that you are serious about paying your bills.

■ **Don't blame the victim**. Tight times can be incredibly trying, so when a creditor calls and harasses you for his money, it is very easy to become angry and vent all your frustrations. You must keep in mind, however, that the reason he is pressing you is that he provided something to you in good faith and now you have violated the agreement. He has every right to press you. If you find yourself becoming upset by what a creditor is saying when he calls, don't lash out emotionally. Tell him you will call back with an answer, and then wait until you have cooled off and developed a logical response.

extended period of solid financial performance. If you are a non profit, you will likewise find it easier to ask for support from funders when you are operating in the black. Charitable donors are much more inclined to invest in vision and vitality than they are to cover debt and dysfunction.

- Do stay close to your customers. Don't get so preoccupied with the numbers that you forget who is paying the bills. Stay tuned to their concerns, their needs, their changing means.

- And, last but not least, don't make the same mistake twice. As Ted S. Frost suggests, "If you're going to get yourself into financial trouble again, at least have enough class to think up some different way of doing it."

Note: An earlier version of this article appeared in the January 1987 issue of Exchange and has been updated by the author for this issue.

Losing Money/ Making Money

by Lynne Meservey

Where have all the dollars gone? You were so sure that the tuition rate you established was competitive, yet fair. You've controlled your expenses. So why isn't your center earning what you expected? It may be that two important factors have not been considered. The first factor is discounting and the second is ancillary programs.

Discounting

Most child care programs offer discounts for employee children, multi-child families, vacations, and/or absenteeism. Often these discounts are deducted from tuition fees prior to recording income. When this bookkeeping procedure is used, the center's financial statements will not contain important information concerning the actual cost of discounting. A $65 tuition fee may result in $57 of actual income after discounting. It's best to have your profit and loss statement show the full tuition amount and to account for each of the discount categories. Ancillary income programs can help recover losses due to discounting.

Ancillary Income

Centers that lose $8 to $10 of income to discounting can recover the loss *and actually improve on it* by offering well planned ancillary programs. Ancillary income is the money centers generate from sources other than normal tuition fees. These programs add diversity and enrichment to educational programming. The added value of ancillary activities can also keep families from withdrawing prematurely.

The working parent prefers programs that provide activities for their children that they have difficulty providing. There aren't many extra hours in a working mom's schedule to take children to dance classes, get haircuts, or to visit the circus when it is in town. Because parents want the best for children, dance, gymnastics, music appreciation, or other enrichment lessons are among the most popular of these programs. Children are also looking for fun and interesting things to do. School-age children respond especially well. Some projects can also be promoted to the public. These may be fundraisers for a charitable organization or promotions that help sell services.

There are four categories for child care ancillary programs — service, enrichment, product sales, and fundraisers. A well-balanced program will appeal to many family needs.

Service programs. Ask yourself, "What services could reduce the demands on busy working parents?" The most effective services will be those that save parents time and money. A survey of parents often produces a list of needs. The programs you choose should have value for a relatively large group of parents. The less staff time to oversee and implement the service, the better. Continually monitor and evaluate the quality and appropriateness of the service, and be sure that it does not detract from normal operations. Typical service programs include: breakfast, parent coffees, developmental testing, vision/hearing/speech assessments, occasional Saturday or evening care, birthday parties, tutoring, or mailing services.

Enrichment programs. Directors are most familiar with ancillary programs like dance, art, music, sports, field trips, movies, speakers, and computer lessons. They appeal to a relatively large number of children and have definite value. When consistent with a center's educational philosophy, they successfully relate to other learning in the center. There should be no pressure on families to participate and, whenever possible, these activities should occur out of view of children who are not part of the enrichment activity.

Product sales. Books, tote bags, t-shirts, and children's photographs are typical products cen-ters sell to parents. Other creative items like toys, pre-made Easter baskets, or letters from Santa may be popular. It's wise to limit product sales in your ancillary program planning. The greatest risk is having a surplus inventory of an item that you can't unload on anyone! On a more positive note, a terrific, creative item can be a very effective money maker. Choose care-fully and wisely and you'll be a winner. Volume purchasing will reduce the cost per item but watch out for overstocking. Inventory each piece and store carefully.

Fundraising. Fundraisers can be a great way to increase income. They require more pre-planning, organization, and lead time, but the returns can be good. Depending on the activity, manpower demands can affect the success of the project. Consider the types of money raising activities that are popular in your community and try to come up with a fresh approach. Be cautious. If a particular organization is already well known for having a big annual bazaar or carnival, you may be wise to develop a completely different idea. People expect to be entertained and to spend money — give them as many opportunities as possible to do both.

Choose dates carefully to be sure they don't compete for participants with another activity. A weekend following a holiday is often a good time. Always plan on an alternate rain date for outdoor functions, or have an indoor facility available. Involve as many others as you can; not only will the extra hands be helpful, but the more people you have, the more the word will be spread about the venture.

Projected Earnings

What kind of return can you realize? Let's face it, some projects are more fun to do and may be less work. Before you choose any program, consider:

- How much of your time will the project take?

- How much staff time will it take?

- What effect will the project have on the day-to-day operation of your center?

- How interested will the participants be in the project?

- What kind of return will you expect for the time and money invested?

- What are the risks involved?

- Can the parent afford the expense?

A mark up of at least 25% should be expected from any ancillary activity, but don't let that limit you in negotiating or setting prices. Supply and demand will guide you in determining the price and the program offered. When considering a project, carefully estimate the time it will take. Is it better to have several smaller, easier projects or one or two large ones? What effect will it have on the operation of the center, teachers, and children if special projects are continually changing routines, room arrangements, and employee workload?

Often a simple, easy-to-administer program produces a better return than one that is more complicated. For example, breakfast programs are fairly easy to administer and provide regular additional income while swimming or dance programs typically offer a much smaller return.

Planning is the Key

Good ancillary programs require good planning. Compare programs and providers before you choose the ones you will use. Ask for written bids and check references carefully. Try to see instructors in action.

Give careful consideration to staffing needs beforehand. Staff must "buy-in" before they can be expected to support your plans and be enthusiastic about them. Involving your staff in the selection process will increase receptivity.

Balance the program carefully. Avoid scheduling two programs at the same time if they are likely to appeal to a wide market. Consider other events, activities, or timing that might affect participation. Perhaps holidays, vacation days, or public school schedules will have an impact on the program.Summertime is often a good time to plan a program for the up-coming school year. Outline the pro-gram and make contact with potential providers. Ask others for referrals. Require providers to be bonded and to produce insurance certificates.

Promotion

Use every resource at your disposal to promote all of your ancillary projects.

Parents and children are a captive audience, so get their attention and support early to build enthusiasm. Several reminders will encourage action — at least three reminders seem to be the key. Use center newsletters, separate invitations, posters, banners, ancillary brochures, and bulletin boards to promote the program inter-nally. Pre-selling tickets or requiring deposits encourages commitment and assures participation. To promote your projects to the general public, send notices to local papers for placement in community bulletin boards. Contests may draw interest prior to the event, as will drawings for attractive prizes.

Repeat business is important. Be sure everything is prepared ahead of time and is organized. Nothing hurts a program more than confusion. It's always wise to ask participants and workers to evaluate each project so that improvements can be made.

And, lastly, have fun. Ancillary projects add variety to daily routines and play a major role in successful child care operations.

Lynne Meservey is vice president of operations for CorporateFamily Solutions in Nashville, Tennessee.

Financial Policies

*"A smart director acts quickly to solve a problem,
an effective director anticipates and avoids problems
by establishing policies and procedures
to deal with the myriad situations
that arise along the way."*

Is Your Salary Schedule Up to Speed?

by Roger Neugebauer

1.

What are we paying for?

Sometimes it's important to step back and ask some really basic questions: *Why are we paying people? What are we expecting to get in return?*

In child care centers, when you hire someone, you could be . . .

- paying for time;
- paying for skills; or
- paying for results.

You need to decide which of these factors you are paying for, because your choice dramatically impacts how you pay people.

If you are paying for time, your assumption is that you are paying for a warm body to fulfill ratio requirements over a period of time. In order to maintain adequate coverage, you would simply need to pay enough to attract and retain staff who meet minimum legal requirements.

If you are paying for skills, your assumption is that people knowl- edgeable and practiced in early childhood education will perform significantly better than persons without training and experience. Therefore, you would tailor your salary schedule to attract well prepared individuals and to reward their continuing acquisition of knowledge and skills.

If you are paying for results, your assumption is that all that really matters is who performs well on the job. You would design your salary schedule to reward those who are effective performers. It is my observation that large numbers of centers behave as if they are simply paying for time. By not attaching any monetary value to skills or performance, these centers get what they pay for — mediocre to poor performance.

On the other hand, the overwhelming majority of salary schedules I reviewed for these articles reflect a strong bias toward paying for knowledge and skills. There is considerable research support for this bias.

The landmark 1976 National Day Care Study concluded that ". . . caregivers with education/training relevant to young children deliver better care with somewhat supe-rior developmental effects for children (Ruopp)." More current research, the 1988 National Child Care Staffing Study, found that teachers with either a bachelor's degree or specialized training in early childhood education at the college level exhibited higher quality care-giving (Whitebook).

Less than 5% of the salary schedules reviewed gave significant weight to on-the-job performance in setting salary levels. Many centers require that employees receive a satisfactory rating before receiving a step increase, but very few awarded significant upgrades for above average performance.

2.

Is our pay equitable?

The premise behind the equity issue is that people should receive equal pay for equal work. There are several ways to evaluate equality of pay — you can compare the pay of a teacher in your center with the pay of people doing comparable work in other professions, teachers in other centers, or other teachers within your own center.

Clearly the pay of child care teachers compares poorly to the pay of kindergarten teachers, for example. Many centers are struggling creatively to take small steps toward narrowing this gap. Only a concerted effort by a broad spectrum of players in the child care arena will make a serious impact.

Equity from center to center is another matter altogether. A center committed to providing quality services certainly wants to attract and retain the best teachers available. One way to do this is to offer salaries above the community average. At least once every two years, you should do a market survey on teacher salaries in your community to make sure you are not falling behind. In addition, you should keep an eye on salaries offered by new centers when they open.

It is also important to be alert to equity issues within your own center. Sometimes when you have a mix of new and long-term teachers, inequities will develop. You may pay two teachers performing the same job with the same level of performance at significantly different levels. This can potentially be discouraging to the lower paid teacher.

3.

Should we offer annual increases?

Centers grant salary increases based on the following factors:

- responsibility;
- longevity;
- cost of living; and
- performance.

It is possible that there still exist a few staff cooperatives where all staff members are paid the same regardless of the job they perform. With these possible exceptions, all centers today offer increased salaries as staff assume new jobs with increasing responsibility within the center.

Most centers also make some provision for granting annual increases based on longevity and/or cost of living. While such increases are viewed as important and expected, the way in which they are administered does raise some interesting questions and consequences.

Longevity salary increases are based on the assumption that the longer persons work in a job, the better they will perform. While this may be true in some professions, there is little evidence to support it in child care. The National Day Care Study found little relationship between years of child care experience and caregiver or child behaviors (Ruopp). The National Child Care Staffing Study found "child care experience is a poor predictor of teacher behavior toward children" (Whitebook).

From these findings we draw several conclusions. If we want teachers' performance to improve, we can't abandon them in their classrooms. We need to provide continuous feedback, regular training, and ready support to help them improve. Using longevity as a reason for raising salaries without any reference to improved performance does not appear to be justified.

Cost of living adjustments are made to compensate for the impact of inflation. If an employee's salary stays the same but the cost of living increases, her salary has in effect decreased.

Not all employees are equally impacted by inflation. Someone earning $30,000 per year is not nearly as impacted by a 5% increase in the cost of bread as someone earning $10,000. However, since the average child care teacher earns just below the poverty level (Whitebook), there is little question that annual adjustments are of vital importance for most employees in this profession.

"Automatic increases assure staff that their value is noted and will be acknowledged in predictable increments at predictable times. In a historically underpaid field such as child care, automatic increases validate the necessity to upgrade salaries for all who work in the field."
— **Working for Quality Child Care**

For a center to guarantee annual cost of living adjustments could be a hollow promise. Every salary increase must be paid for with a commensurate rise in income. If your center gives an across the board cost of living increase of 5% and your income declines 5%, you could be courting disaster. Many centers inject this reality into their personnel policies with statements such as "Every effort will be made to provide annual cost of living raises subject to the availability of funds."

Such cautious promises offer scant assurance to staff members living on the edge of poverty. If the center can't give an annual increase, they will have to wait 12 months for a much needed raise. Certainly being sincere about exploring every avenue to increase salaries is essential. Another small way t oease anxiety is to review financial projections quarterly or semi-annually with the idea of offering smaller, more frequent adjustments. (Of course, then you will have to figure out a way to alleviate the stress on your bookkeeper.)

Determining the amount of an annual cost of living adjustment is not an exact science. Many companies peg their increases to the Consumer Price Index (CPI). The CPI is calculated by the price of goods and services purchased by a family of four with an annual income of $12,000. This index, therefore, has little relevance for families of different sizes or in higher income brackets. But because the majority of child care teachers do earn under $12,000, the CPI is a fairly reliable measure for centers to use as a benchmark.

4.

Should we offer merit raises?

There is much to be said for pay-ing for performance instead of longevity. You want staff who work hard and continue to improve to believe that their contributions are valued. You can show appreciation by frequently observing and acknowledging their good deeds, by providing all the materials and moral support they need, and by publicly praising their performance. However, it is hard to give a clearer, more welcome signal than cash.

Clearly people don't gravitate to child care for its financial benefits. Over and over again, teacher surveys have shown that the true rewards of teaching relate to making a difference in the lives of children. However, at some

• **Merit raises should not be given in place of cost of living increases, but in addition to them.** If raises are only given to exceptional performers, you run the risk of alienating the majority of your teachers who may be performing adequately but not spectacularly. Some centers employ systems whereby teachers with unsatisfactory performance are not given raises, those with satisfactory performance are given small raises, and those with superior performance are given larger raises.

• **Small merit raises may be more harmful than no raises at all.** Giving an employee a token raise for meritorious performance is more likely to induce cynicism than pride. If you are going to award merit raises, they must be perceived as worthy of the effort.

• **A merit raise system is only as effective as the evaluation system upon which it is based.** If you are

---

"Few companies can afford the kind of financial incentive that makes any real difference in the lives of their employees. Most financial rewards are quickly adjusted to. Although management seldom hears, workers make fun of minor increases, cynically tallying the depreciating effect of inflation and taxes."
— David Viscott, MD

---

point, even the most committed teacher will become discouraged if year after year they do a great job for the center but are paid no more than anyone else, or less than teachers in other centers.

If your center is considering granting merit raises, here are some points to consider:

going to base pay on performance, you need to be sure you are measuring performance objectively and fairly. You need to have in place an evaluation instrument that all staff view as valid. (Having their input in its development will go a long way toward establishing its validity.) Those performing the evaluations must be skilled at observing and giving feed-back.

• Annual evaluations for salary determination should not be viewed as a substitute for ongoing employee appraisals. If an employee is to use supervisory feedback to improve her performance, this feedback needs to be frequent, nonjudgmental, and non-threatening. An annual salary evalua-tion goes against all of these guide-lines. Even with a merit raise evalua-tion system in place, you need to regularly engage in giving specific, objective feedback to employees to give them the information they need to improve their own performance.

As a center director, you need to invest your limited resources wisely in order to maintain a stable, high quality organization. We recommend, wherever possible, giving a combina-tion of cost of living and merit raises. You need to bring out the best in your staff by rewarding their great efforts as individuals as well as by doing everything in your power to raise the salaries of all teachers.

References and Resources

Ruopp, Richard et al. *Children at the Center*. Cambridge, MA: Abt Associates, 1979.

Sibson, Robert E. Compensation (*Fifth Edition*). New York: AMACOM, 1990. Townsend, Robert. *Further Up the Organization*. New York: Alfred A. Knopf, 1984.

Viscott, David, MD. *Taking Care of Business*. New York: William Morrow and Company, Inc., 1985.

Whitebook, Marcy. *Who Cares? Child Care Teachers and the Quality of Care in America*. Oakland, CA: Child Care Employee Project, 1989.

Working for Quality Child Care. National Center for the Early Childhood Work Force, 6536 Telegraph Avenue, Suite A-201, Oakland, CA 94609.

Guidelines for Fine Tuning Your Salary Schedule

by Roger Neugebauer

I n one of my first forays into the child care world, some 20 years ago, I applied, unsuccessfully, for a job at a staff cooperative. All employees at New Morning Children's Center were paid the same hourly wage and shared equally in responsibilities and decision making. The team spirit of the place is what attracted me to it.

Even in my brief encounter with the center, it was clear that this team spirit was developing a few chinks. The founders of the center shared a strong commitment to equality of pay and power. However, state licensers looked upon the staff structure with horror and were aggressively fighting it. In addition, as new staff members came on board whose ideologies and priorities did not match the founders, internal enthusiasm for equal pay declined.

Eventually, New Morning gave in to the pressures of capitalism and began paying the cook, the administrative coordinators, and the teachers differing amounts. Eventually, too, it changed its name to something like Preschool Prep Learning Center. Eventually, too, it went out of business.

The moral of this story is never turn down a future publisher who can give you bad press. It also demonstrates that the administration of salaries is not a simple mechanical procedure. Rather, it is direct expression of the values of the organization. How differences in pay are distributed, and the size of these differences, intentionally or unintentionally, communicate what the organization values.

Pay differentials are typically spelled out in a center's salary schedule. In research for this article, we analyzed over 100 salary schedules submitted by Exchange Panel of 200 members. In these schedules, four factors were used to measure the monetary value of employees: responsibility, training, experience, and performance. In this article, I will share with you how centers weigh these factors in developing their salary schedules.

Pay for Responsibility

None of the centers whose schedules were reviewed were staff cooperatives — all centers paid differing amounts for persons carrying out different responsibilities. Pay differences by position are in fact quite dramatic, as can be seen in Table A. A lead teacher typically earns 50% more than a teacher aide, and directors earn 50% more than a lead teacher.

The 1988 National Child Care Staffing Study (Whitebook) also found significant differences in the average hourly wages of center employees:

Director	=	$9.85
Teacher/Director	=	6.38
Teacher	=	5.58
Assistant Teacher	=	4.86
Teacher Aide	=	4.48

In the staffing study results, the pay differentials among teachers is not as dramatic and the differential between teachers and directors is more dramatic than in the *Exchange* survey. The differences may be accounted for by the samples — the staffing study examined 227 randomly selected centers in five cities, and *Exchange* examined 100+ hand-picked centers from throughout the country. The five year time difference may also be a key factor. During these five years, the supply of qualified teachers has decreased, causing an escalation in the wages offered to attract and retain experienced teachers.

In any event, we are not recommending that your center adapt either of these pay patterns. We are simply reporting what is standard practice in the early childhood arena.

What we are strongly recommending is that you take a close look at your own pay patterns. Do the differences in your pay for different positions truly reflect the value you place on these positions? The way you invest your resources in personnel should support your understanding about what it takes to deliver quality child care.

In the salary schedules we reviewed, for example, it was clear that a growing number of centers have identified the lead teacher as a key to quality. In

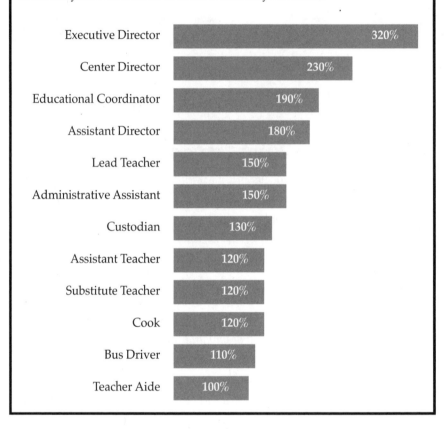

Table A
Early Childhood Salary Relationships

This chart demonstrates the relationship of average salaries for different positions in early childhood centers, using Teacher Aide salaries as the base. For example, the average Lead Teacher salary is 150% of the average Teacher Aide salary. Based on a review of over 200 salary schedules.

Position	Percent
Executive Director	320%
Center Director	230%
Educational Coordinator	190%
Assistant Director	180%
Lead Teacher	150%
Administrative Assistant	150%
Custodian	130%
Assistant Teacher	120%
Substitute Teacher	120%
Cook	120%
Bus Driver	110%
Teacher Aide	100%

these centers, lead teachers are paid anywhere from 65% to 85% more than teacher aides.

Pay for Training

Centers clearly place a value on training. The more training a teacher has, the more she is likely to be paid. However, how training is factored into salary schedules varies considerably. About one in four centers build training into job requirements, but offers no financial incentives. For example, a center might require that a teacher aide have a high school diploma, an assistant teacher have at least two years of college, and a lead teacher have a college degree. In these centers, an assistant teacher with a college degree would earn no more than one with two years of college, and a candidate with only a high school degree would not be considered for an assistant teacher position.

The majority of centers, however, recognize the value of training in establishing job requirements as well as in setting salaries within job categories. In these centers, an assistant teacher with a college degree would earn more than an assistant teacher with two years of college. As can be seen in Table B, typically a teacher with an AA degree will earn 15% more, and one with a BA degree 25% more, than a teacher with only a high school degree. A master's degree only adds another 5% to one's pay.

Some centers place additional value on education that is specifically related to early childhood education. In these centers, for example, a teacher with an AA degree in early childhood education is valued just as highly as a teacher with a bachelor's degree in an unrelated field (Table B).

While the 1976 National Day Care Study (Ruopp) found training relevant to young children was a better predictor of teacher performance than years of education overall, the 1988 National Child Care Staffing Study (Whitebook) yielded more mixed results. In the latter study, it was found that teachers with either a bachelor's degree *or* specialized training at the college level performed equally well in the classroom. In addition, it found that "specialized training at the post-secondary level is more effective in preparing good teachers than is specialized training at the high school or vocational education level."

In the days when the supply of teaching candidates seemed inexhaustible, there wasn't great pressure on centers to pay more to hire teachers with college training. Directors would rationalize their fiscal conservatism by observing that in their experience college trained teachers often weren't well prepared for the real world of child care.

Research findings now make it clear that teachers with college degrees or college level ECE training will typically do a better job. With the returning shortage of qualified teachers, it would be a mistake for centers not to place high value on college education in establishing or refining their salary schedules.

Pay for Experience

Three out of every four center salary schedules we reviewed offered some form of annual pay increases. Increases ranged from 1.5% to 5% annually, with the average falling in the 3% range. These increases tend to be described more as cost of living adjustments than as rewards for improved performance. As was observed in the first article in this series, experience tends to be a poor predictor of teacher performance (*Exchange*, March 1994). Teachers with more years on the job are not necessarily better performers than less experienced teachers. Therefore, centers are probably exercising good judgment in not investing heavily in longevity.

Cost of living increases, on the other hand, are very important to teachers. With salaries as low as they are, teachers have little cushion against the impact of inflation. Slightly less than half of the salary schedules we reviewed stated that there were no automatic cost of living increases. When funds permitted, these centers typically give across the board increases in the range of 2% to 4% to all employees.

Most of the other salary schedules we reviewed treated annual increases

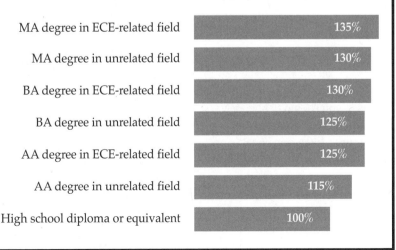

Table B
Typical Educational Differentials

Child care centers typically pay more to employees with higher levels of educational attainment. Using the average pay for high school graduates as the base (100%), the following are the average increases provided for education:

Education	Differential
MA degree in ECE-related field	135%
MA degree in unrelated field	130%
BA degree in ECE-related field	130%
BA degree in unrelated field	125%
AA degree in ECE-related field	125%
AA degree in unrelated field	115%
High school diploma or equivalent	100%

regressively, i.e. the higher your salary the lower your annual increase. In some cases, this is done intentionally. Recognizing how low their entry level salaries are, some centers deliberately gave employees at the bottom third of the salary schedule a higher percentage annual increase than employees at the top third.

In many centers, the regressive nature of their salary schedules appeared to be unintentional. In some, annual increases varied unpredictably from year to year and from position to position. In others, where the center elected to increase all employees' hourly wages by a flat amount every year (typically 10¢ or 15¢), the result is the higher your hourly wage, the lower the percentage your increase will be.

From reviewing salary schedules, we conclude that all centers need to take a close look at their provisions regarding annual increases. First, consider whether you want to lock your center into automatic annual increases for all employees. Especially for your low income employees, automatic increases offer some degree of security. However, if your center is struggling to achieve financial stability, annual increases may not always be affordable.

Second, in granting cost of living increases, you should deliberately decide what your priorities are. Do you want to give an equal percentage increase to all employees, or do you want to give a higher increase to low income employees, or do you want to invest the greatest share of the increases in your top employees?

Pay for Performance

In the first article, we made a case for paying for performance rather than longevity. We suggested granting raises based on how well teachers perform, not on how long they have been at the center.

While a strong case can be made for merit raises, in fact, the concept is not a popular one in this field. Less than one in 15 of the salary schedules we reviewed offer any form of merit pay. Tying pay to performance is often viewed as running counter to the nurturing team spirit we promote in our centers. This case was strongly put by one of our Panel of 200 members (see "No to Merit Pay" box). In addition, many directors are reluctant to attach dollars to performance since measures of performance are so subjective in this field.

Those few centers that do tie pay to performance do so in a variety of ways. The most common approach is a two to four category rating system. One center rates each employee annually as either *unsatisfactory*, *satisfactory*, or *highly satisfactory*. Employees rated unsatisfactory are given no annual increase and are scheduled for close monitoring. Those rated satisfactory are granted a 3% increase, and those rated highly satisfactory earn a 6% raise.

Several of the more ambitious plans we reviewed calibrated their reward systems more finely. For example, employees might be awarded points for attendance, training attended, teaching skills, staff relations skills, and parent relations skills. Employees' annual increases would then be calculated based upon how many points they earned — if they earned 50% of all possible points, they would earn 50% of the maximum possible raise.

One after-school program offered a unique approach. They start all teachers at a low entry level wage. Then, over the course of two years, they rapidly move up those teachers who demonstrate good skills into teaching positions paid above the going rate.

Putting Together the Pieces

Now the hard part. Once you've decided what your center intends to value monetarily in its salaries, you need to translate these values into a usable salary schedule. Here are some factors to weigh in developing or refining your schedule:

Simplicity. Heed *Accounting Law #1* — "Salary schedules inevitably expand to fill every square on the spreadsheet." Resist the urge to make your salary schedule more elaborate than it needs to be. Many small and some not-so-small child care organizations get by with no more than a list of starting salaries for each job category. Every year the director then either decides on giving an across-the-board raise or makes decisions on a one-to-one basis.

Security. The main disadvantage with very simple salary plans is that they fail to provide employees with a long range view. Employees who plan to make a career of child care want to know what they can aspire to — What is the maximum salary they can earn? How can they advance within the center? A good salary schedule informs employees about their career options and opportunities.

Clarity. Some of the salary schedules we reviewed could just as well have been written in Chinese — maybe they were. They were incomprehensible. Give your new salary schedule the man-on-the-street test. Have several of your friends not involved in child care review it. When they can understand it, it's ready to be unveiled at your center.

Flexibility. Some of the salary schedules we reviewed left no room for maneuvering. The steps and levels for all positions were set in stone. Make your plan flexible enough so that you can add positions, upgrade or downgrade positions, or change step sizes without redoing the entire plan.

Liability. Before committing to any salary schedule, you should evaluate the long range worst/best case scenario. What if your salary plan works and you totally avoid turnover? What would your total salary costs be three years from now? Five years from now? Can you afford this?

Relevancy. At the beginning of this article, I observed that your salary schedule should be a direct expression of your organization's values. Sometimes, however, in developing a schedule you get so wrapped up in the mathematics and logistics that values and goals fade into the background. You should analyze your new or your current salary schedule to see if it truly supports your values. Are the positions that are most valuable to your organization properly rewarded? Are the factors you value the most (training, experience, or performance) rewarded the most?

Three Types of Salary Schedules

In developing your salary schedule, you have some choices to make. The

---

One View: No to Merit Pay

It is our policy NOT to give merit increases or bonuses. We are aware that this is somewhat of an unusual policy, but our reasoning is tied to our respect for teachers and our philosophy, which understands that quality education comes from a community of professionals working together to serve the needs of the children and families in its care.

Teachers need to be paid the highest salaries possible for the challenging work they do. Our board of directors makes significant efforts to provide maximum funding for salaries and benefits. Teachers get "rewarded" with knowing the salary increase is maximal (ours has ranged from 6% to 8% per year) and that the board and administration are continually working to provide a place where teachers can practice their profession.

We have no teacher aides in the school, only teachers and head teachers, who have supervisory and administrative responsibilities. We have hired them to do the same job (within job classifications), not to do a "better" job than others. Moreover, we believe that a primary obligation of the professional early childhood administrator is to develop team building skills. ECE teachers need to have the skills to be able to work with peers sometimes under stressful conditions.

If we were to try to reward some teachers at a differential rate, it would be very difficult to make a decision that would accurately reflect the precise truth about who deserved what. Merit pay is by nature exclusionary and we believe counterproductive to building a stable, quality environment in which to teach. No matter what criteria "merit" is measured by, if monetary value is assigned individually, team boundaries are crossed, possibly damaged, and probably discouraged. The hierarchical relationship between the administration and the individual teacher is promoted to the exclusion of the teacher's development of complex, sophisticated, and subtle communication with his/her peers. This is the very communication necessary for meeting the complex, sophisticated, and subtle educational needs of young children and their families. This, in our view, is counterproductive to our goal of respecting our teachers as professionals and contrary to our view of what quality education is all about.

— *Susan Britson, Step One School, Berkeley, California*

salary schedules we reviewed fell into three general categories. One in three of these were very simple or basic plans; most of the rest were traditional salary schedules; and less than one in ten fell into the innovative category.

The basic plans were not much more than lists of positions with starting salaries. In some cases, these spelled out the starting, mid-range, and top of the line salary for each position. While these plans are seldom inspiring, they are probably perfectly adequate for small, stable centers.

What we call the traditional salary schedules are grids with multiple levels and steps. Typically, the columns across the page represent different levels of education (high school diploma, AA degree, etc.), and the rows down the page represent years of employment. In some centers, there is a separate grid for each position, while in others all the positions are covered in one mega-grid.

The advantage of these traditional schedules is that they can be easily understood. People are accustomed to seeing salaries presented in grids and can easily figure out where they currently fit in, where they can progress, and what they need to do to get there (complete that AA degree, survive ten years, etc.).

A possible disadvantage is that the beauty of these plans is often only skin deep. The traditional schedule looks very impressive — it looks organized and standardized, and it fills the page with numbers that appear to have been calculated with great precision. Yet some of the most impressive looking grids we reviewed were seriously flawed. Some had steps that increased

in erratic non-patterns; some had step increases that were so tiny as to be insulting; and one contained math errors that resulted in the assistant teacher making more than the lead teacher after six years.

A few of the schedules we reviewed were innovative. There were some creative attempts to factor in performance, ongoing training, and participation above and beyond the call of duty. Unfortunately, a few of the most creative plans were also some of the most complicated ones — it would take a computer whiz to calculate all

the points and percentages. Overall, however, we appreciated the courage centers demonstrated in blazing new ground with these plans and only wish that we could convince some foundation to fund a study of their impact.

We attempted to capture the best thinking we observed in the 100+ salary schedules we analyzed and present it in two models. These models are presented in Table C, "Traditional Salary Schedule," and Table D, "Performance Based Salary Schedule."

Table C
Traditional Salary Schedule

	I	II	III	IV	V	VI	VII	VIII	IX	X
1	1.00	1.04	1.08	1.12	1.16	1.20	1.24	1.28	1.32	1.36
2	1.02	1.06	1.10	1.14	1.18	1.22	1.26	1.30	1.34	1.38
3	1.04	1.08	1.12	1.16	1.20	1.24	1.28	1.32	1.36	1.40
4	1.06	1.10	1.14	1.18	1.22	1.26	1.30	1.34	1.38	1.42
5	1.08	1.12	1.16	1.20	1.24	1.28	1.32	1.36	1.40	1.44
6	1.10	1.14	1.18	1.22	1.26	1.30	1.34	1.38	1.42	1.46
11	1.20	1.24	1.28	1.32	1.36	1.40	1.44	1.48	1.52	1.56
21	1.40	1.44	1.48	1.52	1.56	1.60	1.64	1.68	1.72	1.76
31	1.60	1.64	1.68	1.72	1.76	1.80	1.84	1.92	1.96	2.00
41	1.80	1.84	1.92	1.96	2.00	2.04	2.08	2.12	2.16	2.20
51	2.00	2.04	2.08	2.12	2.16	2.20	2.24	2.26	2.30	2.34
61	2.20	2.24	2.26	2.30	2.34	2.38	2.42	2.46	2.50	2.54

NOTE: This is an abbreviated model. To save space we have left out Steps 7–10, 12–20, etc.

Before we present these models, a major note of caution is in order: *Do not adapt these models in your center!* These are presented as starting points only. You need to modify these to incorporate your own values, priorities, and fiscal realities.

Model 1: The Traditional Approach

This model is in the form of the standard grid with levels going across the page and steps going down the page. Here is how to modify it to your needs:

Decision 1. What increments do you want to build into your grid? In Model 1, we set the increases for the levels in 4% increments. These increments typically account for levels of education. We set the increases for the steps, which typically account for annual increases, in 2% increments.

We purposely made the steps smaller than the typical 3% increments to provide more flexibility. When increments are large, the center has an all or nothing choice — you either move an employee up to the next step or you don't. With smaller increments, you can decide to move each employee up one, two, or even three steps a year, or you can move them up one step every six months.

One disadvantage with these small steps is that it adds to the size of your grid. If you want to include all staff members on the same grid, you may need to include as many as 70 to 100 steps.

We also chose, for simplicity's sake only, to make the increments for the steps uniform throughout the grid. Thus the salaries of employees at the bottom and top of the grid would increase at 2% for every step. What this means is that employees at the bottom end would receive smaller increases in actual dollars and cents than those at the top. You may elect to reverse this by starting the increments at 3% or 4% at the bottom and gradually reducing them to 1% at the top end.

(Note: Throughout this article we refer to salaries and salary schedules in reference to all employees. Many centers actually pay hourly wages for some employees and annual salaries for others. We are not arguing for or against this classification of employees. We use the term salaries as a generic term for all monies paid to staff.)

Decision 2. What is your base salary, i.e., what is the starting salary for your lowest paid employee? Once you set this entry level amount, you can translate all the increments on your grid to actual monetary amounts. For example, using our grid in Table C, if your base salary is $5.00 per hour, the succeeding amounts in row 1 would be $5.20, $5.40, $5.60, etc. Step 2 amounts would be $5.10, $5.30, $5.50, etc.

Decision 3. How much are you going to reward various levels of education? For example, if we were to take the typical educational differentials from Table B, here is how they would fit into our salary schedule:

High school diploma starts at
 Level I
AA degree would start at Level V
BA degree would start at Level VII
MA degree would start at Level IX

You may elect to value these levels differently or to define the levels differently. Some centers, for example, set levels based on credit hours of college completed. Others factor in CDA status or workshop attendance.

Decision 4. Where do you want to set the entry point for each position at your center? If we were to use the typical position differentials from Table A, here is how they would fit into our model:

Teacher Aide	=	Step 1
Bus Driver	=	Step 6
Assistant Teacher	=	Step 11
Lead Teacher	=	Step 26
Center Director	=	Step 66

As with educational levels, you will need to take the job categories used at your center and place them on the grid based on how you value them.

Decision 5. When will center employees qualify for moving up a step or to another level? Do employees move up one step every year automatically, or only if they receive a positive evaluation, or only if monies are available? Do employees progress to a higher level every time they complete a higher level of education?

Model 2: Performance Based Approach

This model is a variation of some of the innovative schedules we reviewed. It assigns significant weight to a staff member's performance in setting annual increases. Here is how to modify it to your needs, keeping in mind that every point awarded in Steps 1, 2, and 3 is worth 100% of your base rate:

Table D
Performance Based Salary Schedule

How to Use This Instrument: For Step 1, insert the points assigned for the employee's position. For Step 2, insert the points earned for the employee's highest level of education completed. For Step 3, insert the number of points earned first for years of satisfactory performance at your center, second for the years of above average performance, and third for the years of superior performance. Now determine the employee's new hourly rate by completing Step 4.

Step 1 — Responsibility

Teacher Aide	1.00
Cook	1.20
Assistant Teacher	1.20
Custodian	1.30
Lead Teacher	1.50
Assistant Director	1.80
Director	2.30

Step 2 — Training

AA Degree	.05
ECE-Related AA Degree	.10
BA/BS Degree	.10
ECE-Related BA/BS Degree	.20
Master's Degree	.15
ECE-Related Master's Degree	.30

Step 3 — Experience/Performance

Years of satisfactory performance
(add .02 points/year)

Years of above average performance
(add .04 points/year)

Years of superior performance
(add .06 points/year)

Step 4 — New Hourly Rate Determination

Multiply total points earned in Steps 1 through 3 times base rate for center.

_____ points x $_____ per hour = $_____ per hour

Decision 1. What is your base salary, i.e., what is the starting salary for your lowest paid employee? You will use the hourly rate for the base salary in Step 4.

Decision 2. What value do you want to assign to each job category in your center? In Model 2, we have used the differentials from Table A. You will want to modify these to reflect your center's values.

Decision 3. What value do you want to assign to each level of education? In Model 2, we have used the differentials from Table B. You will want to modify these to reflect to your center's values.

Decision 4. How many points do you want to award for different levels of performance? Keep in mind that if you go this route you must find or develop a tool for measuring performance that is viewed by all concerned as fair.

Once you have completed these adjustments, you should test it out. Based on your recent experience, use this format to determine, hypothetically, the salaries of several employees at different levels in your organization. Does this result in salaries that are fair? Does it result in any radical increases or decreases in current pay levels? Can you afford it?

If your test is unsuccessful, keep tinkering with the points or come up with a similar set of steps that fit your needs better.

A Final Caution

Your organization may well have a salary plan in place, so you may not be interested in going through a big production to establish a new one. That is probably a wise decision. However, I would encourage you to at least take the time to review your current schedule against the key points raised in the two articles in this series. Make sure that you are getting the maximum positive impact out of the resources you devote to salaries.

Credits

We reviewed over 100 salary schedules from Exchange Panel of 200 members in preparing the two articles in this series. The following centers' plans were especially helpful :

Central Learning Center, Memphis, TN; Children's Learning Center, Yardley, PA; Children's Programs Inc., Brookfield, WI; Community Children's Project, Jackson, WY; Gertrude B. Nielsen Child Care and Learning Center, Northbrook, IL; Graham Memorial Preschool, Coronado, CA; Gretchen's House, Ann Arbor, MI; Janet Rich Day Care, Rochester, NY; Learning Tree Montessori, Seattle, WA; Moffett Road Baptist Child Development Center, Mobile, AL; The Nursery Foundation of St. Louis, St. Louis, MO; St. Elizabeth's Day Home, San Jose, CA; Wausau Child Care, Inc., Wausau, WI; World Bank Children's Center, Washington, DC.

References

Ruopp, Richard et al. *Children at the Center*. Cambridge, MA: Abt Associates, 1979.

Whitebook, Marcy. *Who Cares? Child Care Teachers and the Quality of Care in America*. Oakland, CA: Child Care Employee Project, 1989.

Designing a Job Classification and Wage Scale System

by Mary Ann Anthony

As the American economy continues to grow, creating unprecedented low unemployment across the country, child care center directors are challenged with recruiting and retaining qualified staff in a shrinking labor market. At the same time, the demand for quality child care has never been higher. In this pressured environment, wage rates are often arbitrary, depending upon how desperate the director is to hire or retain or which staff member yells loudest for an increase. Staff morale and loyalty always suffer in this atmosphere of grab what you can, and turnover increases as staff seek higher wages or fairer treatment elsewhere. So what is the solution?

The answer is to assess the state of your program's current practices and apply rational thought to your job descriptions, wage scale, and salary increment policies to maximize the effectiveness of your salary budget.

What Are the Characteristics of a Good Salary Plan?

■ Establishes wages in a systematic way that everyone can understand

■ Reflects levels of pay in the community

■ Reflects relative worth of jobs in the center

■ Fair and consistent in treatment of employees

■ Built on classification of jobs that recognizes degree of difficulty and responsibility

■ Recognizes education and experience of employees

Why Have a Job Classification and Wage Scale System?

Staff retention. When a clear and definitive career ladder is established, staff can see what it will take to advance professionally and what the rewards will be as they do.

Staff motivation. Staff will have clear incentives to improve their professional qualifications.

Fairness. Because a rational and consistent pay scale related to clearly defined qualifications and job responsibilities is made visible to each staff member in a center, the perception of *deals* and favoritism is eliminated. Though it takes a period of time to fully implement, ultimately staff in the center doing the same job with the same qualifications and longevity will receive equitable compensation.

Improved quality of staff. Staff see the benefit of their own professional development in terms of monetary reward and career advancement. Directors can allocate their precious compensation dollars to get the biggest bang for the buck in terms of staff qualifications.

Enhanced ability to analyze compensation issues. Budgeting becomes easier because wage rates are more predictable. The exercise of comparative wage studies is simplified.

Once you accept the value of having a job classification and wage scale system, there are steps to follow to develop one that reflects the reality of your center. As director, the easy way is to go through these steps in splendid isolation and finish the job in a day or two. However, the staff will accept the plan more readily if the process is participatory. A representative committee of staff members will lend credibility and a sense of openness to the project.

Steps to Getting Started

Do a task analysis and identify the positions and classifications your program needs. This should be done as objectively as possible, without regard for the personalities currently in any of the positions.

Develop job descriptions. These should summarize the information gathered in the task analysis and should consider the following factors:

— Nature of the work itself
— Degree of responsibility
— Responsibility of supervision of others
— Nature of supervision received
— Degree of contact with the public
— Knowledge, skill, or ability required

— Training and experience required

Set minimum qualifications for each position.

— Education
— Experience
— State certification

Classify each position in relation to the others. Develop your ideal functional organizational model and develop a chart which displays your classifications visually.

Survey competitive wages in your community. Consider the relative value of your benefit options when comparing your wages to others.

Establish a wage range for each identified job classification. This is often best expressed as *Low – Mid – High*. Chart this on your classification grid.

Analyze your current employees. Make a list showing their educational level, experience, certification, and current rate of pay. At this point (to protect confidentiality), you will not include your committee.

Determine where your employees fall on your new job classification grid by virtue of their qualifications, NOT by their current job title.

Analyze whether their current wage falls within or outside the new ranges established for their qualification level.

Adjust the pay range for the classification wherever necessary.

Develop a plan to make any necessary adjustments to individual pay rates to conform to the new scale. This could mean phased in incremental increases for staff who fall significantly below the range and position they're in, or it could mean freezing wages for staff who are compensated above their qualification and responsibility level. All new hires will conform to the system from date of hire.

Develop increment policies, considering the following common reasons for granting increases or exceptions:

— Qualifications
— Merit
— Length of service
— Cost of living
— Available resources

Finally, plan to revisit your wage scale periodically to be sure that it still meets your program's needs. Once your plan is established, revision should be a simple process.

It will take some time and a thoughtful plan to eliminate the inequities in your center. Ultimately it should enhance your ability to recruit and retain qualified people. This article has deliberately not addressed the issue of how to pay for an enhanced wage scale. In my experience, an analysis of the competitive wage market and a rationally worked out job classification and wage scale are important tools to use in approaching parents, boards, and other funders for additional salary dollars.

Improved quality of staff. Staff see the benefit of their own professional development in terms of monetary reward and career advancement. Directors can allocate their precious

71

compensation dollars to get the biggest bang for the buck in terms of staff qualifications.

Enhanced ability to analyze compensation issues. Budgeting becomes easier because wage rates are more predictable. The exercise of comparative wage studies is simplified.

Once you accept the value of having a job classification and wage scale system, there are steps to follow to develop one that reflects the reality of your center. As director, the easy way is to go through these steps in splendid isolation and finish the job in a day or two. However, the staff will accept the plan more readily if the process is participatory. A representative committee of staff members will lend credibility and a sense of openness to the project.

Mary Ann Anthony holds a master's degree in child care administration, and has been a director and manager in for-profit and not-for-profit child care since 1977. From 1990 to 1996 she was vice president of operations at Mulberry Child Care Centers, before joining Catholic Charities in Boston as Director of the Child Care Division. There she is responsible for the operation of nine child care centers and four family child care systems, with a budget of $11 million, serving over 1,000 children from low income families. She recently joined the faculty of Johnson and Wales University's M.Ed. in Early Childhood Administration & Leadership program, teaching financial management.

Proposed Staff Qualifications/Responsibilities/Wage Scales

POSITION AND MINIMUM QUALIFICATIONS	SALARY RANGES			RESPONSIBILITIES
	LOW (Starting)	MID (2½ Years)	HIGH (5 Years)	
Assistant Teacher, Level I • 16 years old, no experience, no course • Full or part time	$7.00/hour	$7.65/hour	$8.25/hour	Staff/child interaction, staff/staff interaction, implementing curriculum
Assistant Teacher, Level II • High School Diploma/GED • OCCS Teacher Certified • CPR Certified • 1 year experience	$8.00/hour	$8.65/hour with additional course	$9.25/hour with 3 courses	Above, plus staff/parent interaction
Teacher, Level I • Assistant Level II plus 1 additional course or • CDA with 1 year experience • Literate	$10.00/hour ($19,500/year)	$10.80/hour ($21,060/year)	$11.60/hour ($22,600/year)	Above, plus lesson plans, health and safety, child assessment, behavior management, classroom environment
Teacher, Level II • CDA with 2 years experience or • Associate with 1 year experience or • BA with 6 months experience (OCCS Lead Teacher or higher)	$10.75/hour ($21,000)	$11.60/hour ($22,600)	$12.45/hour ($24,200)	Above, plus responsible in absence of lead teacher
Lead Teacher • CDA with additional courses toward degree and 3 years experience or • Associate with 3 years experience or • BA with 18 months experience	$12.00/hour ($23,400)	$12.95/hour ($25,252)	$13.90/hour ($27,100)	Above, plus progress reports, parent confences, responsible for overall program planning
Mentor Teacher (ECE Specialist) • BA and 6-10 years experinece or • MA and 4-8 years experinece (minimum 3 years in one center, internal candidates only)	$14.00/hour ($27,300)	$15.10/hour ($29,445)	$16.25/hour ($31,600)	Above, plus specialized education duties, mentor less experienced staff, provide training
Assistant Director • Same as Mentor Teacher, but OCCS Director I or II qualified	$14.00/hour ($27,300)	$15.10/hour ($29,445)	$16.25/hour ($31,600)	Supervise lead teachers and teachers, assist director with administrative duties, assume responsibilities in director's absence
Program Director (Center Based) • OCCS Director I or II, 3-5 years experience (center specific) • BA in ECE or related field	$16.40/hour ($32,000)	$17.70/hour ($34,515)	$19.00/hour ($37,118)	Overall responsibilities for program leadership, quality, health and safety, fiscal management
Program Director (Family Child Care) • BA in ECE or social work, 3-5 years supervisory experience				
Provider Coordinator • BA in social work or ECE	$12.30/hour ($23,985)	$13.25/hour ($25,838)	$14.25/hour ($27,800)	Coordinate all activities related to assigned family child care providers
Case Manager • BA in social work or related field				Coordinate and manage all activities relating to assigned clients of family child care program
Director of Child Care Services • MA in ECE, administration, social work, or related field or • BA with MA in progress (additional experience may substitute for MA) • 5-7 years progressively responsible experience in child care, human services • 3-5 years supervisory, admininistration, community organization	$40,000	$47,500	$55,000	Responsible for carrying out agency's mission and for overall operation of all assigned programs, provide leadership and vision to all program staff

Managing Money

Competitive Wage Analysis

Center _____

Date _____

Competitor Name _____

Location _____

Licensed Capacity _____

Employer Sponsored / Subsidized ___Yes ___No

Single Site _____ Multi Site _____

| POSITION | WAGE RATE | | | HOURLY/ SALARY | # EMPLOYEES IN POSITION | BONUS Y/N AVG $ | BENEFITS | | | | | | |
	LOW	AVERAGE	HIGH				VACATION	SICK	HOLIDAY	PROF DEV	MEDICAL ($)	DENTAL ($)	OTHER
ASSISTANT TEACHER													
TEACHER													
LEAD TEACHER													
TEAM LEADER													
ASSISTANT DIRECTOR													
DIRECTOR													
COOK													
SUBSTITUTE													
OTHER (define)													

Please provide other information you learn about this center that may be helpful in determining wage scales.

_____

_____

_____

_____

State-of-the-Art Thinking on Parent Fee Policies

by Roger Neugebauer

here are two fools in every market; one who asks too little, one who asks too much.
— Russian proverb

No one wants to make foolish mistakes when it comes to the tricky business of setting parent fees. It's a difficult balancing act, setting fees high enough to adequately reward staff and low enough to be affordable to families. It's no less difficult setting fee policies that are flexible enough to meet the needs of parents under stress yet tough enough to protect the center from financial hardship.

*To give centers guidance on setting fees and fee policies, we analyzed over 150 fee policies submitted to us by members of the **Exchange Panel of 200.** In this article, we will share some of the best thinking we discovered in these documents.*

A bargain at twice the price: Fee schedules

There is a tremendous variation in the rates early childhood programs charge. In the fee schedules we reviewed, for example, the daily rate for full day care of a four year old ranged from $7.80 to $31.05. These variations reflect regional cost of living factors, staffing levels, competition, family incomes, and outside support.

In the "Fee Relationships in Centers" box (see page 76), you can see the relationship between what centers charge per day for different services. For example, if Your Average Children's Center charges $20.00 per day for full day care for preschoolers, it would charge $25.60 per day for infants, $23.00 for toddlers, and $9.00 for school-agers (after school only). If Your Average Children's Center charges $20.00 per day for full day care, five days a week, they would charge $13.00 per day for half day care and $23.80 for three days a week care.

The relationship among fees for preschoolers, toddlers, and infants is fairly consistent. However, the differential in fees for preschoolers and school-age children attending in the afternoon only varies dramatically.

In some centers, the after-school fees are as little as 15% to 20% less than preschool fees, while in others they are as much as 75% to 80% lower. Part of this enormous differential depends upon whether or not transportation is included in the fees and whether or not the space is being provided at low or no cost. But even when these variables are factored out, fees for after-school care still vary widely. This would seem to indicate that there is not a common agreement regarding the structure and staffing of school-age programs.

Cheaper by the dozen: Multi-child discounts

There is also wide variation in the discounts centers provide for the second and third children from the same family enrolled in a center at the same time. Slightly under half of the policies we reviewed made no provision at all for multi-child discounts. In those that did, the amount of discount varied from 5% to 50% for a second child, and from 10% to 66% for the third child.

Some of the typical policies:

If you have more than one child enrolling in the center, you will receive a family discount. The fee for the second child will be two thirds tuition, and the third child will be one third tuition. — **Colorado Springs Child Nursery Center**, Colorado Springs, Colorado

Parents enrolling more than one child will pay full fee for the youngest child and be given a 10% discount for each other child. — **Ebenezer Child Care Centers**, Milwaukee, Wisconsin

There is a discount for the second child in the family of 20%. A third child could attend at a 30% discount. — **Euclid Avenue Preschool**, Cleveland, Ohio

Most policies are a little fuzzy as to which children get the discount. Some imply that the discount applies to the most recent enrolling child, while a few indicate that the discount is applied to the child(ren) paying the lowest fees.

Fee Relationships in Centers

In analyzing fee variations, we used the daily fees charged for preschool children (three and four year olds) attending full day, five days a week as the baseline. We found that fees charged for different types of services varied on average as follows:

Infants (full day, five days a week)	+28%
Toddlers (full day, five days a week)	+15%
Preschoolers (full day, three days a week)	+19%
Preschoolers (half day, five days a week)	-35%
School-Agers (before and after school, five days a week)	-26%
School-Agers (after school only, five days a week)	-55%

To be or not to be: Charges for absences

The greatest amount of ink in the policies we reviewed was consumed explaining to parents how and why fees are charged even when the children are absent. Clearly, this is an area where centers have experienced a hard sell. Therefore, it is important that the policy statement on absences be clear and persuasive. Here are some of our favorite examples:

We are prepared for each child each day whether the child attends or not. There will be no refunds for days absent. Each family will be allowed two weeks of absenteeism with no charge. — **Hester's Creative Schools, Inc.**, Greensboro, North Carolina

Tuition is the same every payment regardless of days missed due to illness or holidays. Think of this as a yearly commitment for your child, not in terms of days of attendance. — **Breezy Point Day School**, Langhorne, Pennsylvania

To assure that we can provide the highest quality of services, it is essential that the financial status of the center remain stable. Expenses cannot be sufficiently reduced to overcome losses due to absenteeism. Therefore, we must require that each family financially support space guaranteed for your child(ren) even if the child is absent. — **Pow Wow Child Development Centers**, Johnson City, Tennessee

Please note that tuition must be paid in full without deduction for absences. This is because our staffing and other operational expenses are arranged on the basis of fixed enrollment levels and must be met on a continuing basis. Few of the operating costs of the facility are eliminated when a particular child is absent. — **HeartsHome Early Learning Center**, Houston, Texas

Centers struggle to develop absence policies that meet the centers' needs for financial stability, yet are sensitive to the needs of families. About half the centers provide discounts or credits for family vacations and/or extended periods of illness. Here are some of the clearer, more creative policies on "approved absences":

Families enrolled in our 12 month program prior to June 1st of that year are entitled to one free week of vacation. This vacation week is not transferable from year to year. . . . This vacation week is offered on a Monday through Friday service week only.
— **Rainbow Express Preschool**, Lansdale, Pennsylvania

There will be no credit for absences of one week or less. A $45 non-attendance fee will be charged for the second consecutive week of absence and up to four weeks. Your child's place will not be held after the fourth week.
— **Another Generation Preschool**, Sunrise, Florida

The vacation allotment has already been figured into your child's contract at the time of enrollment. Your child's regular rate remains the same every month, regardless of when he/she goes on vacation.
— **Gretchen's House**, Ann Arbor, Michigan

If your child is absent from the center three or more days in one week due to sickness, conditions beyond your control, or preapproved vacation time, your tuition charge will be reduced by 40%.
— **Children's World Learning Center**, Euless, Texas

Some centers waive fees for absences due to a variety of other causes: "in-patient hospitalization," "death in the immediate family," "court-appointed visitation," "center closings due to inclement weather" (only two centers out of the 150+ waive fees for this reason), "parents on maternity leave," and absences "at the request of your doctor."

Pay me now or pay me later: Payment terms

With the exception of drop-in programs which charge after the fact for actual hours attended, centers today require payment in advance. Not too many years ago, collecting after the delivery of services was common, and commonly this resulted in major cash flow stresses as expenses were incurred ahead of income.

A slight majority of centers require payments on a monthly basis. This clearly is the low-hassle route as it minimizes the number of collections that must be made. It also gives a center considerable flexibility in managing cash flow. Most centers divide the annual fee into 12 equal payments, although a few invoice each month based on days of service to be delivered. In some communities, however, parents cannot afford to pay 30 days in advance. Therefore, a significant minority of centers collect on a weekly basis.

Some centers give parents a choice of paying on a weekly, bi-weekly, monthly, or semester basis. In these cases, discounts are given to those paying on the longer term basis.

Most centers prefer to receive payments by check — some even have policies against receiving payments in cash. Surprisingly, only a small minority allow payments by credit cards.

What's up front?: Registration fees and deposits

At enrollment time, nearly all centers collect from parents a registration fee and a deposit.

The primary purpose of these charges is to provide security for the center — to assure that parents are serious about enrolling their children and to cover unpaid fees if a child is withdrawn abruptly.

Registration fees, variously referred to as "application fees," "enrollment fees," and "reservation deposits," range from $15 to $75. We found little correlation between registration fees and service fees — i.e., centers charging the highest fees for child care don't necessarily impose the highest registration fees. For most centers, registration fees are a one-time charge. However, many centers, particularly centers operating on a ten month schedule, impose a smaller "reenrollment fee" every year.

Registration fees are typically non-refundable. One center offers a refund if a child or family encounters an "unavoidable crisis" which forces them to withdraw in the first 30 days. Several centers observed that the registration fee was refundable in special instances "at the discretion of the director."

Security deposits (which are seldom referred to as "security" deposits) range from one week's to one month's fees. Most centers ask a two week deposit and many ask for one month. These deposits are refundable if parents comply with center fee policies. For example, typical statements on deposits read:

At time of registration, a refundable deposit is required. The deposit is refunded if the family gives the director of the center a written notice two weeks prior to withdrawing from the center. If this notice is not received. the family will forfeit the deposit.

— Early Childhood Options in University Circle, Cleveland, Ohio

A two-week deposit is required prior to a child starting the center program, preferably at registration; however, an alternate payment schedule can be arranged if the entire deposit cannot be paid at time of registration. If a child is withdrawn at the end of the program year, the two-week deposit can be refunded. If a child is withdrawing prior to the end of the program year, the two week notice must be given; but deposit can only be refunded if a replacement can be found within that two week period.
— The Children's Center, New Milford, Connecticut

From a center's point of view, registration fees and deposits are necessary for financial stability. However, from a family's perspective, they can add up to a serious hurdle. If a family must pay up front for a registration fee, a one-month deposit, and the first month's tuition, this could run anywhere from $500 to as much as $2,000 per child.

Realizing the cash flow strain this can cause, some centers try to soften the blow. For example, **The Children's Center** (as noted above) offers to work with families to collect the deposit over time. Another alternative, which is used by other services but not by any of the centers whose policies we reviewed, is to ask parents to guarantee their fees with a credit card. In that way, no money would be collected unless the family defaulted on their fees.

With concern, we noted that none of the fee policies we reviewed included a provision for refunding interest accrued on deposits. If your policy does not address this, you may want to check to see if your policies are in compliance with your state's usury laws.

This is the end, my friend: Withdrawals

Most centers spell out fairly specific policies for procedures for withdrawing a child from the program. These policies are designed to give the center adequate notice so it can collect what is due from the outgoing family and find a child to fill the vacancy.

A typical policy:

Thirty days written notice is required to withdraw a child from the program. This enables the center to process an application from the waiting list. Payment is required for 30 days following the withdrawal notice, whether or not the child continues to attend the center during that period.
— Play and Learn Centers, Fort Washington, Pennsylvania

Many centers also spell out specific policies for temporary withdrawals due to family vacations or illnesses. Often a center will place a child on extended absence on a priority wait list so that he has the opportunity to fill the first vacancy when he is ready to return. This issue most frequently arises during summer vacation months. Here is a typical way centers deal with such withdrawals:

Persons signing a 12 month agreement and wishing to withdraw for the summer months of July and August may do so by informing the center director in writing by April 1 and paying the September tuition by June 1. If the child does not return in September, the tuition is forfeited.
— The Children's Learning Center, Yardley, Pennsylvania

All dressed up with nowhere to go: Late pick-ups

This obviously is another hot issue. Clearly, it is a major imposition on teachers when they must wait until a late parent shows up. And it can be anxiety-producing to young children. Most centers have learned that they must be firm about late pick-ups or it quickly mushrooms. Here are some typical policies designed to discourage lateness:

Since the center closes at 6 pm, a late pick-up charge of $5 will be assessed for each quarter hour or fraction thereof that a child is left beyond 6 pm. This fee is payable immediately to the employee who has remained with your child.
— Early Explorations, Encinitas, California

Once the center closes, the teacher who remains with children is paid directly by the parent. Charges are $3 for the first five minutes and then $1 per minute. All payments are to be made by the end of the week. If payment has not been made, First Care will pay the staff member and will add twice the amount to our statement.
— First Care, Inc., Glen Ellyn, Illinois

Most centers also recognize that being totally inflexible regarding lateness places even more stress on families already operating on the edge. Here are examples of policies designed to be less burdensome:

You are allowed three late pick-ups with a maximum tardiness of up to 30 minutes.
— **Pulama Keiki Preschool and Daycare**,
Lihue, Hawaii

If you know you are going to be late, call the center. If is difficult for both your child and staff if a child is left at school without knowing why.
— **Child Care Center**,
Evanston, Illinois

No fees for late tuition or late pick-ups. We trust families will cooperate. Families who are habitually late in paying or picking up their children will be asked to find another early childhood program.
— **St. Elizabeth's Day Home**,
San Jose, California

On average, centers charge 75¢ per hour for late pick-ups, and most policies provide that payments be made on the spot to the teacher staying with the child. **The Reston Children's Center** in Reston, Virginia, imposes progressively stiffer penalties, with the first lateness being charged at $1 per minute, the second at $2 per minute, and the third at $4 per minute. **The World Bank Children's Center** in Washington, DC, even spells out that it is the "center's front office clock" that will be used to define lateness.

The check is in the mail: Late payments

Another chronic problem for child care centers is collections. People in early childhood education usually are not hard-nosed collectors, so late payments can easily get out of hand if not dealt with decisively.

The better fee policies clearly define when fees are due and when payments become late. Typically, monthly fees are due by the first of the month and become overdue by the fifth of the month. Weekly fees are typically due by Monday and are late by Wednesday.

When fees are late, most centers impose late fees ranging from $5 to $20. One center imposes a late penalty of 10%. If parents are late with their fees several months in a row, or fall more than a month behind (two weeks behind in some centers), directors typically reserve the right to disenroll the child (with any deposit being forfeited).

There are two problems with flat charges for late payments. First, once a payment is late and the late penalty has been incurred, there is no incentive for parents to quickly make amends — whether they are one day late or two weeks late, the charge is the same. Charging interest that accrues on a daily basis makes delays progressively more painful.

Second, late charges may violate state usury laws. States limit the amount of interest you can charge for overdue payments. Typically, the limit is in the range of 1.5% per month. Thus, if your monthly fee is $350, the maximum late payment you could charge would be $5. Review your late payment policies in light of applicable state laws!

Here is an example of a late payment policy that clearly has been developed with legal requirements in mind:

It is further agreed that any payment which is in default shall bear interest at the maximum legal rate and from the due date until paid. The promiser hereby waives demand notice of presentation. In the event it is necessary to refer this matter to an attorney for collection, it is mutually agreed that the prevailing party shall be entitled to reasonable attorney's fees and that the venue of any action shall be King County, Washington.
— **Learning Tree Montessori**,
Seattle, Washington

Another way to avoid bad debts is to confront problems early and work out solutions that meet the center's needs as well as a family's. By encouraging families experiencing financial difficulties to let you know in advance about problems they may have with fee payments, you can often work out a schedule of payments that will help the family, but will also assure the center that payments will eventually be made. Here is one center's approach:

If your family should have an unusual or emergency type financial problem that may effect the prompt paying of tuition, please call or stop by the office and talk with the administrator or bookkeeper. Often we can work something out until the crisis or emergency subsides.
— **Kirkmont Presbyterian Preschool**,
Beavercreek, Ohio

Roger's Rules for Effective Fee Policies

1. **Don't sell yourself short.** The fees you charge should be based on what it costs to provide a level of quality you can believe in. If you set your fees to be in line with what other centers in your community charge, you may or may not be setting them high enough to cover your costs. If you keep your fees low because you fear that parents may not be able to afford higher fees, you are resigning your center to a mediocre level of quality. Rather, you should set your fees based on what quality care costs and then work hard to find ways to offer scholarships and discounts for families who truly can't afford your program.

2. **Don't set policies you won't enforce.** It is easy to write tough policies to deal with all your problems. However, policies accomplish their purpose only if they are enforced by real people in real life. The cleverest late pick-up policy is worthless if you lack the commitment to enforce it, or if you only enforce it intermittently. And if you have one policy you don't consistently enforce, it takes the teeth out of the rest of your policies.

3. **No small print, no surprises.** Parents won't be influenced by policies they aren't aware of. At intake, carefully review in person your key policies on withdrawals, absences, late pick-ups, and late payments so parents clearly know in advance what the rules are. Many centers require that parents sign a statement or contract agreeing to these policies and, in some cases, agreeing that they were briefed in advance about these policies.

4. **Watch the tone.** In writing policies it is natural to slip into a negative, legalistic tone. This often leads to policies that are far from family friendly. One manual, for example, stated that it was including a strict late pick-up penalty because "inconsiderate behavior by parents forced us to do this." Don't lecture or moralize. Show respect for parents, assume their intentions are good, and take their perspective into account. State your policies in straight-forward, non-judgmental fashion.

5. **Write policies well.** Some of the policies we reviewed were so garbled that we couldn't understand them. Many were littered with misspellings and grammatical errors. Some of the policies were far too complex — one center's policies on vacation credits took four pages to explain and a degree in mathematics to calculate. After you have written your policies, have them reviewed by people outside your staff — center parents, your neighbors, your grandmother. Then quiz them to see if they understand your policies.

6. **Attend to presentation.** Just as a delicious dinner can be diminished with lousy presentation, the best policies can be undermined if poorly presented. If no one on staff has an eye for graphic design, see if you can find a volunteer among your parents to give you some layout and design advice, or lean on your printer for a little free consultation.

7. **Help parents find help.** Some of our favorite fee policies included advice to parents on how to qualify for public subsidies. We were truly amazed by how few centers' policies informed parents of how they could save money with the federal child care tax credit. Make your policies useful tools for parents as well as your center.

Establishing and Managing
A Tuition Aid Program

by Teresa Vast

*T*he primary goal of a tuition aid program is to help families enroll and keep their children in your center. Tuition aid revenue can also improve your center's financial stability and boost quality. This article explores some of the basic issues in establishing and managing a tuition assistance program — target groups, sources of aid, determining need, and whether to use an external financial aid service.

Tuition Aid Helps Families AND Centers

As an early childhood administrator you know that financial barriers prevent many families from enrolling their children in your center. Among participating families, late and missed payments tell you that many parents struggle to pay the tuition and fees.

Moreover, since tuition revenue comprises an average 87 percent of the typical center budget (Cost, Quality & Child Outcomes Study Team, 1995), low or fluctuating enrollment can threaten your center's financial viability and the quality of your program.

Most directors strive to set prices at affordable levels, often relying on subsidies of donated space, goods, and services, and on the willingness of staff to accept low wages. But even these "bargain" prices are higher than many can afford. Public child care subsidies help some families pay, but many states' authorized payment rates fall short of the tuition and fees (Adams & Snyder, 2003).

To increase financial stability, many providers seek funds from private sector sources to bridge the gap between what families can pay and what it costs to produce a high-quality program. One approach is to raise funds for a need-based tuition aid program.

Setting clear goals and guidelines for such a program will help you both in raising the funds and in equitably awarding aid to families.

Target Groups

In establishing and managing a tuition aid fund, the most fundamental question is "Who do you want to assist?" The answer will depend largely on your program's mission, the communities you serve, and the resources available.

While some programs focus resources on the lowest-income families with the greatest need, others reach out to families with moderate income who also have financial need. Additional goals, such as increasing diversity, can also be addressed within the framework of need-based aid. Since need usually far exceeds aid resources, priorities should be established to ensure aid is distributed in such a way that the purposes are fulfilled.

Some potential target groups include:

Low-income families . . .

■ who do not meet the eligibility criteria to qualify for publicly-funded child care assistance.

■ who receive child care assistance, but must make a larger co-payment than they can afford, either because the child care eligibility formula does not reflect basic living expenses or the rate does not reflect real early care and education prices.

■ who meet eligibility requirements for public child care assistance via a voucher or admission in a contracted center or enrollment in Head Start, but are placed on a waiting list or turned away.

■ whose children may lose early learning opportunities when a parent loses a job and employment-related child care benefits.

Moderate- and middle-income *gap group* families . . .

■ who are ineligible, based on income, for publicly-funded child care assistance, but do not have the financial resources to pay for high-quality early care and education.

When is reduced or free tuition *not* aid?

If a tuition discount or free enrollment is not based on financial need, it should be accounted for separately in the center's budget. Examples include reduced or waived tuition provided as employee benefits (a personnel expense), and sibling discounts available to families regardless of demonstrated financial need (a marketing expense).

Sources of Tuition Aid

Once purposes for tuition aid have been established, you have a strong basis for raising needed funds. A community foundation or *fund development* professional can help you identify promising charitable sources and devise a strategy to meet your program's revenue goals.

While not all revenue sources or strategies are appropriate to every type of program nor available in every area, potential sources for tuition aid include:

■ Charitable grants from community or private foundations or corporations

■ Contributions from the United Way or community service clubs

■ Gifts from wealthy individuals familiar with your program

■ Commercial enterprises operated as a subsidiary

■ Fundraising activities, such as direct-mail appeals to alumni families and community supporters; special events such as concerts, auctions; and occasional or regular sales of specialty items, merchandise, etc.

■ Endowment income: Some programs create an endowment fund to generate interest income, a strategy long-used by colleges, universities, and many private K-12 schools. Once established and adequately funded, an endowment can provide a stable source of revenue for tuition aid.

Finally, tuition revenue itself can be a source of financial aid, usually as a supplement to other sources. Some programs include aid as a standard budget expense category, designating a portion of revenue (e.g., 5 percent) to the tuition aid line item in accordance with their mission and purposes (e.g., to establish a diverse school community).

Managing the Tuition Aid Program

Raising the money is but one step in getting tuition aid to those who need it. Policies and procedures that address who will manage the fund and how the program is implemented are also essential.

Staffing. It takes time and diverse skills to oversee and manage a tuition aid fund. Large and multi-site programs are more likely to hire staff to administer financial aid, while small programs are more likely to add these responsibilities to the director's role. In either case, the added expense should be reflected in the budget.

Financial aid staff need communication and people skills to advise and counsel parents. They also need math and computation skills for reviewing applications and tax returns. They have to keep an eye on the *big picture* of the purposes of the aid and also pay attention to details in tracking data and keeping records. Professionalism is a must in dealing with sensitive and confidential information.

Policies. Written policies and procedures form the foundation of the tuition aid program. They help you to administer the funds impartially and with confidentiality. They must be clear and fair, so that parents, staff, and funders can trust the process and the results. Policies and procedures should address: staff and volunteer roles and responsibilities, outreach activities, application forms and processes, methods for calculating financial need and ability to pay, guidelines for equitably distributing aid, and an appeals process. Guidelines for record keeping, protection of privacy, and use of data should also be included.

Determining Need and Awarding Aid

Early care and education programs are often unprepared for the delicate task of reviewing families' financial information and assessing their ability to pay. The absence of a uniform national method (like those used in college financial aid) adds to the challenge. Many programs have devised sliding scales as a rough measure of ability to pay, but these can vary widely, even within a single community.

As a director, you want to have confidence in your methods and be able to demonstrate effective use of limited funds. Potential contributors may also be interested in knowing that you base aid decisions on valid assumptions.

Colleges, universities, and many private K-12 schools rely on standard methods and forms and an external financial aid service. Their process is a useful guide. Three key questions outline the major steps: What is the family able to pay? How much aid is needed to close the gap between what the family can pay and the program's tuition price? What portion of the

family's financial need can you meet with available tuition aid resources?

■ How much can the family pay toward your center's tuition and fees?

To ensure that families are treated equitably and that limited funds are wisely awarded, a uniform method based on sound economic principles should be used to calculate what a family can reasonably contribute. The formula and process should consider family size, income, assets, and special circumstances reported by applicants on a form you provide, verified with tax returns and other documents. After deducting standard allowances for basic necessities (e.g., food, shelter, taxes, etc.), families can be expected to pay a portion of any remaining income.

One option is to rely on an external financial aid service for the forms, method, and financial need analysis. For more information about issues in determining families' ability to pay, see *Learning Between Systems: Adapting Higher Education Financing Methods to Early Care and Education* (Vast, 2001).

■ What is the financial need of the family?

Once you have determined how much families can pay for early care and education, calculating their *need* for financial assistance is a matter of simple math:

Tuition and fees
– Expected family contribution
= Need

■ What portion of the family's financial need can you meet?

Distributing limited funds is a balancing act. The amount you award to each family will depend on your available tuition aid funds, your program's priorities, the amount each family needs, and the relative need of all families who qualify for assistance. When need outpaces aid, a common method of rationing involves meeting a percentage of need.

Due to the sensitivity of award decisions, it is wise to have a committee or volunteer oversight group to consider the relative need of the various applicants in relation to the program's purposes and priorities. However, all who have access to a family's financial information must maintain confidentiality.

In-house or External Financial Aid Service?

In contrast to other levels of education, no financial aid service currently exists that is geared specifically to early care and education programs and the families they serve. Perhaps this will change in the future when social and financial investments in early care and education expand to match the importance of the early years. Public and private funders may eventually demand the same level of reliability and accountability that financial aid methods now provide in higher education and many private K-12 schools.

There are good reasons to consider using an external financial aid service rather than attempting to handle everything in-house (see sidebar). But there are also disadvantages in using available services. This was clearly demonstrated in a recent experiment in Hawaii in which two foundations provided tuition aid to a dozen preschools with a requirement that all families use the same financial aid application form. Key to this approach was the availability of a third-party method and processing system. The School and Student Service for Financial Aid (SSS) was used for the foundations' experiment.

A project of the National Association of Independent Schools (NAIS), SSS provides financial aid applications and processing services for over 2,300 K-12 schools nationwide; only a handful of early care and education programs currently subscribe to the service. Parents complete a uniform application, send it to SSS, and the schools named by the parents receive the results, including the "estimated family contribution." The schools use the information they receive in calculating need and awarding aid. Costs of the service are paid through annual fees from participating schools ($125) and application fees paid by families ($20). Low-income families are given fee waivers.

Preschools that used SSS gave mixed reviews of their experience:

Advantages:

■ The form and process was helpful in setting up a new tuition aid program.

■ Using the service saved staff time in creating forms and calculating income.

■ The SSS calculations provided results that could be trusted — a useful tool for determining need.

Why Use a Financial Aid Service?

■ Research-based method produces reliable results for making fair aid decisions.

■ Eliminates need to develop a valid method, create forms, and perform complex calculations.

■ Additional training and support is available to service subscribers.

Why Use an In-House Financial Aid Method?

■ Your program has developed forms and methods using valid and current economic research and resources.

■ Your program has dedicated staff with financial aid skills.

■ Your program has access to training and support from a volunteer or consultant with financial aid expertise

---

■ The "estimated family contribution" was useful in prioritizing need and making award decisions.

■ The impartiality of an objective third-party process improved parent-director relationships.

Disadvantages:

■ The parents' financial form was intimidating and difficult for many applicants.

■ Staff had to provide extensive assistance to some applicants, particularly low-income families.

■ The form includes unnecessary questions for families with limited resources.

■ The processing time was too long for the school and parents.

■ The services are geared to 9-month school calendars and limited application periods.

■ The forms and process were more labor intensive than programs' usual practices.

Mark Mitchell, vice president for financial aid services at NAIS, acknowledges that there is room for improvement in making the SSS application more user-friendly and shaping the service to meet the needs of early care and education programs. He notes NAIS plans for a flexible online form that would simplify the process for applicants with low income and few assets, but still capture all necessary data from those with more complex finances. For additional information about SSS, contact Mark Mitchell at (202) 973-9766 or mitchell@nais.org, or visit www.nais.org.

A different kind of "third-party" approach is used by some centers that serve predominantly low-income families receiving public assistance. Rather than submitting families to another application process, they rely on government-administered needs tests. For example, if the family qualifies for a particular level of child care assistance that falls short of the tuition price, the program uses private tuition aid funds to make up the difference between the tuition price and the combined total of the family co-payment and publicly-funded voucher.

Regardless of whether an in-house process or external financial aid service is used, the key is to ensure that aid awards are equitable, based on sound data and reliable methods that clearly establish need.

Looking to the Future

The concept of a community-based financial aid "hub" has sparked interest among advocates nationwide. A centralized financial aid agency, perhaps co-located with a child care resource and referral agency or other family-oriented services, would be a resource for families seeking tuition assistance and could also serve as an external financial aid office for area providers (Vast, 2001). Concentrating expertise and services in a community agency would reduce the burden on providers and increase access for parents — without the stigma of welfare. This could be especially important as funding eventually increases and eligibility for aid expands.

In the meantime, you can develop your center's tuition aid fund. Using the steps outlined here, you could fine-tune your methods and processes, or experiment with a new approach, such as using an external financial aid service. Innovative center directors seeking to maximize their use of available funds and resources could even form a network to jointly establish a financial aid service that is customized for early care and education and geared to their needs.

References

Cost, Quality & Child Outcomes Study Team. (1995). *Cost Quality, and Child Outcomes in Child Care Centers, Public Report*, second edition. Denver: Department of Economics, University of Colorado at Denver, p. 44, table 5.1.

Adams, G., & Snyder, K. (February 2003). "Essential but Often Ignored: Child Care Providers in the Subsidy System." *Occasional Paper Number 63, Assessing the New Federalism.* Washington, DC: The Urban Institute.

Vast, T. (July 2001). *Learning Between Systems: Adapting Higher Education Finance Methods to Early Care and Education, Final Project Report.* Indianapolis, IN: Lumina Foundation for Education, pp. 27-33.

Teresa Vast is an independent early childhood consultant who specializes in policy research and analysis, planning, and program development for nonprofit organizations, foundations, and government. Her projects focus primarily on system planning and financing, financial aid, and professional development systems. Teresa has done extensive research on adapting higher education financing methods to early care and education and has designed and implemented several tuition aid programs. She holds bachelor's and master's degrees in human development from Pacific Oaks College.

Tried and True Techniques for Collecting Fees

Ideas from center directors

Collecting overdue fees is one of those ugly jobs that no center director enjoys. But directors who are lax in collecting fees often are confronted with even uglier tasks —raising fees or cutting salaries to make up for lost revenues due to unpaid fees. Happily, such dire measures can be avoided by adopting and consistently enforcing the following fee collection procedures. These procedures have been employed with great success by the directors listed at the end of this article.

• Spell out fee policies at enrollment

When parents are enrolling their children, they should be informed that the center cannot operate with stability unless all fees are paid on time. Fee payment schedules and procedures should be clearly outlined verbally and then presented to the parents in writing. This discussion should cover not only when and how to pay fees, but also what actions the center will take when fees are late, and what steps parents can take when they are caught in a crisis and know they will have difficulty paying fees in a timely manner. To avoid future misunderstandings and disputes, some centers have parents sign a copy of a fee policies statement (which includes the actual fee for their child) at enrollment.

• Keep in close touch with all parents

Parents who are most likely to fall behind in paying fees are either those who are unhappy with the program and feel little motivation to pay their fees on time or those parents who are experiencing personal difficulties and feel uncomfortable about asking for special consideration. Therefore, one of the most effective steps you can take to avoid fee delinquencies is to maintain good relationships with parents.

If the director keeps in close contact with the parents, she will be able to detect signs of disgruntlement early and deal with them before they get out of hand. Likewise, if a director is on good terms with parents, they will feel more comfortable approaching her if they are in difficult straits and need to make some special arrangements on deferring fee payments.

• Be alert for freeloaders

Directors in several communities have reported instances where a parent will enroll a child in a center for several months without paying the fee and then transfer the child to another center and then to another. Directors try to screen out such parents by checking up on parents who seem overly eager to enroll their children without even seeing the program. In some communities, directors have curtailed this practice by exchanging names of parents who leave without paying fees.

Financial Policies and Procedures

• Make it easy to pay

The more trouble parents have to go to in order to pay fees, the more likely they are to delay doing so. If fees are to be paid to the director, for example, and the director is frequently on the phone or not to be found, this will frustrate parents and result in payment lapses.

Many centers have locked metal boxes with slots so that parents can drop their checks off effortlessly when they come to pick up their children. One center has a desk in its reception area so that parents can sit down and write out their checks. Other centers send out invoices with stamped return address envelopes so that all parents have to do is to slip the check in the envelope and drop it in a mail box.

Still other centers have found that parents appreciate the option of paying fees with a commercial credit card. Such a system gives parents the option of deferring their payments on the credit card. Meanwhile, the center is paid in cash for charge slips it turns in (less a typical 5% service charge) to the bank.

• Collect fees in advance

To encourage the timely payment of fees, most centers have adopted a policy of requiring fees to be paid before service is provided. Some centers require fees for an upcoming month to be paid in full by the first of the month, while others collect fees for the upcoming week on Monday of that week.

From an administrative point of view, collecting fees for a month in advance

is clearly advantageous. With monthly fees, the center's income for the month is known and on hand early in the month. Also there are one-fourth the checks to process. In many communities, however, parents find it difficult to pay for a full month in advance and prefer the weekly fees. Some centers have dealt with this dilemma by establishing a monthly fee policy and then working out biweekly or weekly fees for parents for whom the monthly fees are a hardship.

For those centers that currently collect fees after the fact, we have some good news. Centers that have converted from post-payment to pre-payment policies have experienced little resistance from parents when the reasons for the change were clearly explained.

• Collect a deposit

It is now common practice for centers to collect at enrollment the first month's fee plus a deposit of one additional month's fee. This deposit is held and applied toward the fee for the last month. This policy helps avoid the common practice of not paying the last month's fee when a child is removed from a program.

Be sure to check into applicable state laws regarding the collection of deposits. These laws may require that interest be paid to parents for the deposit while it is in the hands of the organization.

• Enforce late payment penalties.

Many centers have successfully discouraged late payments by charging penalties. A center collecting

fees on a weekly basis, for example, will typically charge a penalty of $5 for fees received later than Tuesday.

Once again, it is important to review your penalty in light of applicable state laws. Some centers have had the legality of their penalties challenged as being interest charged in excess of permitted limits. To avoid this complication, some centers raise their fees by a small amount and offer reduced fees for parents paying on time.

• Offer to deal with problems in advance

All the centers surveyed for this article go out of their way to assist families experiencing temporary financial difficulties. As one director observed, "We don't believe that getting rid of problems is the answer. We try to stick with families having difficulties — we do not want to compound their problems. In ten years we have rarely lost any money in operating this way."

Some centers have a small scholarship fund set aside so that fees for families in crisis can be partially subsidized for short time periods. Some centers lower fees temporarily with the understanding (agreed to in writing) that the amount of the reduction will be made up over a set period of time when the crisis is over. Other centers assist families in securing assistance from public agencies, church groups, or other charitable organizations.

All centers stress from the day parents enroll their children that they will only be able to be flexible in times of family crisis if the center is notified about a problem immediately. If a parent is reluctant to discuss a problem and starts falling way behind in fees, the center may have few options to offer.

• Act quickly on delinquencies

Directors must be vigilant to keep overdue fees from turning into bad debts. By acting immediately when an account becomes overdue, you can often nip a problem in the bud. If you wait too long, the amount of money overdue may become so large that it is almost impossible for a family to pay it off.

If you are reluctant to press parents when fees are overdue, this can also set a dangerous precedent. When people don't have enough money to pay all of their bills, they tend to defer paying whatever bills they can without resistance. If they know they can pay their fee to your center a week late without any consequence, they are more likely to do so.

It is especially important to be vigilant as summer approaches. This is often the point at which delinquencies occur. Parents planning to move or withdraw their child for any other reason may be tempted to avoid paying their final bills knowing that they soon will have no need of your services.

For a parent who is late only rarely, a written notice of delinquency will probably suffice. However, for chronic late payers, immediate personal contact may be required. Those who make a practice of not paying bills on time are not likely to be influenced by form letters, no matter how threatening.

When contacting a delinquent parent, it is important not to show anger or disrespect. Work at maintaining the dignity of the parent, and your dignity will remain intact.

• Offer repayment options

If a parent falls behind, it may not be the best strategy to insist that the overdue amount be paid in one lump sum. Centers should negotiate a realistic repayment plan with parents of limited means. If a parent is experiencing financial difficulty, he may be unable to pay off a large debt all at once; but he may be able to pay it off gradually by paying a little extra with every fee payment. Or parents may agree to take out a loan in order to pay off the debt.

• Have parents sign a promissory note

When parents agree to pay delinquent fees of a substantial nature, you should follow up on their expressed willingness by asking them to sign a promissory note. A typical promissory note establishes interest amounts for late payments and specifies that all collection costs are the responsibility of the debtor. (Standard forms for promissory notes can be purchased at most office supply stores.) A key advantage to having a signed promissory note is that it fixes the amount owed, thus strengthening your case if legal action is required.

• Minimize bad check losses

Bounced checks are not a serious problem for small businesses that know their customers well. However, from time to time all centers have customers' checks returned by the bank. Several procedures can be implemented to minimize losses from bad checks. First, before depositing checks, make sure that they are signed, that the date is correct, and that the printed and written amounts are correct. Second, try to deposit checks on the same day that they are received — this reduces the possibility that checks will be returned due to insufficient funds or because an account was closed. Third, when checks are returned, notify parents immediately to give them the opportunity to pay in cash or to deposit additional funds into their account.

• Sue in small claims court

In extreme cases, some centers have found it necessary to sue parents in small claims court to collect delinquent fees. The advantage of suing in small claims court is that they operate informally — lawyers aren't required; both parties simply discuss the case with a judge. There are some disadvantages, however. First, when a case is scheduled, the center may be required to have a representative in court, possibly for a full day, waiting for the case to be heard. Second, winning a judgment by no means guarantees that you will collect the debt, as the court itself has no means of enforcing its decisions. One center has found it necessary to go to the local sheriff to have judgments enforced. The act of going to small claims court may have more impact than the collection of a single debt. If parents know that you are willing to go to court, they may be less likely to push you to that extreme.

• Stop providing care

The ultimate penalty, when all remedies have been exhausted, is to stop providing child care for families who fail to pay their fees. Most centers have seldom, if ever, found it necessary to exercise this option, as its mere threat is often sufficient to produce action. Other centers, in extreme cases, have refused to accept children for care until parents paid overdue fees and have achieved positive results with such steps.

While this laundry list of fee collection procedures may seem a bit extreme, having them in place does make a difference. Centers that consistently enforce the early steps in the process seldom need to use the sterner measures. Centers that demonstrate a willingness to go all the way seldom experience losses.

To conclude with a positive example, one large center that implemented fee collection procedures such as these has not lost a single penny in delinquent fees in five years.

Credits

The following center directors provided ideas for this article: Tracy Altzeni, Apple Tree Children's Centers, Urbandale, Iowa; Phil Roberson, Swan Lake Children's Center, Bartlesville, Oklahoma; Charles Wilson, Magic Years Learning Center, Webster, Texas; Elizabeth Schilling, Creative Child Care, Columbus, Ohio; Jeanne Sasaran, Loma Alta Preschool, San Diego, California; Carl Staley, United Day Care Services, Greensboro, North Carolina; Charlene Richardson, Child Development Center, Chula Vista, California; and Margaret Bridgers, Margaret Ann Nursery School, Lexington, Kentucky.

How Centers Spend Money on Quality

by John Morris and Suzanne Helburn

Is there a difference in the budgets of centers providing better quality care? What do their budgets look like compared to centers providing lower quality care? Data from a recent study — *Cost, Quality, and Child Outcomes in Child Care Centers* (CQO) — allowed us to construct budgets comparing center cost breakdowns (see Table 1 on page 91) by quality of service provided.

Briefly, we found that better quality centers spend more per child on staff wages, staff benefits, and administrative salaries and benefits than centers providing lower quality. There is little overall difference in costs per child on other expenses such as for facilities, materials, and food

Furthermore, the higher labor and management costs per child carry through to proportionately higher total cost rather than to a different distribution of costs. The higher total cost per child was also reflected in proportionately higher total revenue, so that good quality centers offset higher total cost per child with higher total revenue. However, on average, surplus or profit per child did not differ significantly between lower and higher quality centers, indicating that there is little financial reward for pro-viding higher quality. We did find differences in finances by level of quality among the three sectors of for profit, independent non profit, and church-affiliated centers that raise questions about the prevalence of mediocre care in general in the industry.

About the Study

The CQO study involved an in-depth study of 401 child care centers in four states: Los Angeles in California, Colorado, Connecticut, and North Carolina. Extensive financial and quality data were collected in the spring of 1993 on a random sample of 50 for profit and 50 non profit centers in each state through on-site inter-views with center directors or owners and day-long observations by trained observers of two randomly selected classrooms where possible — one infant/toddler and one preschool room.

Process quality — emphasizing health and safety characteristics, caregiving, developmentally appropriate activi-ties, and children's interactions with each other and with adults — was measured through three widely used observation instruments: the Early Childhood Environment Rating Scale (ECERS, Harms and Clifford, 1980) or the Infant/Toddler Environment Rating Scale (ITERS, Harms, Cryer, and Clifford, 1990); the Caregiver Interaction Scale (CIS, Arnett, 1989); and the Teacher Involve-ment Scale (TIS, Howes and Stewart, 1987).

ECERS and ITERS observations are scored from 1 to 7 based on about 35 aspects of quality. We used an average

Table 1
Budgets for Higher and Lower Quality Centers
(Values Per Child Hour and Annual Figures)

Expense Category	Per Child Hour		Annual Values	
	Higher Quality	Lower Quality	Higher Quality	Lower Quality
Classroom staff wages*	$1.18	$0.93	$157,999	$118,423
Classroom staff benefits*	0.22	0.15	29,381	18,590
Administration salary and benefits	0.37	0.29	36,791	27,823
Staff training	0.01	0.01	1,526	1,060
Contract labor	0.03	0.03	3,618	3,160
Occupancy	0.28	0.23	38,352	30,645
Food cost	0.09	0.09	12,395	12,417
Insurance	0.03	0.03	3,685	3,753
Other operating cost	0.18	0.16	22,490	20,152
Overhead	0.01	0.03	2,291	3,266
TOTAL COST*	$2.38	$1.94	$306,874	$237,726
TOTAL REVENUE*	2.44	2.00	315,626	253,132
Surplus or deficit**	$0.06	$0.06	$8,752	$15,406
Total donations	$0.23	$0.20	$26,560	$19,988
FTE children			70	66

*Significant difference at 5% level.
**Annual mean surplus is affected by extreme values in size of center.

of these individual scores to score each room. An overall index of quality was constructed for each center combining scores for both observed rooms as well as for the CIS and TIS scores. Like ECERS and ITERS, the overall index was scaled from 1 to 7.

The scale is interpreted as follows:

1 — Inadequate: Health and safety needs not met; no warmth or support from adults observed; no learning encouraged.

3 — Minimal: Basic health and safety needs met; a little warmth and support provided by adults; few learning experiences.

5 — Good: Health and safety needs fully met; warmth and support for all children; learning in many ways through interesting activities.

7 — Excellent: Everything in "good" plus children encouraged to become independent; teacher plans for children's individual learning needs; adults have close relations with each child.

To study differences in center costs among lower and higher quality centers, we divided centers into two groups. Centers were categorized as providing higher quality if either their average ITERS and ECERS score *or*

their overall quality index score was 4.5 or higher. Other centers were classified in the lower quality category.

By this criterion, 148 centers provided higher quality and 253 provided lower quality.

Budgets for Higher and Lower Quality Centers

Table 1 shows budgets for higher and lower quality centers in two ways. Columns 1 and 2 give costs, revenue, surplus (profit), and value of donations per child hour, and columns 3 and 4 give annual budget estimates for the average center.

In order to provide a more accurate estimate of the effect of quality, it is necessary to eliminate the effects of other cost factors — in particular, regional differences, the impact of profit status, and of differing age compositions of children served.

The figures in Table 1 represent mean values, holding constant region and profit status (for profit, independent non profit, and church-affiliated). Although the percentage of center FTE composed of preschool children affects cost per child, it does not have much effect on average cost comparisons between lower and higher quality centers. Asterisks identify figures that show statistically significant differences in the two quality groups.

Higher quality centers served slightly more children (70 FTE compared to 66). The budgets reflect the study's findings that higher quality teaching staff, better adult-child ratios, and lower staff turnover (implying higher wages) lead to higher quality care. Both staff wages and staff benefits were significantly higher in higher quality centers. They totaled $1.40 per child hour in the higher quality centers but only $1.08 in the lower quality centers.

The study also showed that administrator tenure at the center and prior experience, as well as their effective involvement in curriculum planning, lead to higher quality. Table 1 shows that administrator salaries and benefits totaled 37¢ per child hour in higher quality centers and 29¢ per child hour in lower quality centers. (This figure includes an imputed salary for owner-operators who reported no salary and salaries and benefits for all owners, directors, and curriculum coordinators.)

The study also showed that indoor square footage per child was positively related to quality and the budget shows a similar difference, although this difference is not statistically significant. Other than occupancy, other non-labor costs were almost identical in the two groups and combine for less than 20% of the total cost.

Total cost and total revenue were both significantly higher in higher quality centers, both by 44¢ per child hour — that is, on average, the higher quality cost about 20% more than the lower quality centers. Interestingly, there was no difference in surplus per child hour of 6¢ per child hour. The two columns showing annual surplus do appear to show a higher average surplus in lower quality centers despite their slightly smaller size.

This appears to be the effect of a small number of very large and profitable mediocre centers. It does not appear to be indicative of the situation for most centers. In general, these results seem to indicate that higher quality centers can recover their higher costs through higher revenues, but, on average, there were no financial gains from higher quality.

Sector Differences

We also investigated possible differences in the cost of providing quality by centers with different ownership and found such differences among church-related centers, secular non profit centers, and for profit centers.

Not too surprisingly, for profit centers showed the lowest labor costs ($1.42 for higher quality and $1.15 for lower quality) and secular non profits the highest ($1.96 and $1.75). Perhaps more interestingly, higher quality church-related centers had almost the highest labor costs of all ($1.94), while labor cost per child hour for lower quality church-related centers were among the lowest ($1.23).

A similar difference between higher and lower quality centers was apparent for non-labor costs. Higher quality church centers spent 18¢ more per child hour on non-labor costs than lower quality church-related centers. By contrast, higher quality for profit centers spent only 9¢ extra and higher quality secular non profit centers actually spent 14¢ per child hour less on non-labor costs than lower quality secular non profits. Nearly all of these differences were in occupancy costs, not program. Regardless of quality, for profit centers had higher non-labor costs than either group of non profits.

These differences may reflect differences in subsidies. Higher quality secular non profits received 16¢ per child hour more than lower quality secular non profits, almost the difference in costs. Even among for profits, the higher quality centers averaged 5¢ per child hour more subsidies than lower quality non profits, adding to the difference in costs. Among church-related centers, however, the lower quality centers received 12¢ per child hour more subsidies.

The bottom line was that lower quality church-related centers, with a total cost of $1.54 per child hour, were the cheapest source of child care in the study, and they generated a surplus averaging 10¢ per child hour. For profit centers averaged about $2.00 per child hour ($2.20 for higher quality and $1.86 for lower) and provided the lowest cost (not necessarily the lowest fee) high quality care. The secular non profits and the higher quality church-related centers averaged over $2.40 per child hour.

What may be happening in the church-related center sector is that some churches are subsidizing parents' affordability at the expense of quality, while others promote quality and are very similar, financially, to other non profit centers. In the secular non profit sector, better quality centers seem to have higher donations than lower quality secular centers, but otherwise there is not much difference in finances within this sector.

Conclusions

1. There is a cost to improving quality in child care, but it is small except in church-related centers.

2. Higher quality centers put their extra dollars into labor and management primarily — not facilities, supplies, or program.

3. The higher cost of providing quality was offset by higher revenue — that is, one can provide higher quality without a financial penalty, but there is little financial reward.

4. Higher quality centers were no smaller than lower quality centers.

5. For profit centers provided the cheapest higher quality care and churches provided the cheapest lower quality care.

6. Lower quality church centers received higher subsidies than higher quality church centers, and may be focusing on affordability for parents more than quality.

7. Compared to lower quality secular non profit centers, higher quality secular non profits received more subsidies, but their costs (including subsidies) were similar, suggesting an efficient allocation of subsidies to provide quality — that is, the subsidies seem to have gone to the right centers within this group.

8. The quality within sectors is not related to cost in secular non profit centers. Higher quality increases cost only modestly in for profit centers. There is a large difference in cost for quality in the church sector. These extra costs are covered by extra revenues, except in the church sector. If this is the case, why don't centers in the secular non profit and for profit sectors provide better quality on average? Perhaps there is a shortage of highly skilled directors.

References

Arnett, J. (1989). "Caregivers in Day Care Centers: Does Training Matter?" *Journal of Applied Developmental Psychology*, 10, 541-552.

Harms, T., & Clifford, R. M. (1980). *Early Childhood Environment Rating Scale*. New York: Teachers College Press.

Harms, T., Cryer, D. , & Clifford, R. M. (1990). *Infant/Toddler Environment Rating Scale*. New York: Teachers College Press.

Howes, C., & Stewart, P. (1987). "Child's Play with Adults, Toys and Peers: An Examination of Family and Child Care Influences." *Developmental Psychology*, 23, 423-430.

John Morris is professor of economics at the University of Colorado at Denver. He served as economist on the **Cost, Quality, and Child Outcomes Study** *as principal investigator of numerous projects examining the economics of various social services, in particular, of child care.*

Suzanne Helburn is professor emerita of economics at the University of Colorado at Denver and was the coordinator and one of the principal investigators for the **Cost, Quality, and Child Outcomes in Child Care Centers Study** *on which results of this article are based. With Barbara Bergmann, she is co-author of* **America's Child Care Problem: the Way Out** *(Palgrave for St. Martin's Press, 2002).*

Managing Money

Fundraising Strategies

*"The components of a successful fundraising effort are a
program effectively addressing a recognized need,
an audience of donors sympathetic to the cause,
and a strategy that brings the donors
and the program together."*

Where the Bucks Are: Sources for Funds to Grow Your Child Care Business

by Keith Stephens

S tarting a child care business and building it up into a profitable operation requires entrepreneurial skills, hard work, determination to provide a quality service, respect for the consumer, and good luck. And, in most cases, it requires an infusion of money from the outside.

Finding the money you need to finance the process of growth can be a frustrating, fruitless experience unless you do your homework. Prior to hitting the streets looking for money, you need to put together a solid business plan which spells out where your business is headed, how you will do it, benchmarks for judging your progress, and why you will be successful. No one will give you money unless you can assure them of what you expect to accomplish — and can demonstrate a reasonable expectation for a solid, profitable return.

Then you need to identify likely sources of money. There are a wide range of financing alternatives to consider, but each is best suited to businesses at different growth stages. People get in trouble when they pursue the wrong source at the wrong time. Your chances of success are improved by concentrating your energies on a source that is likely to produce results. To help you sort out what sources make the most sense at what point, I have discussed below characteristics of the most common sources of funds for a for profit child care business.

Tapping Friends and Relatives

Friends and relatives are the money source of first and last resort for entrepreneurs just setting out to make their mark in the world. When all you have is a dream, it is very difficult to attract investments from conventional sources of money. As enthusiastic as you may be about your dream, potential investors will primarily be looking at economic return. Weighted heavily against you are the all too familiar statistics showing that most new small businesses fail. As a result, those starting from scratch must turn to the people who are most likely to be supportive — friends and relatives.

Advantages:

- **Friends and relatives are most likely to be receptive** to your plans because they know you and have more reason to be confident that you will succeed.

- **The money will come with fewer strings attached.** Since people close to you will invest in you on faith, they are not likely to insist on placing formal restrictions on how you use the money — or on how you run the business.

- **Most often they will invest for equity only.** This means that you will not be encumbered by a tight repayment schedule or interest payments.

- **You will probably not suffer serious economic repercussions** if your business doesn't pan out and you don't repay the money. Friends and relatives are much less likely than bankers or investors to press for repayment.

Disadvantages:

- **The emotional pressure can be overwhelming.** You don't want to fail for the people who are closest to you. The personal embarrassment is greater if your business is failing and you are losing the money and the respect (you assume) of the friends and relatives who were counting on you. For example, if you lose $50,000 borrowed from your parents and it turns out this was their retirement fund, the emotional cost involved can be very, very high. In many cases, complete alienation results.

- **You are not likely to raise as much money** via this route as you would from conventional money sources, unless you are one of those rare individuals blessed with rich

---

> ### Table 1
> ### Types of Business Financing
>
> Child care businesses utilize outside financing for two general purposes:
>
> **To finance the business itself:** Money needed for the total operation of the business in order to facilitate growth. This article explores options available for this purpose.
>
> **To purchase real estate:** Financing required for the purchase of land and real property. The real estate serves as collateral. A wide range of real estate financing vehicles are available, such as conventional bank mortgages, loans from insurance companies, and investments made through limited partnership arrangements.
>
> There are two general types of financing available:
>
> **Equity investments:** Money that is invested in your business in exchange for a share of the ownership. Money is invested with the expectation that a return will be realized in the future as the value of one's share of the business appreciates.
>
> **Loans:** Money advanced to a business with a formal repayment schedule. Return is realized from interest charged for the use of the money.

---

relatives who are eager to part with their money. On the other hand, while the $50,000 to $100,000 that is the most that you are likely to secure from friends and relatives will not enable you to launch a national chain, it should be sufficient seed money to start a single center.

Other Considerations:

In most cases, it is best to treat money raised from friends and relatives as an investment in the company. Give everybody stock in the company. If your business is successful, everyone will get a stock dividend or be bought out by someone else (hopefully at a nice profit). If the business fails, they will have gambled and lost.

On the other hand, if for some reason you desire to retain 100% of the stock, you would want to treat the money received as a loan with an agreed upon repayment schedule and rate of interest. While this will place you under a stronger obligation to repay the money, it will enable you to exercise full control of the business.

Finding an Angel — a Private Investor

An angel is a wealthy individual who you persuade to invest in your business. This approach is similar to convincing a friend to invest, although — since this individual will not necessarily know you personally — your personal credibility as well as that of your business plan will be subject to much tighter scrutiny.

Advantages:

- **A private investor will be more emotionally removed** from you than a friend or relative. Your relationship can operate in a more businesslike fashion, without the emotional undercurrents of a personal relationship.

- **An angel will probably not insist on gaining control** of the business. Most likely he or she will not have the time or inclination to become immersed in everyday decision-making.

- **You are likely to have access to more money** from a wealthy individual than from friends and relatives.

- **An angel will not necessarily be looking for a quick return**, so you will not be pressured to generate dramatic profits immediately. More likely, the private investor will be looking for a reasonable return three to seven years in the future when you sell the business or go public.

Disadvantages:

- **A private individual will be harder to win over** than friends and relatives. You will need to prove yourself and the viability of your plan.

- **He or she will want more protection.** One way to structure a more attractive deal for a private investor is to offer preferred stock. A preferred class of stock could offer many privileges to this individual:

a stated rate of return, some preference upon liquidation, some preference in terms of dividends (that he/should would receive dividends before you did, for example), the right to move from preferred stock to common stock, or the right to pick up voting privileges to more actively protect his/her investment if the business is not doing well.

- **More documentation and more legal work will be involved** in putting the transaction together.

- **The final arrangement will likely be much more tightly structured** than one with a friend or relative. There will be more restrictions on how you spend the money and run the business, such as frequent reporting on your progress, participation in approval of the budget and major fixed asset purchases, limits on expenses, and limits on your salary.

Other Considerations:

How do you find an angel? By talking to your banker (most larger banks have something akin to an executive banking section for wealthy individuals), your lawyer (particularly lawyers in bigger law firms which have contact with affluent individuals), your accountant, and representatives of trust companies and investment management services (that manage assets for other people); by going to the right business meetings and belonging to the right community organizations; and by advertising in the business or classified section in the newspaper. In all these ways you will be seeking referrals which will lead you to an individual who is willing and able to put up the kind of money you need.

Making a Private Placement

A formalized method of securing private investors is the private placement. Under this procedure, you go out to the business or investment community with a business plan and offer to sell stock in your company. Typically the purpose of a private placement is to attract money from a number of people beyond your inner circle of friends and relatives.

A private placement is a less rigorous procedure for selling stock than a public offering. The rules governing private placements are less involved, and the disclosure requirements less stringent. However, there are specific limitations on how much can be raised in this manner, and who can invest. You will need to consult your lawyer regarding rules and regulations defining these limitations.

Advantages:

- **You are spreading the risk.** By selling shares in your company to a number of investors, the degree of risk each one is being exposed to is less than if one individual was making the whole investment. People may be more willing to invest if they know that others are willing to do so also.

- **A greater amount of money can be raised**, in most cases, through a private placement than through private individuals.

- **You can retain final control.** While you are selling shares in your business in order to generate capital, you can normally retain at least 51% of the stock yourself.

- **This is a long-term investment.** Investors are typically looking for a payoff coming not from annual earnings but from resale of the company either to someone else or to the public through a stock offering (so their 3% share in a $1,750,000 company becomes 3% of a $10,000,000 sale). Normally, investors expect a return in a three to seven year time frame. Thus there will not be pressure to achieve an immediate high level of profitability. However, there will be the expectation that the company grow steadily and significantly.

Disadvantages:

- **This is not a do-it-yourself project.** You will need to hire a lawyer to prepare a form of prospectus known as a private placement memorandum. In this document you spell out for prospective investors the nature of your company and the business that you are engaged in, the key people in your company, your future plans, your past financial performance and future financial projections, and your money needs.

- **This is not an appropriate vehicle for a small business** planning for modest growth. Even if you perform most of the paperwork and legwork yourself, legal fees can run anywhere from $10,000 to $20,000. With this built in cost of raising the money, it means that for raising anything under $200,000, this would not be a practical vehicle. This is not for single centers looking to add one or two locations. It is more applicable if you are operating three or four centers profitably and can present a creditable plan for growing significantly.

Table 2
Financing Under Different Stages of Development

Stage of Organizational Development	Likely Financing Sources
Start-Up Stage • Organization is only in the idea stage. • No service is being delivered. • This represents a high risk investment. • A limited source of funds is available.	Self, friends, or relatives Private sources
First Stage • Organization is now delivering a service. • It has proven that it can sell in the marketplace. • Profitable operations are still at least two years away.	Venture capital Private placement
Second Stage • Organization is up and running. • It is marketing its service with a degree of success. • It needs funds for expansion.	Venture capital Private offering Public offering Bank
Third Stage • Organization is running well. • It is generating steady profits. • It needs additional capital to continue its rapid growth.	Public offering Bank
Mature Stage • Organization is running well. • It is generating steady profits. • It has been able to manage in both up and down business cycles. • It generates sufficient cash flow to handle most of its working capital needs. • Its services are well accepted by the marketplace.	Bank Insurance company Public offering

- **This is not an appropriate vehicle for a new business.** Typically you need to be up and running in order to establish credibility. In some cases, primarily in the high tech arena, it can be a vehicle for start-up, but in this case you will need a strong sell on yourself.

- **This is a time consuming process.** It will require that you take time away from your business. This means that you must be able to set your business up in such a manner that it can run without you during this period. If not, you may see your business go down the drain before you get the investment to make it grow.

- **You must be prepared to lose** the time and money you invest in the process. There is a high likelihood that the deal will fall through. Therefore, the legal fees and the time you invest in the effort will go for naught.

Other Considerations:

Once your private placement memorandum is complete, you can conceivably sell it yourself by tracking down likely prospects and pitching it to them on a one-to-one basis. You are more likely to experience success, however, if you enlist professional assistance. Often you can find a small local brokerage firm, a local investment banking firm, or a local financial management firm that is willing to take on the sales effort for you. What they end up doing is placing your shares with their clients. Financial planners, who have emerged in the last few years, are a good vehicle for taking your plan and presenting it.

Keep in mind that any investment professional will expect a commission in the 5% to 10% range. In addition, you must recognize that they see a multitude of plans. You must make yours stand out from the crowd. Finding a lawyer who is experienced in doing private placement deals will be most helpful here.

Borrowing From a Bank

Your friendly neighborhood banker is often the first person you think of when you need money. Unfortunately, you are likely to discover that this friendliness is only skin deep when you come asking for money to grow a business. While banks have tremendous assets at their disposal, they are not inclined to risk these assets on any business that is not already well established. However, at various stages in your growth, bank financing is feasible and desirable.

Advantages:

- **Banks are easy to find.** Bankers love to have deals brought to them to look over. (It's amazing how positive they are at the first interview, how difficult they are to deal with after that, and how cold they are when they turn you down.)

- **The methodology for dealing with banks is clearly defined.** From the very start, it is clear what banks will lend money for, what hoops you will have to jump through to get it, and how the deal can be structured.

- **Banks can be very helpful** to you in your business. They have trained people who look at numerous businesses and see how they perform. They routinely analyze your financial statements and compare them with other industries.

If you can see these comparisons and the financial ratios they develop on your business, this can be quite useful to you.

- **Banks have several financing vehicles** to employ: working capital loans when you need more money in your business, and have the profitability to support it; asset financing when you want to grow your business, but need money to buy new equipment, etc.; real estate construction funding when you want to construct a new facility or remodel your old center; and mortgage financing when you want to purchase or refinance your property.

- **The amount of money obtainable is limited only by your ability to qualify.** Loans can range from $500 personal loans to commercial loans for billions of dollars. Most independent banks will be limited to the $200,000 to $300,000 range, but this should meet the needs of most center operators.

- **You don't have to give them part of your company.** Banks are not equity investors, they are lenders. They will insist upon a tight repayment schedule, not a share of your business.

Disadvantages:

- **Banks are very conservative.** Banks are tightly regulated and closely scrutinized, and this forces them to be conservative. A banker is thinking at all times, "What can go wrong?" We, as entrepreneurs, think of all the things that will go well. It is important to know how a banker thinks and tailor your presentation accordingly.

- **Banks rarely give long-term loans.** You can get term loans in the three to five year range, but seldom are they willing to go beyond that (with the exception of mortgages). A common procedure is to write a loan with a five to seven year payment schedule, with a single large payment at the end of every year. This gives them the leverage to review the loan every year to determine if it should be renewed.

- **Banks will closely monitor your business.** They will periodically want to see your financial statements and, if you start falling behind, will ask for more frequent and detailed reports. This can become onerous if your record-keeping is haphazard or done in an unconventional way.

- **Banks are professionals at collecting money.** In the event you fall behind, they can make it reasonably difficult for you.

Other Considerations:

When evaluating your loan request, bankers will take a close look at the three C's of banking: *character, credit,* and *collateral.* Is the person running the business competent and trustworthy? Does the business have a solid credit history? Are there sufficient assets in the business to secure the loan? Almost always, you will be asked to provide a personal guarantee.

These criteria tend to work against businesses just starting out, or those that are struggling. In addition, the stipulation that investments be secured by hard assets can be a problem in child care where there is no inventory, no receivables, and few tangible assets

(outside of property) which a bank would view as marketable.

Pursuing Venture Capitalists

In recent years, most of the glamour in venture capital has gone to high tech industries. However, now that growth in this area has leveled off, venture capitalists are looking around for other hot industries. And child care is one industry that has started to attract their attention.

Companies that venture capitalists find appealing are not yet at the bankable stage. Sometimes they are start-up companies, but more likely they are already organized and just starting to show a potential for dramatic growth. What these companies need is an infusion of money to turn this potential into a reality.

Advantages:

- **They will help you grow.** Because venture capitalists are in the business of growing companies, they have talent on hand to assist you in managing your business. They are going to be actively involved in protecting their investment.

- **Venture capitalists can make substantial investments.** Because of all the investigative work that goes into making investment decisions, they are not interested in any deal for less than $250,000. Venture capital is not a viable source of money for small companies. It is only a realistic possibility for a business with aspirations of becoming a regional or national chain with around 50 centers.

Disadvantages:

- **Venture capitalists are hard to find.** They are not on every street corner like banks. However, lists are available from *Inc.* and *Money* magazines.

- **Dealing with a venture capitalist can be an intimidating process.** They won't know you, and won't have any confidence in what you can accomplish. You will need to convince them that you are worthy of their trust.

- **You will need to sell them on the child care industry** as well as on your business. They won't share your dream. When you say *child care,* they will say *insurance problem.* You will have had to do your homework well to make a convincing case for them to invest in a soft service industry that they won't understand.

- **You will have to give away a big hunk of your company and you will be under the gun to perform.** They will want seats on the board of directors, and they continually will want to know what is going on. You can retain control, but only if things are going as planned. In all likelihood, they will insist upon provisions that will improve their influence over the company if things don't go well.

Other Considerations:

A venture capital firm is absolutely going to want to know "How are we going to get out of this deal?" If you can't demonstrate to them, with a high degree of certainty, that within three to five years they will be able to walk away from the deal with a healthy profit, they won't even talk to you.

They are not looking for dividends paid out of profits. They're looking for the return that comes from building a company and then disposing of it. The return they expect from any one investment is in the range of 50% to 60% per year. In other words, if they put in $1 million they would expect $10 million back at the end of five years.

Approaching Insurance Companies

Insurance companies are not a likely funding source for garden variety child care businesses. The financing vehicles they prefer are suited to massive real estate investments. For the most part, insurance companies won't even talk to you if you're looking for less than $1 million. On the other hand, if you are an established regional chain needing $12 million to build 20 centers at $600,000 apiece, an insurance company would be an appropriate vehicle for arranging for that investment in one fell swoop.

While insurance companies will consider some equity arrangements, they are primarily interested in real estate deals. Like banks, they are not risk takers; but because of the size of their investments, they can sometimes offer better interest rates, and they can be somewhat more flexible in how they structure the deal.

Making a Public Offering

A public offering is a vehicle for mature companies that want to finance growth or a change in ownership. This is a route that would only make sense for regional or national chains with 50 or more centers looking to raise at least $10 million.

Investors in a public offering would be interested in a return on earnings — your profitability is going to determine what price you can get for your stock.

You could have a public offering for a start-up venture, but you would need one of the regional or national broker-age firms to work with you on it, and it is unlikely that you could sell them on the idea. On the other hand, a public offering would be an appropriate route if an individual had built up a chain of 50 centers and wanted to sell them, yet wanted to stay involved in the day-to-day management.

Keith Stephens, a CPA, is the former president of Palo Alto Preschools, once the country's largest privately owned child care chain, and past president of the National Association for Child Care Management.

Keys to Success in Raising Funds

by Roger Neugebauer

Exchange *magazine has surveyed over 100 child care centers about their successful, as well as their unsuccessful fundraising projects. From the experiences of these centers, the ten factors described below have emerged as keys to successful fundraisers.*

Define Your Purpose

The willingness of staff members, parents, volunteers, and members of the community to give their support to a fundraiser will be enhanced to the extent that the need for funds is clear and important. People need to know that their contribution of time, talents, or resources will make a difference.

Therefore, before launching a fundraising effort, a center should assess whether it is truly necessary and, if so, for what purpose. This intent should then be identified at the outset of any appeals for support. Centers have found that the more specific the purpose can be defined the better. It is easier to generate support for "constructing an outdoor climbing structure" than for "building up the contingency account"; it is more inspiring to contribute towards a "scholarship fund" than towards "general operating expenses."

In child care, fundraisers often have important secondary purposes as well. Centers often utilize these projects to provide publicity for the center and to enhance parent involvement. These purposes should clearly be identified at the outset, also, so that the project can be organized in such a way as to ensure their accomplishment.

A common pitfall here is when a secondary purpose is really the main purpose. Centers sometimes use fundraisers as a device for getting parents involved. This can unnecessarily waste the precious time of parents and can backfire when the parents realize their efforts do not accomplish anything of importance.

Set a Goal

Centers have found it beneficial to set a target amount to be raised each year. Having a financial goal helps planners to gauge the magnitude of the effort required, and to decide on the type of activities which are appropriate.

A center needing to raise $500 would not establish a thrift shop, nor would one requiring $6,000 schedule a bake sale. Having a specific dollar goal is more likely to instill confidence in potential donors that the center knows what it's about. Once the goal is set, it can also help focus volunteers' efforts if they are kept informed about the progress toward that goal. Some centers even post a chart at the center, much like the thermometer of United Way, which shows volunteers how close they are to accomplishing the goal.

Fundraising Strategies

Know the Audience

Who is likely to contribute to your center? The type of fundraising projects a center implements should be appropriate to the project's potential audience.

If your center is known by individuals in your community who have abundant financial resources and who believe in what your center is doing, the direct approach may be best. Contact them, explain your need, and ask for a donation. If, on the other hand, your program is known and supported primarily by individuals with scant financial resources, asking for donations may not be realistic. Instead, it may be more appropriate to offer some goods or services in return for people's contributions.

In planning this type of fundraiser, the potential audience needs to be examined even more closely. Who is the potential audience? What goods or services are likely to be of real interest to them? How much are they likely to contribute? You are operating on shaky ground if you cannot answer these questions with some certainty before planning a fundraiser.

Make it Fun

Select a project that staff and parents are excited about. Most fundraisers depend heavily upon the volunteer work of staff, parents, and board members. The amount of effort these people are likely to invest in a project relates significantly to the extent they are excited about it.

If the chairperson of a fundraising committee decides that a raffle will be the solution to all the center's financial woes, but parents are none too eager to hustle prizes or tickets, chances are the raffle will fizzle.

Build on Strengths

Try to select a fundraiser that builds on the skills that already exist in the center. Personnel in child care centers have expertise in areas such as child development, child nutrition, children's activities, and parent education.

Examples of fundraisers capitalizing on such skills include children's entertainment series, gymnastics classes, babysitter training and referral, cookbooks for children, and parenting workshops. A child care center should be most effective and efficient in organizing fundraisers such as these. In addition, such a project can showcase the skills and services of the center to potential supporters and customers.

Look for Repeaters

Centers surveyed noted several reasons for selecting fundraisers that can be repeated on a regular basis. First, the center can learn from its mistakes. Errors which were made the first time in planning, publicizing, and putting on a project can be eliminated in future reruns, thus saving on wasted energy and resources.

Second, the project will not need to be organized from scratch every time. Press releases, flyers, costumes, booths, or publicity strategies developed the first time can simply be refined rather than reinvented.

Third, the more often a successful project is run, the more effective publicity will be.

Be Cost Effective

Centers can fall into the trap of thinking that any project that brings in money is worthwhile. However, such reasoning fails to consider the value of staff and volunteer time expended in raising the money.

People's time should be considered as a valuable resource. It should not be squandered on fundraising projects that generate a small return on time invested.

To calculate the return on time investment (R) of any project, simply deduct all expenses (E) incurred in putting on the project (including the value of paid staff time) from total income (I) of the project, then divide the remainder by the total number of hours (T) spent by staff and volunteers on the project:

$$\frac{I - E}{T} = R$$

To illustrate, consider the case of a spring fair held by a nursery school in New England. This school's staff and parents donated about 475 hours of time (T) planning, publicizing, setting up, and operating the fair — and expended $250 in center funds (E) for booths, food, and publicity in order to raise a total of $850 (I) for the center. Plugging this into the formula, it can be seen that for every hour invested in this project the center earned $1.26 in profit:

$$\frac{\$850 - \$250}{475 \text{ hours}} = \$1.26 / \text{hour}$$

Even though the project was a *success* in terms of raising a significant chunk of money, the return on the investment of volunteers' time was dreadfully low. Bake sales and dinners are often equally wasteful of volunteers' time.

On the other hand, other fundraisers described by directors interviewed for this article brought returns of anywhere from $25-150/hour. Given the fact that such cost effective projects are quite realistic, a center should certainly think twice about engaging in any project which will return less than $20/hour.

Publicize Aggressively

Centers that have the most success with fundraisers are those which have mastered the art of getting the right message to the right people at the right time.

The first step in an effective publicity campaign is clarifying what is being *sold*. If the fundraising project is a direct appeal for donations, what is being sold is the cause — people are being asked to give money to a cause they believe in.

For an indirect fundraiser, such as a raffle, a bake sale, or a dinner, it is the product or service that is being sold — the chance to win, the cookies, or the meal. The *message* of all publicity should concentrate heavily on what is being sold.

This right message must also reach the right people. Often in membership drives and appeals for donations, certain professionals — such as doctors, who are deemed most likely to contribute to the center — are singled out for calls.

Likewise, a center which offers a noon luncheon in a downtown area sends flyers around to offices in the neighborhood to alert people who eat lunch out. Effective publicity has much less to do with *how much* than it does with *where*.

Centers with sound ongoing fundraising campaigns also take great pains to develop extensive lists of known supporters. Included on this list should be former parents, staff, and board members; those who have visited the center; and those who have attended or contributed to past fundraisers. For every fundraiser, this group should be sent a special announcement.

Maximize Publicity

At the outset of this article, it was mentioned that publicity can be a secondary purpose of fundraisers. In fact, every time you embark on a fundraising initiative you should analyze the publicity opportunities the fundraiser offers. That way you will get extra mileage out of the time and resources you invest in the fundraiser.

A classic example of a missed opportunity occurred when a New England center provided child care at a Women's Fair. The center set up a variety of activities in a corner of the auditorium where the fair was being held. Children were so happy and fully engaged that fairgoers stopped and enjoyed observing the children at the *play area*. This could have provided extremely beneficial publicity with a highly appropriate audience. However, nowhere in the area was the name of the center posted.

Thank Contributors

After every fundraiser, the center should send a thank you to all who contributed to the project — those who planned it and volunteered time to make it happen, as well as those who donated money, goods, or services. The thank you typically includes a final report on the results of the fundraiser — "We reached 110% of our goal," "We were able to finance remodeling of the infant room," etc. Some centers keep donors on their mailing list for the center's newsletter.

Circles of Support

by Kathy Hines

During a job interview, I was once asked how I liked being a professional beggar. The image of fundraising as panhandling permeates our world, yet it couldn't be farther from the truth. A beggar offers nothing in return for your support. A fundraiser offers concerned constituents an opportunity to invest in a cause. Chances are, a beggar won't ask you whether you'd prefer your loose change to support food purchases or bus tokens. A successful fundraiser works with donors to make sure mutual needs are met. When was the last time you received a thank you note, annual report, or donor newsletter with a return address of "corner of 7th and Main"? A fundraiser recognizes the importance of cultivating relationships, not simply to ensure a repeat gift, but rather as an acknowledgment of the donor's interest in and concern for the organization.

The constituency from which our donors are drawn is one of our most valuable organizational resources. By taking the time to properly identify and clarify who your constituents are, fundraising efforts can be maximized. A model called "constituency circles" has been developed by The Fund Raising School Center on Philanthropy at Indiana University. The following steps will help you to map out the circles for your own child care center.

Let's start with brainstorming. Write down each type of person, group, or business who has ever had any type of connection with your center. The more categories you come up with, the better. For the time being, don't concern yourself with questions about the appropriateness of your list items. Just let your imagination flow. A sample list might look like this:

- Students

- Parents

- Teachers

- Board of directors

- Grocery store where we buy our snacks

- Playground equipment manufacturer

- Snow removal service

- Donors

- Volunteers

- People who came to open house

- Parents of alumni

- Anyone who saw the article on our center in the Hometown Child Care Newsletter

- People interested in education

- Bakery where we went on a field trip

- Store where we buy art supplies

Once you've finished your list, draw a series of four concentric circles on a separate sheet of paper. These circles will provide a map of your constituency, showing your closest connections in the very middle and radiating out as relationships weaken. Use the following guidelines to place each group on your list into a category. Each of the four circles represents a piece of your constituency:

- **Primary stakeholders.** Located in the very middle, this group represents people who have the closest relationship with your child care facility, those who are most invested in its mission and success. They will include your board of directors, staff, and current major donors.

- **Lesser stakeholders.** This category includes active participants, such as parents and families of current students, active volunteers, and other donors.

- **Casual participants.** These groups have a connection with your center but it is not as strong or as current as those in the previous categories. Examples might include parents of alumni or vendors (snow removal service, stores that you patronize).

- **Similar interests.** These people have a connection with your center by a similarity of interests which could lead them to be more closely involved. Perhaps they attended an open house, requested information, or are known to support other child care centers in the community. Your ties are not as direct, but you are aware of a common bond.

The primary stakeholders are the nucleus of your child care center. These people have the closest relationships, the greatest investments, and the highest level of commitment to your success. It is their responsibility to draw the outer circles in closer, whether by setting an appropriate example, providing motivation, or advocating on your behalf.

Common fundraising wisdom states that before embarking on a fundraising campaign you must have financial commitments from your board of directors. The constituency circles demonstrate that reasoning. If those who are closest to your center are unwill-ing to support it, how will you persuade those whose connections are weaker to get involved?

The circles are also a tool for prioritizing your efforts. With the myriad of responsibilities facing any center director, it is unthinkable that each prospective donor can be approached with the same amount of effort.

Accordingly, work from the middle out. It will be easiest to fold in those who have close, recent, and direct connections with your child care center. This is not to say that time shouldn't be spent cultivating the outer rings as well. Just be certain that you don't overextend yourself, developing elaborate schemes to entice those with minimal connections before you've secured the ones closest to you. Similarly, choose an appropriate solicitation technique for each circle. The time it takes to meet personally with the innermost rings will be worth the effort. The numbers are smaller, the connections are stronger, and you want to focus on continuing to build those relationships.

As you move farther out, it's appropriate to reduce the level of personalization. For instance, while letters to previous donors should always be ≠personalized as much as possible, a mail solicitation to all subscribers of a local child care newsletter can be mass produced.

It is also essential to spend time determining what motivates each circle of your constituency. Parents are looking for quality education for their children. Local businesses may be motivated by understanding the ultimate benefits this education offers to the community. The list of motivations will be as varied as your constituents.

Take the time to find out what they are. Ask your current donors why they contribute. Ask potential donors what appeals to them. And, always, talk to your colleagues about their experiences at their own centers. Don't be afraid to customize the message you put out. Your center meets many needs of many people. Use that variety to your advantage.

You'll play many roles as you raise funds. Become a storyteller while you relate tales of your center's success; a businessperson while presenting the overall financial picture; a negotiator as you determine how to match your needs with the desires of your donor; an educator as you explain child development while touring the classroom. But, as long as you have clarified your goals, believe in your mission, and respect the needs of your constituents, you won't ever be a beggar. Leave the tin cup at home and start circling.

Kathy Hines is the fund development associate at the High/Scope Educational Research Foundation in Ypsilanti, Michigan. She is a member of the National Society of Fund Raising Executives.

Securing Funds Through Grant Writing

by Fredalene D. Bowers

Funding is always a concern for child care centers. It doesn't matter whether the program is nonprofit or for-profit, privately owned or corporate-sponsored, large or small, there never seems to be enough money to cover personnel expenses and purchase equipment and materials. Most child care directors depend on federal or state allocations, parent fees, and fundraising to meet financial needs. The idea of securing additional funds through grant writing is often not a consideration because the process seems overwhelming, and often the director is not aware of grants as a source of additional funding.

If your program is seeking additional funding, grant writing might be your answer. This article will address two aspects to securing funds through grant writing: first, how to apply for grants and second, where to apply.

Understanding the Grant Writing Process

Grant writing is not as difficult as many people believe. Although there are courses on grant writing, very few people start their career with the goal of "becoming a grant writer." Most individuals become grant writers out of necessity — they need to maintain their current funding, they need to secure additional funding to supplement current funds, and/or they want to introduce new programs. The following are some tried and true tips to help the beginning grant writer.

Top 10 Tips:

10 — Assess your chances for success

It is best to start small where competition is not so stiff. Before you begin to tackle the proposal, find out how much money is available and how many grants will be funded. It will be easier to secure a local or state grant for 5-, 10-, or 20-thousand dollars than a federal grant where millions of dollars are available but only fifteen proposals will be funded.

9 — Get to know your funder

Funders have a reason for funding projects. No matter how great you think your idea is or how much your program will benefit by the funding, if your goals do not match the funder's goals, you are wasting your time by applying. Many federal, state, and private funders have a "Pre-Proposal Conference" or "Bidders Conference" to identify the purpose of the funding, the amount of funding, the number of grants to be awarded, and guidelines for submitting the proposal. If possible, attend these in person. You may be able to meet the funders or their representatives. If you can't attend, many funders will mail, within ten days to two weeks, the questions and answers addressed at the conference. Knowing your funder is important. Your success rate *increases 300%*, if you know your funder (CD Publications, 193-94).

8 — Set up a proposal library

There are many commonalities when writing a proposal. All proposals require information about your organization: the history, mission statement, staffing patterns (organizational chart), job descriptions, number of children served, ability to carry out the proposal, current staff resumes, and program demographics. This information is called "boilerplate material." Start files for boilerplate material and continually add items (e.g., current statistics) so the material is at your fingertips when you need it.

7 — Follow the directions exactly and pay attention to details

Grant writing is not a creative activity. The funder is looking for an innovative project, not innovative or creative writing; therefore, it is essential that you follow the directions exactly. Most proposal formats are similar; an abstract or summary (if proposal is over ten pages), a table of contents, a problem or need statement, goals and objectives, target population, project methodology/work plan, organizational capability, evaluation, budget, and appendix/attachments. Read and reread the directions, then follow them: number of pages, headings, size of margins, format, etc. It is also extremely important to pay attention to the deadline. If the proposal is due by 4:00 p.m. on September 30, allow enough time for delivery by mail or plan to hand deliver it, if this is acceptable to the funder.

Read the guidelines carefully so you know how the funds are to be used (and how they cannot be used). Many small grants cannot be used to purchase equipment. So no matter how badly your program needs a new computer or copier, don't write those into the budget. When I asked participants at a recent grant writing workshop to brainstorm innovative projects to fund, one participant responded " . . . textbooks because our school does not have up-to-date textbooks." As I told the group, most funders will not provide money for textbooks since this is the responsibility of the school. However, if the proposal is for a course using innovative techniques and strategies, you may be able to purchase textbooks with some of the grant monies.

Methodology or Work Plan

Be very specific in writing your methodology section. This is where grant writing often falls short. You may know what you want to do but your funder does not, so include all of the relevant details. State exactly how, when, what, and who will be involved. Use the narrative format to explain your proposal. It is better to include more details here than less. Remember, the reviewer/funder has no idea what you are thinking, so be specific. Include your goals and objectives separately. Most funders want the objectives written in measurable, behavioral terms such as "to increase," "to improve," or "to expand." Avoid objectives that begin "to understand" which cannot be measured and are not behavioral objectives.

The goals and objectives can be identified in a timeline or PERT (Program Evaluation and Review Technique) Chart. This format includes the goals and objectives on the left, the responsible party (to carry-out the goals/objectives listed next), then a timeline with the expected completion date identified.

6 — Emphasize experience and qualifications

This is your opportunity to "toot your own horn." Briefly discuss your history in the field: "Our program has over ten years of experience in the field of child care and maintains a reputation for providing high-quality, developmentally appropriate programming." You might also address the educational level of the director and teachers. If your program has completed an evaluation or parent survey, discuss the positive aspects of the evaluation/survey.

If possible, use the appendix/attachments to include newspaper clippings of your program, support letters from parents/families, and photographs of relevant activities.

5 — Seek support from local and state politicians

This is when politicians become your best friends, especially if you are seeking local or state funding. Contact your legislator's aides to discuss ways to fund your idea or project. The function of legislative aides is to help the constituents — that's you! Ask your state representatives about discretionary funds (once called "WAMs" or "Walking Around Money") used to support programs or projects in their area. These are small pots of money, but it might be just what you need to begin a new project.

Don't be shy about inviting local and state representatives to visit your program. If you do receive funding, send photos to your legislators, or better yet, invite the legislator to visit your program, along with a photographer from the local newspaper. Legislators love to have their pictures taken with worthwhile community projects. Market your program and activities so your political leaders and your community understand and support your program.

4 — Use current statistics and data

Support your request for funds with statistics. Use statistics from newspapers or journals to support your proposal. Local agencies are also good sources of statistics:

Contact the job center/employment center; departments of public welfare, health, education, and/or labor and industry; extension office; county courthouse or human services office; school districts for additional information. The Internet is a wonderful tool for grant writing, with statistics at your fingertips. Use search engines for information on children and families. Current national statistics on children and families can be obtained from the Children's Defense Fund (www.childrensdefense.org). When using statistics and data, compare your program with local, state, and/or national statistics to make a case for funding.

3 — Collaborate and cooperate

These are sometimes referred to as "The Big C's" for funding. Funders want to stretch the dollars as far as possible, and the best way to do this is for agencies/programs to work together. There are many benefits to collaboration — more innovative ideas, more individuals willing to provide support letters, sharing resources, and providing in-kind match. In-kind match is often required and may be either cash or support services and goods. Cash match is actual dollars, which is often difficult because most agencies are financially strapped. Support services and goods are defined as individual volunteer service and donations of office space or supplies. I have provided in-kind services for grants as a volunteer child development consultant, at the rate of $100 per hour for 20 hours (July 1-June 30), thus an in-kind match of $2,000. You may find financial experts, business executives, and secretaries willing to volunteer their time as a match.

Include on your advisory board some *movers and shakers*. These are individuals who may have connections for funds, individuals who have expertise in grant writing, and/or individuals who can serve as consultants for your program and for your proposal.

2 — Proofread and recalculate

This is essential. The proposal is your sales pitch — it's the "Pick Me." It is extremely important to proofread, especially if you have more than one writer. The writers may have very different styles, so one individual needs to be responsible for the final copy. Also, have a staff member read the final proposal. By the time you get to your final copy, you have read and rewritten the proposal so often that you *read over* the errors.

Budgets

It is important to work with a fiscal person to ensure that your figures and calculations are correct. I reviewed one proposal where no personnel benefits were included. That program would have been very surprised if they had received the requested amount, only to find out they couldn't offer the anticipated salaries because the grant was $10,000 short in monies to pay benefits.

1 — Learn from rejection

If the funder did not love your proposal as much as you had hoped and fails to fund it, do not be discouraged. Contact the funder and request a critique or debriefing about why your proposal was not successful. (Sometimes funders will meet with the unsuccessful applicants individually.) Using their feedback, rewrite your proposal and resubmit for the next funding cycle or seek another funding source. Always save your proposals; they can often be recycled. Remember, the funder *wants* to give away the money as long as your proposal matches their goals, objectives, and requirements.

Where to Look for Grants — Start Locally

We have all heard the phrase "Success breeds success." Therefore, in order to be successful at grant writing, the best way is to begin small. Look for local or state grants. On the local level, many social service organizations fund community-based projects; check your local Kiwanis, Rotary Club, Jaycees, Lions Clubs, and others. Women's organizations such as the Zonta Club, American Association of University

Women, and Junior Women's Civic Club may also fund projects. Some counties have Human Services Development Programs which allocate small sums to community organizations. Local businesses may provide funds for community projects through mini-grants; contact retail stores such as Wal-Mart, banks, and grocery stores.

The State Level

On the state level, use the Internet to locate information on grants from the departments of public welfare, health, education and/or labor and industry. If you can't find information this way or you don't have access to the Internet, try calling the department directly and talk with personnel to garner information about locating funding sources.

State and National Foundations

State and national foundations are an excellent source of grant monies; however, they are often harder to obtain since they are more competitive. The best way to find funding sources to match your purpose, your interests, and/or your geographic region is through the "Foundation Center." This is an independent national service organization that provides an overview of private funding foundations. Information about the center can be accessed at www.fdncenter.org. Another source for funding opportunities is CD Publications (www.cdpublications.com). This is an excellent publication (although fairly expensive, $369 per year) with newsletters covering everything from housing to education. Check out the Children & Youth Funding Report Newsletter. This report publishes 24 issues per year and covers grants, foundations, research, and reports in the field. A free, 14-18 page sample newsletter can be accessed from their site.

Federal Funds

The "Federal Register" is the grandfather of all federal grants. This publication provides notices of funding availability (NOFA) issued by all agencies of the federal government, and all regulations and guidelines. Although expert grant writers use this publication regularly, novices may find it a bit overwhelming. The cost of a subscription is expensive, over $300 per year; however, many libraries carry subscriptions.

These are just a few suggestions to get you started as a grant writer and to paraphrase Dr. Seuss (1990), "Today is your day. You're off to Great Proposals! You're off and away!"

References

Bauer, D. G. (1994). *Grantseeking primer for classroom leaders.* New York: Scholastic.

CD Publications. (1993-94, Winter). *Federal Assistance Monitor Grant Update Bulletin* [Brochure]. Silver Spring, MD.

CD Publications. *Children & Youth Funding Report.* [Online] Retrieved July 19, 2004, from www.cdpublications.com.

Ferguson, J. (1992). *The grantseeker's guide to project evaluation.* Alexandria, VA: Capitol Publications Inc.

Government Information Services. (1993). *111 secrets to smarter grantsmanship.* Arlington, VA.

Seuss, D. (1990). *Oh, the places you'll go.* New York: Random House.

Fredalene B. Bowers, Ph.D., a former preschool teacher and center director, is an Associate Professor of Child Development and Family Relations at Indiana University of Pennsylvania, in Indiana, Pennsylvania. She was also a grant writer and program coordinator for at-risk children and families and grant reviewer for state and local grants. She presents state and national workshops on grant writing and a variety of child development topics.

Fishing for Dollars in Philanthropic Waters

by Anne Mitchell

Every child care director, at some point, has confronted the fact that parents (even well-off ones) just can't pay enough to support good child care services. The savvy director is always looking for new sources of funding and evaluating whether they're worth pursuing. If we could become a United Way agency, would the effort be worth it? What could we do as a fundraiser besides another bake sale? Is buying lottery tickets a good investment? Somewhere in this process, the idea of soliciting foundations comes up. Probably right after you hear that some national child care group just got a multi-million dollar grant from You-Name-It foundation, you think: "Why couldn't we do that?" This article is for you.

First, let's be clear that foundations are not now (or ever) going to be the direct source of funding that solves the compensation-affordability problem. Foundations are not — and never will be — the main source of funding for any child care center's operation. The direct services or general operating expenses of any organization are almost never supported by philanthropy. The role that foundations play in a field is something like what an entrepreneur does — improve, expand, and innovate. The difference is that foundations do this indirectly through the work of those organizations they fund, rather than directly as an entrepreneur would in operating a business.

Foundations are looking for innovative solutions to problems, promising approaches to improve on current methods, or expansions of successful programs that address a problem. Expanding services for families (adding or starting new programs), improving practice through professional development, linking child care services with other services families need are all examples of child care ideas foundations might consider supporting.

Foundations correctly believe their role in child care is to help the field solve problems and address current needs, not to become a direct funder of services. Given that cautionary note, foundations can and will fund child care if you approach the right ones in the right way.

The Philanthropic Landscape

Philanthropy comes in many forms, from individual donors to national foundations. This article focuses on philanthropic entities (foundations and corporations) that might support local child care projects. If you want to know how to find major individual donors, that's another story (actually, a set of unique and non-replicable stories). Understanding something about the types of foundations and their basic characteristics can help you identify the right ones to consider pursuing.

All foundations are legal entities designed to give away money for particular purposes to other non profit entities. Many were established with the funds from one individual, one family (or extended family), or one corporation. Others are collections of funds bequeathed by many different individuals and families. Some foundations are restricted to supporting certain types of work or particular geographic areas — either by the will of those who gave the money or the wishes of the current trustees.

Foundations can have a national, regional, and/or local focus in their grantmaking. Some national foundations also have a local grantmaking program to benefit the community they reside in. Community foundations are usually collections of trusts and bequests that are restricted to a specific community. Community foundations often have the word "community" or "area" in their names, e.g., the Rochester Area Foundation or the Marin Community Foundation.

Corporate foundations (or a corporation's annual charitable giving) focus mainly (or solely) on those communities where the corporation has worksites and employees. Community foundations and corporate foundations with a local focus are probably the most likely to support local child care projects. National foundations with a diverse local grants program may also be supporters.

Foundations can legally only give money to certain types of organizations — almost always a non profit corporation which has tax-exempt status (a 501(c)3 organization). Most non profit child care centers would qualify, but for profit centers generally cannot receive funds directly from a foundation. However, associations of providers such as a family child care association or a for profit directors' association can qualify if the association is incorporated as a non profit and has tax-exempt status.

Generally a foundation establishes a set of program areas, priorities, or strategies that guide its grantmaking. Child care is unlikely to be a distinct program priority all by itself, but child care easily fits into a broader area — such as child and youth development, community building, strengthening families, early education and school readiness, or prevention — which are typical philanthropic program areas.

In larger foundations, each program area is the responsibility of an individual program officer. Smaller foundations may have only one staff person who covers all the areas. In some cases, one of the foundation's directors manages the grantmaking as a volunteer. Knowing whether there is a program area where child care would fit and which foundation staff person handles the area where child care fits are essential pieces of information to have.

Foundations generally make grants based on thoughtful, well-written proposals that directly address the specified issues within a program area. Sending a proposal — no matter how brilliant the ideas in it might be — is not the best way to introduce yourself to a foundation. Very few foundations will read and respond to proposals sent "cold." Some foundations do not accept unsolicited proposals at all — they will return them unread — because they only fund projects that are developed at their request by organizations they select.

Others only accept short letter proposals that follow a specified format. Before you make a move, you must know how each foundation approaches grantmaking and what its requirements are for applicants or grantseekers.

What Foundations Fund

Given that foundations will not underwrite your center's parent fees, what will they support? Answer: Improvements and innovations that solve child care problems and benefit the wider community. Professional development is a good example. If the community lacks infant care, a proposal from a group of centers to collectively train their infant care teachers in a manner that would institutionalize an infant care course in the community college might be a fundable proposal. Building the infant care rooms might be fundable if you could find a foundation that supports capital projects, so called "bricks and mortar."

Another example is collaborations to expand services. If the community's Head Start grantee and a child care center(s) wanted to jointly provide comprehensive all-day early education, a foundation might fund the planning and start-up phase of such a venture.

Fundraising — no matter whether it is selling raffle tickets or writing a grant proposal — is not begging. You are offering someone an opportunity to support a worthy organization or project and, in the case of a foundation, an opportunity to give away money that the foundation is required by law to give away. Successful fundraising is the combination of four elements:

- a credible, trustworthy person

- with good ideas for feasible projects,

- that match the foundation's goals, and

- will be carried out in an organization that is financially solid and well managed.

Technically, grantmaking is the act of one organization making a grant to another organization. Actually, successful grantmaking is the result of positive human interactions — the foundation officer and the grant seeker establish a working relationship based on good communication and mutual trust that leads eventually to the approval of a grant.

Foundations fund people — people they know, people they trust, people with good ideas. Child care center directors who are active in their community are more likely to encounter potential funders in situations where relationships can be established — such as at community meetings or events — than directors who only venture out to attend an occasional conference with their early childhood colleagues.

Getting Started

Many people think the first step is to make a list of all the geographically appropriate foundations that have any history of "giving to early childhood." On the contrary, the place to start is with ideas (although research on funders may be needed later). The goal is to make a match between your good ideas and a foundation's goals. Matchmaking is done by people — your ideas will be shaped and changed

(improved, hopefully) through your interactions with the foundation officer.

Begin by developing some ideas for projects that would benefit your organization and the wider child care community. This can be done alone, but often goes faster in a small group (if everyone is clear on the task). You might get the local directors' group to brainstorm ideas. After you get a list, pick out the three or four ideas that seem most feasible and write a one-page description of each idea. The "who, what, where, when, why, how" approach used by newspaper reporters is a good way to start. Write down what the project is, why it is needed, who will do it, how long it will last, what results it will have, and what it will cost.

Because human relationships are important in philanthropic fund raising, another good method for getting started is to think about your own networks and contacts in terms of potential funders. Are any of the people you already know potential funders — that is, connected in some way with corporations or foundations? What about your board — who do they know? Some of your board members may well know philanthropic leaders and be willing to discuss child care with them and introduce you to them directly.

Finally, think about your staff and parents. Some of them may have networks that include potential funders. Don't underestimate your parents. One source of corporate funds for child care is the AT&T evelopment Fund. A child care provider must be recommended by an AT&T employee to access these funds, which are

available for child care improvement and expansion in AT&T communities.

Chances are, if there's a community foundation in your area, you've heard of it. If not, look in the phone book or go to the library. There are a number of published sources of information about foundations that can help you find those in your geographic area that might consider a child care related request.

Your local library may have the current year's *Foundation Directory* published by the Foundation Center, an information clearinghouse on foundation and corporate giving headquartered in New York City. This directory contains entries for close to 12,000 foundations, giving brief descriptions of their mission and history, total assets, annual grant total, size of an average grant, types of organizations supported, contact information, and any restrictions. *The Directory of Corporate Giving* has similar entries for over 2,000 corporate grantmakers. If your library does not have these directories, you can contact The Foundation Center directly at (800) 424-9836. They will refer you to the nearest Foundation Center Library or to a Cooperating Collection.

Another way to access information about The Foundation Center is on the Internet (http://fdncenter.org).

The process of seeking and receiving foundation funding takes time and effort. Think carefully about whether the process is worth the reward before you start. If it were easy, everyone would be doing it. In fact, some child care center directors have successfully negotiated the foundation waters and are willing to share their lessons. A follow-up article will chronicle the actual experiences of child care center directors who have received foundation grants, including their tips, advice, and pitfalls to avoid.

Anne Mitchell is the president of Early Childhood Policy Research, an independent consulting firm specializing in policy research and planning on child care/early education for government, foundations, and national non-profit organizations. She can be reached at awmitchell@aol.com via the Internet.

Keys to Maintaining a Good Banking Relationship

by Keith Stephens

> **A** bank is a place where they lend you an umbrella in fair weather and ask for it back again when it starts to rain.
> — Robert Frost

Many child care operators probably share Robert Frost's cynicism about banks. They may remember with bitterness how when they were getting started every bank in town turned down their loan requests. Now that they have a profitable venture going, these same bankers are eagerly soliciting their business. But if times get tough, they may just disappear.

While such cynicism may well be warranted, in the long run, it is not productive. A bank can be such a valuable asset for a small or growing business that it is in every operators best interest to invest time in developing a positive working relationship with a bank.

Selecting the Right Bank

Not all banks are the same. You should shop for a bank that best meets the special needs of your business. Some suggestions:

• **Find a bank that specializes in your business**. Different banks specialize in different areas: real estate, small business, international lending, service industries, capital goods industries, etc. You will get much better service from a bank that is used to doing business with your type of business.

Advertisements by banks in your local newspaper's business section often spell out the types of business they are soliciting. A bank's annual report will contain a statement of purpose and lists of offices, departments, and board members. This can yield insights into a bank's specialties. And finally, by talking to other local child care professionals and small business operators, as well as to your accountant and lawyer, you can benefit from their experiences in dealing with a variety of local banks.

• **Look for a small local bank**. Unless you manage a large or growing child care business that is looking for a multi-million dollar loan (banks typically are prohibited from making loans in excess of 10% of their total capital — thus a small bank will not be able to handle a multi-million dollar loan request), your interests will probably be best served by a small bank.

Small banks offer a number of advantages. In order to remain competitive with larger banks, they must try harder to attract customers, i.e., they strive to excel in their service. In addition, they can be more flexible in putting together financial packages. And finally, you will have more clout in a smaller bank where your account will be more important to the success of the bank. You will get to know more of their key decisionmakers.

• **Find a bank that is close by**. As a matter of sound internal controls, a child care business should be making deposits on a daily basis. In that case, the proximity of the bank will be an important factor.

That is not to say that the nearby branch bank is always your best bet. When checking out a nearby bank, be sure to ask these questions: Does it have a commercial lending department? Do its hours fit your needs? Are its fees competitive? Will it provide immediate credit on your deposits?

- **Consolidate your banking**. Some business people spread out their banking at a number of banks. Their theory is that when it comes time to ask for assistance, they will have a number of ready alternatives.

I am much more inclined to recommend focusing on one bank. A bank will price your transactions based on how much business you do with them. You want to be as important a customer as you can possibly be.

Developing a Positive Ongoing Relationship

Banks' decisions are made by people — not by computers, formulas, and financial statements. When the time comes that you need help from a bank, you are much more likely to get a fair hearing if you know the decision-makers on a personal basis than if you are a stranger.

This not only applies if you are looking for a loan, but also when you encounter little difficulties. For example, let's say you make a mistake that causes your account to be overdrawn. If you are only a number to the bank, chances are they will bounce the overdrawn checks, thus aggravating those you made the checks out to. On

the other hand, if you have a friendly representative at the bank, she may call you up and give you some time to cover the overdraft before taking action.

It takes time to build personal relationships at your bank, but it is time well invested. To start with, introduce yourself to the bank president, the branch manager, and/or the head of the commercial lending department. Keep them posted from time to time on how your business is doing. There is a lot of turnover at banks, so the higher up your personal relationships, the better.

It is especially important to build a good working relationship with your account officer, the bank official who is in charge of your business at the bank. This person represents your company within the bank to other officers and loan committees, as well as outside the bank when creditors call for references. Therefore, you want this person on your side as an advocate.

There are many steps you can take to improve relations with your account officer. Use your daily deposits as an opportunity to keep in touch with her. Put her on the mailing list for your center newsletter. Send her announcements when you pass important milestones, receive positive press coverage, open a new center, receive center accreditation, or hire key new people.

Devote some time to helping your account officer better understand your organization, as well as the overall child care business. Share with him articles (from trade journals as well as business publications) that support the strength of this growing industry. Invite him out to see your center or

centers in action. Enlighten him on your organization's niche in the child care market.

Show your appreciation for her hard work by introducing her to other business persons who may be interested in opening accounts with her bank. If your account officer has been especially efficient in handling your needs, you should send a letter to the bank president conveying your pleasure.

On the other hand, if you are having difficulty with your account officer, you may consider asking for a new one before decisions are made about your account that are difficult to reverse. This can be risky because you may alienate your current officer. But if the relationship is deteriorating, it may be necessary.

Getting a Loan

When the time comes that you need money, you will want to present your case well. Keep in mind that your account officer will not be reviewing your request in isolation, but along with many other requests competing for the bank's money.

Since a banker, like anyone else, is likely to take the course of least resistance, you can increase your chances of success if you make his work easier — if you present him with a proposal that is thoughtful and complete. Presenting a complete proposal not only makes the bank officer's work easier, it also shows that you have thoroughly researched what you propose to do. Likewise, when he inevitably asks for something that was not included, your fast response will demonstrate the urgency and seriousness of this request, and will convey the impression that you are organized. If he has to call you every day for information, and you are slow to respond, you will create the impression that you have something to hide.

You should expect that the bank will review your proposal carefully. If there are any problems or discrepancies, point them out and provide explanations up front. Don't cross your fingers and hope that they won't be found, because when they are, your credibility will suffer.

Your loan request package should answer the following basic questions:

How much money do you need?
Don't go in with an inflated figure, hoping to negotiate down to a satisfactory amount. Start with what you want exactly. All your documentation should support your request for this amount. This will demonstrate that you have done your homework and are not making a frivolous request.

How will you use the money?
The clearer you can be about what you will do with the money, the better the banker will understand your proposal. If you can spell out that his money will be used to purchase tangible assets such as computers or playground equipment, all the better. If the money will supplement general operating funds during an expansion phase, be as clear as possible about how this extra operating capital will insure increased profitability in the future. When and how will you repay the money? In the final analysis, a bank will lend you money not because you

are a good person, nor because your business looks good, but because they are con-fident they will recoup their money with interest. A vital part of your proposal, therefore, will be to demonstrate that you have the ability to pay them back.

You will need to supply a current income and expense statement, a balance sheet, and a cash flow projection for the duration of the loan. If you are a small business, a sole proprietorship, a partnership, or a closely held corporation, you will need to supply personal financial information as well.

While banks will accept financial statements that you prepare in house, they tend to give more credence to statements that have some third party seal of approval. Their first choice would be CPA-audited statements, their second choice CPA-reviewed statements, and their third choice CPA-compiled statements (where a CPA takes the numbers that you provide and compiles them into standard financial statements).

No matter how complete a package you provide, the bank will take your numbers and put them through their own financial statement analysis. Some banks will give you these results if you ask. This will help you understand your own numbers better, and will give you some idea about what the bank considers important.

For example, a bank may analyze such factors as *margin management* (what are your controllable expenses, what does it cost in addition to your fixed costs); *working investment* (the rate at which you collect and pay bills); *solvency*

(how liquid your assets are, what kind of cash flow you are generating); *debt capacity* (how much debt your business can reasonably carry); and *sources of equity* (how much trade credit, bank credit, and personal credit you have).

After You Get a Loan

Bankers hate surprises. After they have loaned you some of their money, they want to hear (1) that you are doing what you said you were going to do and (2) that your financial projections are coming true. Keep them posted on your progress with at least quarterly updates. Don't make them come to you for a status report.

If your numbers are not working out, or if something is going wrong with your plans, your banker will want to know about it early. You may be reluctant to share bad news, but it is better to be up front about problems. If you are, the bank may be willing to reschedule your payments to help ease you through the tough time. If the first they know of your problems is when you fail to make a payment, they will be considerably less conciliatory.

With an investment of a little time, your banker might hand you an umbrella just when you need it most.

Keith Stephens, a CPA, is the former president of Palo Alto Preschools, once the country's largest privately owned child care chain, and past president of the National Association for Child Care Management.

Fundraising Success Stories

"Nothing gets your creative juices flowing better than learning about others' success stories."

Putting the "Fun" Back in Fundraising

by Dawn Marie Barhyte

One of my favorite fundraising moments happened years ago during a sweltering July when as a co-director I decided to host a Christmas in July rummage sale with water games at my center. The local firehouse loaned us a dunking booth. Staff, parents, and children alike, giddy with excitement, lined up to take a shot at "dunking the director." Fortunately, it was summer; because I spent a lot of time in the water. The children cooled off by snacking on snow cones and trying out our makeshift water slide. Parents and staff were good sports getting into the fun by boomeranging water balloons at each other. We managed to make a profit with the summer sale. More importantly, it was a fun day that allowed us to make new friends; kids channeled some energy while cooling off; and we shared priceless, lighthearted moments that enriched our allegiance to each other. We also gave members of our community a break from the heat. They'll be more likely to support our organization in the future through word-of-mouth referrals and future fundraising. When it comes to child care, our name will be fresh in their minds.

Consider expanding your role to include the fundraising hat and you'll see that the possibilities are endless!

Directors as Fundraisers

Directors are in a key position to give centers an overall boost by holding fundraisers. It is no secret that many centers are operating on a shoestring budget and could use additional revenue. As state and federal support decreases and budgets continue to shrink, there is growing pressure to supplement budgets with monies from other sources. Fundraising can provide a solution and boost your bottom line.

Today many child care centers around the country are turning to fundraising as lucrative moneymakers and so can you. While it may seem intimidating and time consuming, fundraising can lead to solid financial support, making it well worth the effort.

The Many Purposes of Fundraising

Although raising money is the primary reason to hold a fundraising event, it's not the only one. You can also:

- raise the profile of your center
- cultivate community support for your organization
- foster a sense of community spirit
- boost staff morale
- harness the creative energy of your staff
- create a sense of shared purpose that can unify staff and promote camaraderie

Holding a successful fundraiser is a lot like running a small business; it requires the same time and effort and both share the goal of making a profit. While fundraising can be demanding, it is possible to streamline the process and maximize results.

Before You Fundraise

Before you begin fundraising activities, you need to:

- be clear about what you hope to accomplish
- identify your target audience
- identify organizational resources available to produce the event

- clarify why you are raising money
- decide how the money will be used
- evaluate the benefit to your organization

If you are looking for some fresh ideas or some novel ways to spruce up your existing fundraising campaign, this article will offer tips to achieve your fundraising goals and to capture your fair share of available monies to subsidize your program. The reality is you'll be juggling a host of other responsibilities while coordinating a fundraiser; but no matter what your fundraising goals are, fundraising can be fun!

A Fundraising Idea

Host an art auction utilizing volunteers and art donated and designed by staff, parents, local artists, and your center's children. To ensure a good turnout, do it on a weekend and provide free child care that evening. You are guaranteed a captive audience. For the little ones' enjoyment keep it interactive by setting up a classroom with an assortment of open-ended art materials and age-appropriate projects that can be completed in an evening. Auction off art for a fair price to the highest bidder and you'll undoubtedly make a profit. Ask local artists to serve the refreshments and mingle with your audience.

When working as a co-director for a child care center, I found members of my local art league were thrilled to be included, to have an opportunity to showcase their works, and perhaps make a sale. Parents wanted to purchase their children's creations, too. Staff and children's self-esteem and morale were high as they watched their treasures being sought after.

We raised some funds that came in handy when planning our direct sales campaign.

Select the Ideal Fundraising Program

- determine how much money your program needs to raise
- identify available resources (volunteers, cost, time)
- boost community awareness (through media and word-of-mouth)
- conduct a cost-benefit analysis to determine if the potential benefit of the event is worth the time, money, and effort required to carry it off
- schedule fundraisers throughout the year to avoid competing with other organizations' fundraising events
- know your target audience (income level, purchasing habits, giving)

While there are many fundraising options to choose from, product sales are consistently the most effective and financially-rewarding approach to fundraising. In the article "Fundraising Fundamentals: Elements for Raising Money through Product Sales," the Association of Fundraising Distributors and Suppliers said research has found that 75% of Americans and eight out of ten parents will purchase fundraising products each year. The vast majority of sales are made to relatives, friends, and co-workers.

Today there are hundreds of fundraising products and programs available that maximize an organization's financial return and minimize the time investment of volunteers and staff. Better still, many products have stood the test of time and are reasonably guaranteed to succeed. These compa-

nies will work closely with your organization every step of the way to help volunteers raise funds.

From my experience it pays to spend a little more to make more. Maybe you can learn from my mistake:

As junior volunteer coordinator of a community hospital we compiled apple cookbooks to be sold at our annual Apple Fest. We didn't do well even though we were giving away free apples which were donated from a local farm. The cookbook recipes were first-rate, but the presentation was ho-hum. Had we invested some money in printing the cookbooks with a more professional look, I think we would have done better. As a result of our haste and frugality, we had to store hundreds of unwanted cookbooks.

Choosing a Fundraising Company

Russell Lemiex, executive director of the Association of Fundraising Distributors and Suppliers suggests focusing on five key areas when choosing a fundraising company.

How long has the company been in the product fundraising business?
Companies with a track record are more likely to anticipate and meet an organization's needs.

What services does the company offer and how much do they cost?
Depending on groups' specific needs, services (e.g., incentive programs, kick-off parties) can improve efficiency and financial success.

How will the company handle problems that arise?

Discuss how the company will handle unforeseen problems that occur (e.g., incorrect or damaged products). *What is the company's reputation?* Ask for a list of references and check them out. Talk to peers about the company and your local representative.

Are they a member of the Association of Fundraising Distributors and Suppliers? For a free list of Association of Fundraising Distributors and Suppliers offering products and services in your state and community, write 57775 Peachtree-Dunwoody Rd., Atlanta, GA; call (404) 252-3663; or e-mail afrds@assnhg.com.

Hosting a Fundraising Event

Special events can be organized as an alternative method of raising capital. You don't have to be a fundraising professional to pull one off, either. The advantages of events are:

■ they are fun and entertaining
■ they foster good public relations
■ your dollars are available on the spot

Potential disadvantages are:

■ they require a committed group of volunteers, time, and effort to organize
■ they require an initial outlay of funds

To offset costs host a fundraising event to raise cash so you can then choose a more costly event. It's a win-win.

Here are some fundraising companies and resources to get started:

■ Cookbook Publishers, Inc. — the first company to reproduce recipes as a unique fundraiser — (800) 227-7282 • info@cookbookpublishers.com

■ Current — cards, wrapping paper, snacks — (877) 665-4481• currentfundraisercustomerservice@current.com

■ Dutch Mill Bulbs — imported guaranteed-to-bloom bulbs at below-garden shop prices — (800) 533-8824, ext. 226 • www.dutchmillbulbs.com

■ Mr. Fundraising — helping hundreds of loyal customers since 1969 sell quality fundraising products — (800) 637-3828 • www.mrfundraising.com

■ EkidsFundraising.com — quality snacks from chocolate to popcorn (888) 474-5900 • help@ekidsFUNdraising.com

■ Fundraising Depot — one of the oldest and largest selections to choose from — (800) 327-0322

■ Itsmyartwork.com — does amazing things with children's art, transfers designs on note cards, bookmarks, etc. — (877) 300-8922 • sales@itsmyartwork.com

■ Morris Cookbooks — customized cookbooks; typesets collected recipes — (800) 445-6621 • www.morriscookbooks.com

---

For organizations with a dedicated group of volunteers who enjoy the social nature of sponsoring such events and are up to the challenge, these can be a good choice. They usually generate good press coverage and ticket sales can be robust. Keep in mind that the more unusual your fundraising ideas, the more people will support them. Good ideas are good cash generators, too. Use this list to spark your imagination and provide inspiration for your group as you plan for events and activities. Appeal to your staff and volunteers' whimsical side and get creative!

A Host of Fundraising Events

Food-and-Drink Events: These range in scope and price. Savor the possibilities by featuring a basic meal like a pancake breakfast or unlimited bowls of spaghetti. Particularly popular now are wine-tastings, luncheons with fashion shows, dinners featuring ethnic foods, and tea parties.

Holiday Bazaar: Set up a delightful and tantalizing selection of homespun crafts and goodies just in time for the winter holidays. Ask teachers, staff, and parents to contribute. Charge admission and hold raffles for prizes donated by local merchants. Get local cable stations or radio stations to advertise and you'll double your profits.

Auctions: Hold an auction with goods and services that are donated by local merchants. Useful services such as babysitting, dog walking, tutoring, yard work, haircuts, and manicures are all community favorites.

Bake Sales: Home baked goodies can't be beat. Have parents and staff bake cookies, pies, cakes, and brownies to sell. Add an extra flair by choosing a theme, such as baked goods from around the world. Consider charging a small entrance fee and give awards for the best pie, cookie, or cake and then auction it off to the highest bidder.

Cook-Offs: Novice chefs are going to line up to compete for the best apple recipe, chili, or cookie. You decide on a theme and contestants pay to compete. Invite families in your center to taste and rate the dishes. Ask for a donation at admission.

Bingo Party: Always popular and entertaining, this event is run in the traditional manner. You charge a set fee per card. Instead of money for prizes, give away donated merchandise from local merchants.

Book Sale: Another old favorite. People are sure to donate books and book lovers are sure to buy them. Have community members bring in old books that you then sell for a buck a book.

Book Fairs: An excellent way to promote the importance of reading

between parent and child. The best time to hold a book fair is in the fall when you hold a parent-teacher night or an open house.

Raffles: Raffles are a fun and simple way to raise cash and one bound to earn you an enthusiastic reaction from the community. Ask local businesses to donate prizes and hold the drawing at a special event.

Rummage Sales: One person's junk is another person's treasure. Although a huge undertaking, rummage sales are a good way to generate cash. Hold the event in the fall or spring when people traditionally clean out their closets. Involve your families by asking them to donate their used toys, books, and clothes to benefit the center. Try making up theme baskets with the help of your staff like gardening lovers' or cooks' delight.

Engraved Bricks: People like to leave a lasting impression, so give them an opportunity to leave their mark. Sell engraved bricks or ceramic tiles that will be used in your center's walkway or playground.

Pet Show: Pet lovers are notorious for wanting to show off their beloved buddies. Charge an entry fee and get donated prizes from pet stores and local vets for categories such as best dressed, cutest, most charming, and best trained, just to name a few.

Collectible Cookbooks: Is your cheesecake recipe to die for? Are your friend's brownies deliciously decadent? If so, others might think so, too. Compile staff, parents', and friends' recipes and make up a customized cookbook to sell at one of your fundraisers or community events.

There are many organizations that will help you produce a charming keepsake.

Art Show and Auction: Invite community members, relatives, and parents to view artwork created by your staff and children. Charge an entrance fee and hold an auction to raise money. Consider using original artwork to create note cards, bookmarks, and calendars to sell.

Carnivals and Street Fairs: These kid-friendly fundraisers will build your visibility. More than being money-makers, they are a *friend*-raiser. Tie it in with a local festival to boost attendance and profits. My town has an Apple Fest every fall that has over 200 craftspeople. We have a special section just for children, complete with games, petting zoo, sand art, face painting, and a puppet show. It's great fun for the community to get to know you and your services at this family-friendly event.

Costume Parties: Choose a theme or an occasion such as Halloween and send out invitations to families and post fliers around town (e.g., post office and library) to increase community awareness. Charge admission for the masquerade as well as for the refreshments, which you can have donated to cut costs.

As we all know, it costs money to run a high-quality early childhood program. More money in our budgets could mean new classroom supplies, enrichment programs, outdoor equipment, and staff development. With effort and know-how, you can create a fundraising campaign that will support your program and its future — and have fun in the process!

For More Information

Blasius, C. (1995). *Earning more funds: Effective, proven fundraising strategies for all non-profit groups.* Fort Wayne, IN: BC Creations.

Burke, M. (1993). *Creative fundraising.* Menlo Park, CA: Crisp Publications.

Ciconte, B. L. (2004). *Fundraising basics: A complete guide.* Sudbury, MA: Jones & Bartlett.

Finn, M. (1982, September). *Fundraising for early childhood programs: Getting started & getting results.* Washington, DC: National Association for the education of Young Children.

Joachim, J. (2003). *Beyond the bake sale: The ultimate school fundraiser book.* New York: St. Martins Griffin.

Mintzer, R., & Friedman, S. (2003). *The everything fundraiser book: Create a strategy, plan events, increase visibility and raise the money you need.* Avon, MA: Adams Media.

Weisman, C. (2000). *Secrets of successful fundraisers.* St. Louis, MO: F. E. Robbins & Son.

Dawn Marie Barhyte is a freelance author who has been published widely. She writes frequently on early childhood topics, child development, and parenting issues. For over 20 years she met the needs of children and their families co-directing, teaching, and coordinating children's programs. She continues her commitment to children and touches their lives through her writing.

Directors' Fundraising Hits

Ideas from center directors

The following is a representative selection of the best fund-raising ideas which have been contributed to **Exchange** by child care directors.

Auctions for Fun and Profit

Jan Silverman (Lucky Lane Early Childhood Center, St. Louis, Missouri) shares how her center plans an auction which has been their most successful fundraiser. The auction is planned and implemented by a committee of board members. It is held at a local hotel and those attending pay $40 each to participate in the evening's festivities.

The evening begins with a silent auction of small items, valued at less than $100. The excitement builds with dinner and a live auction.

A catalog listing the 300 items — including trips, dinners, and other things donated by the community and parents — goes home with the children a week before the auction. Trips, condos, and autographed sports equipment stimulate high bidding. Each board member is encouraged to bring a full table of guests. In past years, the center has netted close to $16,000.

The **YWCA Drop-In Children's Center (Watsonville, California)** raised over $5,000 with an auction. The auction was organized by a committee of ten volunteers which started working five months before the event. Most of their time was spent on canvassing parents, friends of the center, and local merchants for the several hundred items donated.

The auction was held outdoors on a Sunday. Participants were allowed to view the items from 10 am to 1 pm, and the auction itself lasted from 1 pm to 6 pm. A wide range of items are big hits at auctions. At the Watsonville auction, the big item was a wedding package which included a minister's services, a place for a reception, a photographer's services, a cake, and a honeymoon in San Francisco.

The Summit Child Care Center (Summit, New Jersey) raised $11,000 with a "Vacation Auction." A parents' committee sent out requests to over 1,000 resorts around the world. Seventy-five vacations were donated, ranging from hotel rooms in Europe and Hawaii to weekends at private summer cottages.

A center in New York City raised $18,000 auctioning off gift certificates for up to $500 to department stores.

The **Brownie Preschool (Alexandria, Virginia)** featured season tickets to the Washington Redskins and a catered dinner for eight in the bidder's own home.

Other less sensational, but highly popular, items include babysitting services, meals at restaurants, food, furniture, antiques, housecleaning services, and hairdressing.

All centers agreed that the key ingredient to a successful auction is a lively auctioneer to keep it entertaining and to loosen people up. Most centers used a professional auctioneer (some of whom donated their time).

Several centers had a dinner or party in conjunction with the auction. The **Brownie Preschool** held the auction during a buffet luncheon for which $4 per person was charged. Several centers noted that providing free wine and beer during the event had a positive effect on the size of bids.

Another essential ingredient is recruiting enough volunteers to handle all aspects of the auction. Considerable time and energy is required before the event to solicit items; to collect and transport them to the auction site; and to label, catalog, and display them. The day of the auction people are needed to direct traffic, to haul items back and forth, to collect money, to assist the auctioneer, to serve refreshments, and to answer questions.

Mary K. Parker, from the **YWCA Drop-In Center**, reported that about 20 parent volunteers were needed for their action. She stated that without the support of these parents before and during the auction it would not have been possible. **Dr. Lois Ferrer**, from the **Brownie Preschool**, also recommends having center people on hand to provide activities for children of attendees.

A variation on the typical auction is the silent auction. Items in the auction are displayed, either at the center for a week or during a social event. Bidders write out their bids and submit them in a sealed envelope. When the envelopes are opened, the item is awarded to the highest bidder.

Raffles! Raffles! Raffles!

Raffles have been utilized by child care centers to raise anywhere from $400 to $18,000. Regardless of the scope of the raffle, there are two essential ingredients to success: attractive prizes and an aggressive sales force.

Most centers try to have at least one big prize to catch people's attention and a number of smaller prizes to increase participants' chances of winning something.

The **Fallbrook Child Development Center (Fallbrook, California)** had a raffle with 32 prizes — the top one being $100 worth of gasoline.

The **Sweatt-Winter Day Care Center (Farmington, Maine)** raffled off a wood stove at a county fair.

The **John E. Boyd Center (Fall River, Massachusetts)** has found handmade wooden toys and color televisions to be popular items at its annual raffle. Other big draw prizes include quilts, afghans, get-away weekends (free babysitting, free resort hotels, free meals), and three-minute supermarket dashes.

A 50/50 raffle is one of the easiest fundraising ideas used by **Jennifer Ramey (Turtle Mountain Head Start, Belcourt, North Dakota)**. The center prints tickets that include a space for name, address, phone number, and the date of the drawing. The tickets are sold for $1 each. Parents and staff find it easier to sell and keep track of tickets in books of 10. Before the raffle, decide on a goal, say $500. When the goal is reached and the drawing is held, the winner gets half — $250 — and the center gets half — the remaining $250.

The **Androscoggin County Head Start** operates a "20-20 Club Raffle." A limited number of participants contribute $1 per week for 20 weeks. Each week a name is drawn and $20 is awarded. At the end of 20 weeks, a party is held at which $850 in additional prizes are awarded.

Getting parents, staff, and board members to sell tickets is probably the hardest aspect of a raffle. Some centers offer incentives to ticket sellers. The **Fallbrook Center** offered a free automobile tune-up to the parent selling the most tickets.

Other centers offer incentives to ticket buyers. The **Fallbrook Center** made an arrangement with a local pizza house whereby anyone buying a $1 ticket received $1 off on a pizza of their choice.

Before setting a raffle in motion, centers need to take care of two administrative issues. First, a check should be made with local and state authorities to be sure the proposed raffle complies fully with all relevant laws. Second, a sound system for distributing tickets and collecting stubs and money needs to be set up. Tickets should be given directly to the parents and not sent home with their children.

Annual Membership Drive

For the past several years, the **Ossining Children's Center (Ossining, New York)** has held very successful direct mail membership drives. The first year, the drive raised $4,000 for the center; by 1980, the proceeds had increased to $7,000.

The project was launched the first year by sending letters to 12,000 community residents selected from the phone book. The following year, letters were sent to all residents who gave money the first year. In addition, all parents, teachers, and board members were asked to submit names of additional prospects.

Now the letters are sent out to about 1,000 residents each year — including all doctors in the area. This letter is sent out in April, with a follow-up mailing in early December (timed to coincide with the end of the tax year.)

The mailing package consists of a form letter and a return envelope. The letter is signed by the president of the board, and it lists the names of all board members. It briefly describes the center and explains why it operates a deficit each year. Their support is requested in making $5, $10, $25, or $50 donations. The bulk of the donations are for $10. Donors are sent thank you letters which invite them to attend the annual meeting.

Sally Ziegler, the center's director, believes that a key to the drive's success has been active maintenance of the mailing list. Every year, anyone who has not given in two years is culled from the list. In addition, board members and parents are asked every year to contribute new prospects' names for the list.

"Friends" Donate to Center

Church of the Saviour Day Care Center (Cleveland Heights, Ohio) has organized a donation fund and named it "Friends of the Day Care Center." Staff members and parents give to the director, **Alice Licker**, the names of individuals who they think might be willing and able to give money to the center. She sends them a two-page letter which describes the program, lists the items that donations are used for (equipment and scholarships), and invites them to become "friends." This letter tends to be most effective at the end of the year when wealthy individuals often need to increase their tax deductions. Ms. Licker writes a letter of thanks back to each contributor and often encloses a piece of children's artwork.

Previously, this fund has brought in about $750, with the largest single contribution being $250. Other centers have received gifts of as much as $5,000 and have found that they can go back with success to the same contributors year after year.

The Whateverathon

Capitalizing on current interest in endurance-type events, many centers have successfully employed marathon spinoffs for fundraisers.

The **Spanish Educational Development Center (Washington, DC)** sponsored a ten-mile jogathon. Staff, parents, and friends who agreed to run in the race went to their friends and collected pledges to donate a certain amount for every mile they completed in the race. After the race, the runners collected over $1,000 from these pledges for the center.

There are many variations on this theme. The **Pinewoods Center** and other schools associated with the **Association for Retarded Citizens (Troy, New York)** raised $20,000 with a swimathon; the **Parent Child Center** **(La Salle, Colorado)** sponsored a walkathon; the **Refreshing Spring Child Care Center (Schenectady, New York)** held a bikeathon; and **Indiana County Head Start (Indiana, Pennsylvania)** undertook a 24-hour danceathon.

The directors of these programs had several recommendations to those interested in attempting whateverathons. First, the event itself should be carefully prepared for. If there is a course to be traversed, it should be laid out very clearly, with rest and refreshment points, distance markers, course officials, etc. Advice from local athletic associations may be valuable here.

Second, emphasis should be placed on actually collecting on pledges. One center was able to collect less than one-third of its pledges. This director suggested collecting the money at the time the pledge is made.

Third, make provision for all eventualities. Have medical personnel on hand, clear the route beforehand with the police, and set a rain date.

Evenings With Experts

From **Betsy Newell** of the **International Play Group (New York City)** comes the idea of offering evenings with experts. For example, an authority on antiques could offer a session to which participants could bring their own antiques for identification and appraisal.

Other possibilities include presentations by experts on restoring furniture, wine tasting and selection, identifying and appraising china, making bagels, investing in gold or stocks, using make-up, treating back problems, making Christmas decorations, jogging, and self-protection for women. Sessions could also be held at noon, with sandwiches provided.

Presenters would be asked to donate their time, so the major costs would be for providing sandwiches at noon or for renting a room if free space is not available. Staff time would be required for recruiting speakers, arranging space, and securing publicity.

Tickets could be sold for a single session or at reduced rates for a series of sessions. If an average of 50 individuals paid $5 per session to attend four sessions, the center would realize $1,000, less expenses.

Thrift Shop Yields Big Results

A profitable thrift shop has been operated for several years out of a storefront in downtown Boca Raton, Florida, by the **Florence Fuller Child Development Center**. The shop's inventory is primarily donated by the center's 700 members in the community who send in a steady flow of furniture, clothing, jewelry, and antiques. In addition, manufacturers are asked to donate their seconds.

The shop is operated and staffed by volunteers. The volunteers are trained in advance and are required to visit the center so they know what they are working for. On a yearly basis, about 60 to 75 volunteers work in the shop.

The expenses of the thrift shop for rent, utilities, transportation, and one part-time staff member average about $1,000 per month.

Harry Lippert, the center's director, initially devoted a great deal of time to setting up the shop. Now that it is operational, it requires less than two hours a week of his time.

The gross monthly income of the shop has been averaging $3,500, with a profit after expenses of $2,500. In addition, the 60 to 70 weekly customers are encouraged to visit the center. Many do and end up making donations to the center. In 1980, the thrift shop exceeded $100,000 in sales for the first time; and, after expenses, it yielded $72,000.

After reading about the thrift shop in *Exchange*, **Jan Lucas** had the **Westend Day Care Centre (Portage la Prairie, Manitoba)** set up a thrift shop. With the profits, the center was able to buy its own building.

Night on the Town

The **Summit Child Care Center (Summit, New Jersey)** raised $20,000 in 1980 from a unique dinner and dance fundraiser. About 60 "hosts" throughout the community invited from 4 to 40 couples to have dinner at their houses. Those invited included the hosts' friends as well as other couples recruited by the center.

After dinner, a theme dance (disco last year) was held at the child care center. For the full evening's entertainment, couples were charge $30.

As an added feature, hosts submitted their menus in advance to be published in a "Night-on-the-Town" cookbook which was sold that night and thereafter. The event has been held annually for several years.

Most arrangements are handled by an eight-person (non-board members) volunteer committee. This committee starts nearly a year in advance recruiting hosts, recruiting couples, and assigning them to hosts, planning the dance, cookbook, etc.

The hosts contribute their hospitality as well as the food (sometimes over $500 worth) for which they can claim a charitable tax deduction. Last year, the total cost to the center for running the event was $750. Staff time involved in the planning was minimal.

Retha's Carry Out

Patty Siegel reports that one of the best fundraisers for her children's day care center, **Pacific Primary (San Francisco, California)**, is the cook, **Retha Green**. She has enabled the center to purchase much of its kitchen equipment, including a freezer, by operating a unique carry-out service for parents.

Every Friday, Retha bakes chocolate chip and oatmeal cookies and sells them to parents when they pick up their children. The cookies sell for $1.50 per dozen. About 50 families take advantage of this offer every week. Once every three months, she makes complete homemade chicken dinners and sells them to parents for $3 per person. Parents are required to order these dinners in advance.

In response to the reputation Ms. Green developed for her exceptional cooking, the center also compiled for sale at $3 each a cookbook of her most popular offerings. Because of what the center's children commonly asked their parents at mealtimes, the cookbook was entitled "Why Can't You Bake It Like Retha Does?"

Children's Entertainment Series

A number of centers offer a children's entertainment series as an ongoing fundraising activity. Some centers run movies for children in the center on four consecutive Saturdays, or one Saturday a month during the school year. Other centers offer them during school vacations when parents are often most eager for ideas on what to do with their kids.

As a variation, centers could offer puppet shows, skits, gymnastics lessons, dance classes, swimming, field trips, story hours, craft sessions, or any combinations of these.

Tickets to the events could be sold singly or at a reduced rate for the entire series. The advantage of offering a series instead of single events is that nearly the same amount of time and energy would go into preparing and publicizing one event as would go into a series. Tickets could also be sold at the door.

One or two volunteers could be put in charge of setting up and running each event, while a separate committee would be in charge of publicity and advance sales.

No-cake Bake Sale

The **Jewish Community Center Preschool (Tampa, Florida)** netted $300 with little effort by holding a no-cake bake sale. In lieu of asking parents to buy supplies, bake cakes, and staff a booth for a bake sale, parents were asked to send in a donation of $5 or more.

Trip to Bermuda

A successful raffle of a trip for two to Bermuda for four days and three nights — air fare and hotel included — added to the fund-raising efforts of **Mt. Hope Day Care Center (Providence, Rhode Island)**. **Elizabeth Adams** reports that a board member knew of a local travel agency that gives away two trips a year to a community agency.

Last year, they received the trip to Bermuda. After a two month effort of selling tickets for $1 each or six for $5, a drawing was held and the center was $2,500 richer. The only cost involved was buying the raffle tickets.

Special Lunches

Olga Scharninghausen (Oak View Nursery School, San Rafael, California) adds variety to the daily routine and raises money at the same time. Before the school year begins, several special unches are scheduled throughout the year — about one a month. The school does not serve lunch, so this is a special treat. The typical menu is hot dogs, chips, orange juice, and ice cream for $2.

Parents sign up and pay for the lunches at the beginning of the year. Parents are reminded of the special lunch a week before — so that if they did not purchase it, they can include something special in their child's lunch. A few days before the lunch, a mother is recruited to buy the food. You could also vary the menu with pizza or tacos. Almost 100% participation raises $1,000 and provides lots of fun, too.

Mini Fiesta

Judy Morris (First Presbyterian Child Care, San Antonio, Texas) combines fundraising and fun for children, parents, and teachers. Every spring, they hold a mini fiesta for the children — two hours one evening.

All activities are planned with the children in mind — pony rides, an obstacle course, the renting of a space walk, throwing pennies in a jar, etc. The center closes one hour early, and families come to eat dinner and try all the activities. Tickets are sold — 25¢ each or five for $1 — to be used for activities and food. Examples — pony rides for four tickets or juice for two tickets.

Parents and teachers supervise all activities and the cooking. The menu includes food that children like — fajitas, nachos, chalupas, fruit, and juice or soda. The door prizes are contributed by local businesses. The center posts a list of needs for the evening — food, paper products, or balloons to decorate the center. All parents sign up to contribute something.

Judy reports that the fiesta is lots of work, but lots of fun for all involved. The families and friends of most currently enrolled children come, in addition to some former families and church members (150+). The money raised — $2,000 — is used for the needs of the center or staff enrichment.

Car Smash

Anyone who has ever had car troubles has probably had the urge to smash a car. Many centers raise funds by giving people the opportunity to take their aggressions out on automobiles. A junked or about-to-be-junked car is towed to a field or vacant lot near a busy street or to the booth area of a fair. A big sign is put up offering passersby the opportunity to take two whacks at the car with a large sledge hammer for 50¢. Aggressors must pay a premium ($1 or more) if they want the first swing at the windows or headlights.

A variation on the theme used by one center was to have people pay to paint graffiti, designs, or whatever on an operational VW. At the end of the day, the painted car was sold to the highest bidder.

Usually it is possible to get a junk car donated. The major problem is the clean up. A center will need to have a flatbed truck available to haul the car away at the end of the event. In addition, volunteers will be needed to clean up the broken parts. If 200 individuals pay 50¢ to violate the auto, the center will net about $75 after expenses.

Haircutting

In **Chapel Hills, North Carolina**, a group of hair stylists gave haircuts at a city street fair and turned the proceeds over to the **Warrenton Child Development Center**. **Faith Becker**, the center's director, reports that the hair stylists were recruited months in advance, and posters plugging the event and the stylists' business were put up city wide several weeks in advance. The haircutting took place for ten hours on a Sunday. Refreshments were provided by the center to those waiting to be served. There were also hair products on display which customers could purchase.

The cost to the center was minimal as the hair stylists paid for the posters and the parents donated the refreshments. Staff time in organizing the event and setting up the booth was estimated to be about 30 hours.

The customers were charged the going rate in Chapel Hill of $15, or a lesser rate if they could not afford this. The center netted $250 from the event. Ms. Becker reports that they could have raised more if they had had more than the two stylists to service the long lines that waited throughout the day.

Kids' Calendar

Many nursery schools and child care centers publish and sell calendars. The **Parent Child Center (La Salle, Colorado)** prints a calendar with the pictures of the center's children on their birthdays. The **New England Home for Little Wanderers (Boston, Massachusetts)** prints full-color paintings by children on every page of their calendar. Other centers feature pictures of children engaging in center activities, drawings by young children from different countries, pictures of various scenes in the community, recipes for each month, and children's activities. Some centers also sell advertising space to local businesses. Others list on the appropriate dates coming events of community organizations.

Designing, laying out, and printing calendars can cost anywhere from 25¢ to $2 per calendar. The actual cost will depend upon the amount of copy design that has to be paid for, the quality of paper used, the number of colors used, and the number of calendars printed. These costs can be reduced if the center lays out the

calendar itself and if it can get local technical schools or insurance companies to donate the printing.

If 300 calendars costing 50¢ each are sold for $2 each, the proceeds would be $450. On the other hand, if 25 business ads are sold for $50 each and 100 community events are listed for $2 each, the 300 calendars could be distributed free and the net proceeds would be $1,300. In either case, having the calendars in 300 homes would provide considerable publicity for the center.

House Tours

Mt. Zion Presbyterian Child Care Center (Mt. Zion, Illinois) raised $1,200 by selling 500 tickets, at $2.50 each, for a tour of five local houses. On the tickets was printed a map showing the location of the five houses along with a brief description of each house. On the day of the tour, ticket purchasers were free to visit these houses in any order between the hours of 2 and 5 pm. They were asked to take off their shoes upon entering the houses. No guided tours were offered — rather, people were free to explore the houses on their own.

The houses selected represented a variety of styles and features. The tour was held in December so that the families' Christmas decorations were also featured. Other organizations have pursued specific themes in their selection of tour houses.

For example, solar houses, renovated old houses, or houses with creative children's rooms or kitchens have been highlighted.

Owners of the homes were given the opportunity to stay and keep an eye on their homes or to go out and leave volunteers from the center in charge. In either case, **Elsie Mills**, Mt. Zion's director, recommends having one person stationed in each open room in each house to handle problems and answer questions.

The center provided free babysitting for participants at their center while the parents were touring the houses. After the event was over, all the homeowners visited each other's houses and then went to a potluck organized by the center. At the potluck, an instant evaluation of the event was made to help in planning the event for the following year.

Costs to the center for the project were less than $50 — for tickets and publicity. Since this was taken on by the board as their project, little staff time was expended on the project except on the day of the event. One person on the board took charge, but many board members volunteered considerable time — selecting and recruiting homes, developing informational publicity releases about the homes, and selling tickets. The day of the tour 20 to 30 volunteers were required to staff the houses and the center.

International Food Feast

A new twist on the standard dinner fundraiser is an evening with an international flavor. The basic format is to have a series of booths set up around a central eating area. Each booth offers desserts and entrees from different countries. Participants at the feast can move from booth to booth selecting a meal with samplings from any variety of countries. Cheeses and wines from each country could be offered as well. Recipes for all the foods could be made available for sale.

To add to the festivity, periodic performances could be given featuring music and dances from the various countries. For excitement, there could be a raffle or door prize for a trip abroad. The trip could be donated or offered at a reduced rate by a local travel agency which might also be persuaded to provide travel posters to decorate the booths and to use in advance publicity in return for permission to set up a booth at the event.

Tickets could be sold to the event which entitle the purchaser four free "samples." The profitability of the event would depend upon the food being donated by parents, staff, and friends. An organizing committee would need to prepare for the event about six months in advance. The night of the event 20 to 50 volunteers would be required to set up, maintain, and clean up the booths. Major expenses would include rental of a hall, purchase of plates, tableware, etc., and payment for entertainers.

Fairs! Fairs! Fairs!

The following is a collection of ideas on running successful fairs submitted by Exchange readers:

Organizing Ideas

Fairs are often inefficient as fundraisers because they require so many hours of volunteer time to organize and put on while yielding only a modest income. To avoid continuing an ineffective event year after year, a center should keep reasonably careful records of income, expenses, and volunteer hours expended for the event. One nursery school kept such a record and found that 65 individuals had invested over 500 hours in order to net $625 from a fair. If each volunteer had instead contributed only $10, they would have raised more money with no labor.

- In planning activities, care should be taken to provide a mix of activities which appeal to adults and children of all ages. If the fair is going to be aimed more narrowly at adult interests, thought should be given to providing child care during the event.

- Centers have found that fairs tend to be most successful if they are held outdoors since they can attract the interest of passersby.

- To begin developing a fundraising mailing list, have people register for a drawing at the fair. Compile the names and addresses of those registering and send them notices of future fundraising events.

- Don't forget the publicity value of the fair. Be sure to have big signs clearly identifying your center and describing your services, and have plenty of your brochures on hand for interested parents.

Activity Ideas

- **Dunking booth.** Local celebrities are perched, one at a time, on a seat suspended over a water tank or swimming pool. People pay to throw baseballs at a target which, when hit, triggers a mechanism to dump the celebrity into the juice.

- **Used toy sale.** Parents and the center itself donate used but usable toys for resale at low prices at the fair.

- **Marble racer.** Using V-shaped corner boards and blocks, a parent constructs a marble racer on which two marbles pursue separate but equal twisting crisscrossing paths downhill to the finish line. Due to the amount of work involved, this should be constructed sturdily for reuse in future fairs as well as by children in the school.

- **Craft booths.** One area is reserved for tables for craftspersons to sell their wares. The center makes its money by charging a $15-25 fee for rental of each table. Crafts sold should be screened beforehand to ensure that goods offered are varied and of good quality. Some centers also rent tables to local merchants (such as florists and book dealers) to peddle their wares.

- **Miniature golf.** A challenging nine hole course is set up for junior and senior golfers. The object is to hit golf balls over, around, and through a variety of obstacles to hit nine targets. Obstacles could include drain pipes, ramps over children's swimming pools, old tires, bricks, string fences, chairs, and balloons.

Children's Style Show

For the past several years, **Kingsley House** in **New Orleans, Louisiana**, has held a style show in which all the center's children participate. Each year, two teachers and an aide are appointed to coordinate the event. They choose a theme (such as "King Tut"), plan appropriate decorations, and recruit parents to help decorate, sell tickets, and bake food for sale at the show.

Children can wear anything — swimsuits, shorts, nightgowns, etc. The parents write up a description of the outfit, which need not be handmade, and one mother reads this description as the child walks down the walkway during the show. Children also become involved by drawing some of the murals for the show.

Since the food and most of the decorations are usually donated, expenses are few. The three staff coordinators spend a good deal of time in preparing the show, and parents volunteer considerable time.

Margaret LaBlance, the center's child care director, reports that the original purpose of the event was to have an enjoyable social event for the families. Now it not only provides a fun event that all look forward to but it also raises some money (approximately $450) for special classroom activities.

The Christmas Gift Wrap

From **Nancy Travis** at the **Southern Regional Education Board** comes the suggestion of operating a gift wrap service. Secure permission from a large department store or, better yet, a shopping mall to set up a gift wrapping booth on their premises during the weeks prior to Christmas. In setting up the space, be sure to use tables which are high and wide enough to provide a comfortable work area and to put up highly visible "gift wrapping service" signs which state clearly who the proceeds are for.

During store hours, have two or three workers on duty for a four or five hour shift basis. Charge customers a set rate on the basis of package size, but leave the door open to charge a negotiated

rate for oversized or odd-shaped items. Be sure to make arrangements with the store owner on a safe overnight storage area for your materials.

Sufficient wrapping paper, pre-tied bows, and scissors would be needed to wrap 100 or so packages per day. The cost of these materials could be reduced by buying paper in bulk (on rolls with a cutter bar) or by seeking to have items donated (boxes from a bakery or department store, for example). The major commitment would be in terms of volunteers to plan the event and staff the booth — for a two-week stint, a total of 260 to 280 person hours could be required. If on the average ten packages were wrapped an hour during a two-week period, the net proceeds would be between $750 and $1,000. In addition, the center could receive considerable publicity by giving the center's brochure to every customer.

Community Scholarship Fund

Utilizing a $4,000 United Way grant, the **Day Care and Child Development of Tompkins County (New York)** has established a cooperative day care scholarship fund. Families experiencing short-term financial distress are potentially eligible for scholarships on a sliding fee scale basis to enable them to keep their children in child care during their crises. Applications, which are accepted from any of the Council's 11 centers or 200 family day care homes, are screened initially by a Council staff member who also checks to see if the person would be eligible for alternative forms of assistance. Qualifying applications are then reviewed for final approval by a committee of participating child care directors.

While expenditures are minimal, considerable Council and providers' staff time is required to solicit funds and screen applicants.

Parents, children, and centers all benefit from there being a continuity of care, instead of disruption, during crisis periods. Although it is too early to tell whether the Council will find it beneficial as well as possible to expand the scholarship fund, it would seem that such a collaborative project focusing on the needs of families should be of interest to a number of funding sources (unions, businesses, civic groups, and wealthy individuals).

Ice Cream Social

The **First United Methodist Day Care Center (Erie, Pennsylvania)** raised $1,200 by sponsoring an ice cream social. Most of the money was raised by sending out two tickets, selling for $1 each, to the 600+ families of the congregation of the church in which the center is housed. Many church members sent in money for the center even if they did not plan to attend. Most sent in donations of $5, although one $100 donation was received. Since the social was timed to coincide with a local arts festival in a park one block away, there were also some tickets sold at the door.

The event was held on a Wednesday in June from 6 to 8 pm. About 350 individuals attended in person. Many sales were also made on a carry-out basis. Parents brought home sundaes after picking up their child at the center. Elderly persons from a nearby senior citizens' high-rise brought home ice cream for their friends who were unable to attend. The event was advertised on the radio, in the local newspaper, in the center's newsletter, and in church.

The center's director, **Karen Morey**, reported that minimal resources in terms of time and money were required. Less than $100 was spent for the ice cream, tablecloths, disposable dishes, and refreshments. Cakes were donated, and five people spent one hour picking strawberries for topping. About 50 to 60 person hours were required for the entire project — about half for staffing the event while in progress and half for planning and setting up.

Challenge Grants

Many child care centers have been able to double their fundraising income by having businesses and foundations provide grants to match the monies the centers raised locally.

For example, a child care center in Pennsylvania raised about $500 with a fundraising event and then went to a local business and got it to contribute an equal amount to the center. Many foundations utilize this matching strategy in what are often referred to as "challenge grants." The Kresge Foundation provided a grant of $75,000 to the **John E. Boyd Center (Fall River, Massachusetts)** to construct a new facility with the condition that the center raise a matching $75,000 through their local fundraising efforts.

The intent of challenge-type grants is to maximize the impact of scarce charitable funds, as well as to ensure the commitment of and support for the recipient agencies. Generally, organizations making these grants require that the recipient agencies raise their matching funds primarily from donations and pledges from individuals and organizations in their own communities. Funds from government agencies and foundations usually do not qualify.

In some cases, funding sources have required that centers raise their entire matching share before the challenge grant is made. Other centers have received funding on a dollar-for-dollar basis. For example, a funding agency might reserve a specific amount of money for a center; and for each chunk of money the center raises, the agency makes a matching contribution until the reserved funds are exhausted.

Centers have found that a commitment to a challenge grant can be helpful to their local fundraising. They find that people are more inclined to make pledges or donations when they know the center will, in effect, receive $2 for every $1 they contribute. The reverse may also be true. Local businesses that do not have formal challenge grants may still be more inclined to give money to a center if that center asks the business to match whatever they can raise rather than asking for a flat 100% grant.

A Weekend With Buchwald

The **John E. Boyd Center for Child Care and Development** in **Fall River, Massachusetts**, raised about $10,000 when Art Buchwald donated his services for a weekend. **Kathleen Harrington**, from the center, set this in motion by writing a personal letter to the humorist describing the current needs of the center, the history of the center, and some of the crazy incidents which were part of its history (such as when the center was temporarily housed in an armory and they had to convert a military latrine into a Raggedy Ann bathroom). She concluded that if he would let her share with him the story of the center, there would be parts he could make hay with.

As a result, Buchwald offered to come to Newport, Rhode Island (near Fall River), for a weekend to do what he could for the center. The center took full advantage of this offer. Into the weekend they packed a press conference, an appearance on a radio talk show, a dinner, a "lecture" at an historic mansion owned by Salve Regina — Newport College followed by a cocktail party at another of Newport's famous mansions, a sail on Ted Turner's yacht "Courageous," and a tennis match between Buchwald and local celebrities. All proceeds from these activities were donated to the center, as Buchwald waived his normal $6,000 speaking fee and the use of the mansions was donated.

Exchange does not recommend that centers bombard Buchwald for repeat performances but offers this as an example of how to secure support from local, area, or national celebrities.

Weekly Bingo Game

The **Shelley School**, a child care program serving 18 mentally retarded children in **Raleigh, North Carolina**, has raised as much as $27,000 in one year for its building expansion fund by operating a Bingo game. For two years, the school hired an outside Bingo operator to run the games five evenings a week. The school received a percentage of the profits from these games.

Lately, under new, stricter state legislation, the school has recruited volunteers to operate the game one night per week. Under the new rules, the school has been raising about $500 per month from Bingo.

To oversee the game, the school has set up a Bingo committee. This committee registered the game with the local sheriff as required. An initial investment of about $1,000 was made to purchase Bingo equipment. Space, tables, and chairs to accommodate 100 to 125 players per evening were rented in a community building. A separate account was set up to maintain solid financial records on the project. Once the game was organized, little time has been required from center staff and parents for the ongoing operation.

Evelyn M. Turner, the school's director, observed that, while the benefits to the program have been invaluable, there have been drawbacks. Some organizations in the community ceased or lessened their support to the school either because they objected to the gambling aspect of Bingo or because they believed the school needed less support considering its Bingo revenues. She stresses that any program considering Bingo as a fundraiser must weigh this potential lessening of community support.

Warning: Bingo games are strictly, but diversely, regulated in every state. Check applicable laws and procedures in your state before launching a Bingo fundraiser.

Annual Tag Sale

Everything from pianos to tennis rackets is sold at a tag sale by the **Day Care Center of New Canaan (Connecticut)**.

According to director **Margaret Easley**, the center has netted over $2,000, plus a great deal of publicity. Planning started four months before the event with a parents' dinner prepared by the center's children. At the dinner, parents signed up to work on one of six tag sale committees. Two parent/board member co-chairpersons, recruited to oversee the project, met periodically with representatives from the committees to plan and coordinate activities.

- A publicity committee (3 people) distributed posters as well as placed a newspaper ad appealing for donations of furniture, appliances, clothing, glassware, toys, books, and other salable used items. It also contacted, with great success, local real estate agents and professional tag sale promoters for leads on large scale donations.

- A heavy moving committee (2 people) collected heavy items donated.

- A set-up committee (10 people) brought in and set up tables donated by a church.

- An understaffed tagging committee (12 people) spent five long evenings putting price tags on all donated items.

- A selling committee (8 people) ran the sale and collected the money.

- And last, but far from least, a clean-up committee (10 people) spent several days cleaning out unsold items.

The event took place on a Saturday from 9 a.m. to 3 p.m. in a gymnasium which the public school board allowed the center to use free of charge. The center also held a bake sale and a plant sale in conjunction with the sale and raised an additional $200 to $300.

Current Stationery Sales

Current, Inc., a mail order stationery company, offers a 45% discount on all its products for agency fundraisers. The **Cal Poly Children's Center (San Luis Obispo, California)** has found this a simple, yet productive, way of raising money.

The center distributes Current catalogs, provided free by Current, to the 40 families it serves, as well as to friends of the center. Twice a year it collects orders from everyone and sends them to Current. Those ordering pay the full catalog price, but when the center places the order, it gets the 45% discount. It collects abut $500 in orders

each time from which it raises $225. **Missy Dannenberg**, the center's director, reports that it only requires two volunteers about an hour to fill out the order and then to sort the items when they arrive.

Gymnastics Program

The **Groton Child Development Center (New York)** runs a gymnastics program for children aged 2½ to 12. Up to 200 children can enroll for $2 per week for 10-week fall and spring sessions. The center employs a gymnastics director and four instructions (at $4 hour) to run two one-hour sessions weekday evenings and Saturday mornings.

Children are grouped by age and ability with a ratio of one instructor per group of five children. The program is operated in the gym of the local elementary school. In return for

the use of the space, the center buys the school additional gymnastics equipment. **Brenda Benson**, the center's director, reports that the program raised about $1,000 for the center.

Concert Tickets

Elizabeth Adams (Mt. Hope Day Care Center, Providence, Rhode Island) has been successful in bringing several groups together to raise funds for her center. A local retirement home donated refreshments and the use of their large dining room for a concert by the Brown University Glee Club (which appreciated an opportunity to perform).

Tickets were sold to the residents of the home and the parents enrolled at the center. The only cost involved was printing the tickets. The $1,500 raised assures that this event will be repeated again.

Fundraising Ideas That Work

by Roger Neugebauer

Fundraising is often looked upon as a necessary evil in child care. Centers engage in fundraising to bring in the extra funds needed to ensure a basic level of quality.

*But fundraising need not be a burden. A survey of **Exchange Panel of 200** members disclosed many fundraisers that are not labor intensive, that are fun, that build team spirit, and that provide positive visibility.*

This article will share a variety of panel members' successful fundraising ideas. In addition, it will provide some tips for success that you can use as guidelines in developing your fundraising plans.

Sales

The most common form of fund-raisers is the sale of products or services to parents and community members. Such fundraisers can range from a thrift shop bringing in profits approaching $100,000 a year to a bake sale netting less than $100. However, no matter how large your project, you need to take care to secure all necessary permits and pay all applicable taxes.

- **Consignment sale.** The **Harmony Schools** in Hopewell, New Jersey, raised $500 in a consignment sale. Parents brought in good condition items of need for young families, such as clothes, strollers, and cribs, and the center earned a percentage of each sale.

- **Paper cut-outs.** As a fundraiser for the Child Abuse Prevention Fund, the **Ebenezer Child Care Centers** in Milwaukee, Wisconsin, sold paper cut-outs of children. Families included their name on each cut-out they purchased, and the cut-outs were displayed like paper-doll chains around the centers.

- **Class pictures.** A professional photography company took pictures of the centers' children, and **Rainbow Chimes** in Huntington, New York, realized 50% of the profits of the sale of the pictures to parents and grandparents. The organization raised $4,000 with this project.

- **Spa days.** As Mother's Day gifts, the **Beginnings Child Care Center** in Lake Worth, Florida, sold "A Day at the Spa" for $90. The spa day included a Swedish massage, mineral pools, saunas, and a deep cleansing facial, all donated by a local resort.

- **Gourmet coffee.** The **Willow Woods Child Development Center** in Kansas City, Missouri, made $400 by selling gourmet coffee to parents. The center purchased 22 flavors of coffee wholesale in single pot packs and sold them prior to the holiday

Tips for Fundraising Success

1. **Make sure it's time efficient.** People's time is a valuable resource and should not be squandered on fundraising projects that generate a small return on time invested. Successful projects generate anywhere from $25 to $150 per hour of time invested. Any project that generates less than $10 an hour should be viewed as a poor investment. For example, a few parents at the **Bethany Early Childhood Learning Center** in Highland Park, Illinois, raised over $2,000 wrapping gifts at holiday time with a minimal investment of time.

2. **Sell what people already plan to buy.** It is easier to sell someone something they already intend to buy than to create an interest. **Brooklyn Heights Montessori School** in Brooklyn, New York, for example, sells Christmas trees and clears between $10,000 and $12,000 per year. The **Gresham Heights Learning Center** in Gresham, Oregon, sells take-home spaghetti dinners. Parents pre-order the dinners, and then the staff makes spaghetti, sauce, garlic bread, and salad and packs it in to-go boxes.

3. **Make it an annual event.** There are several advantages to turning a successful fundraiser into an annual event. Usually the second time you do a project you can benefit from all the organizing that went into the initial effort — it will take less time and you won't repeat your mistakes the second time. In addition, if an event becomes an annual tradition, people will look forward to it, and set aside time and money for it. For example, **St. Rita's Child Care Center** in Dayton, Ohio, has held its auction every year for the past 11 years. Probably the longest running benefit for an early childhood program is the Westport Handcrafts Fair, an annual benefit for the **Westport Weston Cooperative Nursery School** in Westport, Connecticut, this year being held for the 30th consecutive year.

4. **Build on your strengths.** When thinking of a fundraising idea, you should think first about sticking to your knitting. Think of a project where you can use the skills and experience your organization already possesses. For example, the **Illinois State University Child Care Center** in Normal, Illinois, organizes and sells first aid travel kits for cars. **Children's for Children** in Cincinnati, Ohio, sponsors a one day early childhood conference for local caregivers which brings in about $3,000 per year.

5. **Team up with other organizations.** Sometimes a small child care organization can participate in a large fundraising project by joining forces with other local organizations. In Colorado Springs, the city, the library district, the park department, and the **Care Castle** intergenerational child care center are developing an intergenerational garden where flowers will be planted in memory/honor of grandparents, parents, and grandchildren. In Lansing, Michigan, several community organizations, including **St. Vincent's Home for Children** and the **Community Nursery School**, cooperate in sponsoring an annual raffle. By joining forces, they are able to offer prizes as big as automobiles.

6. **Make it unique to your organization.** To make for an appropriate and memorable fundraiser, tie the project into a unique feature of your organization. The **Fruit and Flower Day Nursery** in Portland, Oregon, for example, sells "Fruit and Flower" holiday baskets as a fundraiser.

7. **Tie it to a celebration.** Major events in the history of your organization present high profile opportunities to raise funds. For example, the **Early Childhood Enrichment Center** in Shaker Heights, Ohio, used the occasion of its 20th birthday to set up a 20th Anniversary Endowment Fund for scholarships. **St. Michael's Day Nursery** in Wilmington, Delaware, used the celebration of its 100th anniversary to raise over $300,000.

8. **Capture the PR value of your fundraiser.** Fundraising projects can increase the visibility of your organization in addition to generating funds. In the long run, the heightened recognition from a fundraiser may be of more value than the funds raised. For example, when the **Fairfax-San Anselmo Children's Center** in Fairfax, Virginia, conducts its annual fundraiser, it hangs a banner over a city street announcing "Annual Back to School Haircut Marathon" along with the center's name.

season in their centers with a minimum purchase of 50 packets.

- **Supermarket coupons.** The **Children's Learning Center** in Yardley, Pennsylvania, earns from $100 to $200 per week from the sale of supermarket certificates to parents. The center pays $950 for every $1,000 in certificates it buys from two local supermarkets.

- **Candy sales.** Every March, the parents at **Children's Discovery Center** in Toledo, Ohio, sell candy in time for Easter. In 1995, candy sales resulted in a profit of $9,500.

- **Book/toy store.** Every October, the **Harper Learning Center** at William Raney Harper College in Palatine, Illinois, holds two book and toy sale days at their center. Parents recruit local vendors and sales representatives for national companies to set up tables in the center's lobby. The center receives from 15% to 40% of each company's sales, resulting in a profit of from $1,000 to $3,000 per year.

- **Plant sales.** Twice a year, **Smoky Row Children's Center** in Powell, Ohio, earns $1,000 from the sale of plants. In November, the center sells poinsettia plants; in the spring, it sells bedding plants and hanging baskets.

- **Art auction.** The **Monadnock Community Day Care Center** in Peterborough, New Hampshire, raised over $10,000 with an art auction. The center approached local artists and asked them to donate one piece of art. The art was sold in a formal auction at the city hall.

- **Hoagie sales.** Periodically, the **Crafton Children's Center** in Pittsburgh, Pennsylvania, raises money by selling hoagies to parents. The staff prepares the sandwiches in their own kitchen and realizes a profit of 50% on all sales.

Events

Events can combine pleasure with profits. They can be fun, but they also can be a lot of work. Centers have experienced success with fundraising events as ambitious as golf tournaments and as modest as a morning tea.

- **5K run.** This year, the **Hi-Hello Day Care Center** in Freeport, New York, raised over $9,000 by sponsoring the second annual Waterfront 5K Run/Walk. A professional race organizer took care of managing, measuring, and timing the race. The center was in charge of promotions, registrations, refreshments, and prizes. In addition to the 5K run and the non-competitive 5K walk, the center also organized short fun runs for children.

- **RockerThon.** An annual event of the **Great Beginnings Christian School** in Canoga Park, California, is the RockerThon. Staff members secure pledges and try to rock for up to 24 hours (one year, five teachers lasted the whole time). The center has raised from $1,000 to $4,000 a year with this event.

- **Children's concert.** The **Good Samaritan Hospital Child Care Center** raised $500 by sponsoring a concert by Hugh Hanley. The center aid the performer's minimal fee, booked an auditorium, and sold tickets in the community.

- **Gala dance.** By holding a dinner dance for two consecutive years, the **Springfield Day Nursery** in Springfield, Massachusetts, has been able to raise over $55,000 for a scholarship fund. The black tie affair is held in the ballroom of a local hotel.

- **Fashion show.** For five years, the **Samaritan Child Care Center** in Troy, New York, has sponsored a children's fashion show. The event is held in the auditorium of a local community college. Children from the center, walking with their parents, model clothing provided at a discount by a local store. Local businesses pay for ads in the program. The event generates proceeds of around $4,000 a year.

- **Wine/food tasting.** In Fremont, California, **Tri-Cities Children's Centers** has sponsored "Tri-City Treats" for eight years. Area restaurants and wineries set up tasting booths at the local Hilton hotel. Mayors of area towns act as judges for the food and wine and award plaques to the winners. A newspaper provides all the publicity, a community college provides musical entertainment, and other businesses underwrite all other event expenses. As a result, the child care organization makes 100% profit on ticket sales, with this year's proceeds exceeding $10,000.

Games of Chance

Lotteries, bingo, and raffles raise large amounts of money for educational and charitable activities in this nation. Early childhood organizations often have difficulty justifying participation in these high stakes ventures. However, centers have found many creative ways to raise funds with fun, low key games of chance.

- **Chinese auction.** The **Children's Space** in Salem, New Jersey, had a fun evening with a Chinese auction. Parents and staff solicited donations from local merchants. At the event, these donated items were displayed on tables with a bowl for each one. Participants buy tickets and place them in the bowl for each item they would like to win. At the end, one ticket is drawn from each bowl to determine the winners. Last year, the auction netted over $1,500.

- **Raffles.** Many organizations use raffles as fundraisers, either separately or as part of other activities. For example, the **Marriott Child Development Center** in Bethesda, Maryland, raised $2,500 by raffling weekend hotel packages donated by their corporate sponsor. The **Euclid Avenue Preschool** in Cleveland, Ohio, holds an annual Mother's Day Raffle in which "gifts for mother," such as dinners at nice restaurants, manicures, a dance cruise, and a night of babysitting, are the prizes.

- **Egg hunt.** The owners of a jewelry store came up with a creative way to help the **Fairfax-San Anselmo Children's Center** in Fairfax, California. The store filled 1,000 plastic Easter eggs with jelly beans. In 20 of these eggs, they also inserted gemstones. In one egg, they inserted a 21 carat diamond (in honor of the center's 21st anniver-

sary). The eggs were displayed colorfully in the jewelry store's front window. The center mailed invitations to 3,500 people on their mailing list and that of the jewelry store encouraging them to join the egg hunt by buying an egg for at least a $3 donation.

Appeals

Sometimes the easiest way to raise money is to ask for it directly. What you are selling is the value of your service to the community. Success depends as much upon the reputation of your organization as it does on the means of making the appeal. Before launching a major appeal, be sure to check out all applicable rules and regulations.

- **Letter/phone appeal.** In Madison, New Jersey, the **FM Kirby Children's Center** raised $10,000 for a playground through an appeal for donations. A letter was mailed to all parents. Then one parent in each classroom called all parents who had not responded and reminded them that any donation, no matter how small, would be welcomed.

- **Care shares.** When the local Kiwanis Club in Cannon Beach, Oregon, adopted the **Cannon Beach Children's Center**, it came up with the idea of selling local residents "Care Shares for Quality." Shares were sold for $20 donations. Donors received official looking stock certificates.

- **Annual letter.** For 24 years, the board of the **Calvin Hill Day Care Center** in New Haven, Connecticut, has been sending out an annual appeal for donations. Each board member mails anywhere from 5 to 15 letters asking for a donation in any amount. This letter brings in about $5,000 a year.

- **Deposit donations.** One way **Early Childhood Options of University Circle** in Cleveland, Ohio, raises money for its scholarship fund is to ask parents to donate all or part of their deposit when they leave the program. Most parents have forgotten they made the deposit and gladly donate it to the fund.

- **Newsletter appeal.** The board newsletter of **Long Beach Day Nursery** in Long Beach, California, is used as a fundraising as well as a communication tool. The newsletter, which is mailed four times a year to 2,800 individuals, includes a progress report on the organization's three centers, a list of recent donors, a wish list of items the centers currently need, and a reply envelope for sending in donations.

- **Adopt an item.** In Fort Worth, Texas, the **St. Stephen Presbyterian Day School** periodically displays pictures of items the center needs along with their prices. Center parents and church members "adopt" an item by donating the price of a specific item.

Ask and Ye Shall Receive: A Primer for Large-Scale Fundraising

by Patricia Berl

In the past, large-scale fundraising activities went hand in hand with non profit organizations. Today, in an increasingly competitive and challenging business environment, every center, whether large or small, non profit or proprietary, single or multi-site, can benefit from a well-orchestrated fundraising campaign.

For child care directors, executing a successful fundraising plan can generate needed funds for daily operations or program expansions. Equally important, effective fundraising strengthens a center's image in the community and expands its market presence.

Fundraising in the 1990's will be a significant factor in maintaining the economic viability of many child care centers. Escalating costs of quality child care services necessitate supplementing income from parent tuitions and state and local subsidies.

Many centers are already turning to private individuals, corporations, and foundations who give over $10.5 billion annually to charitable causes. As the child care industry expands, competition for the funding sources will intensify. Directors must be prepared for the fundraising challenge ahead.

Before you embark upon a fundraising campaign, consider the primary axiom of fundraising:

Successful fundraising lies in blending your organization's goals with the interests and needs of the community.

An effective fundraising plan takes into account six key elements. These are:

- Gifts — the amount of money you are seeking to raise

- Prospects — the people in your community who have both an interest in and a potential for contributing to your cause

- Opportunity — the benefit that is directly bestowed upon the donor as a result of giving

- Appeal — the urgency, immediacy, and inherent attraction of your proposal

- Timing — the time frame within which you seek contributions or make an appeal

- Resources — the financial and human potential you have available to commit to fundraising activities (this includes planning time and management time for board, paid staff, and volunteers)

Much has been written about the psychology of fundraising. Professionals carefully consider three basic questions: who to ask, when to ask, and how much to ask for. A simple analogy of cookie jar economics illustrates the basic elements of strategic fundraising.

Successful fundraising lies in blending your organization's goals with the interests and needs of the community.

Think back to when you were a child and desperately wanted a cookie. Unfortunately, at three years of age, you could not independently obtain the cookies (gift) which were safely tucked away in a container on the top cupboard shelf. To fulfill your need, you naturally sought any family members (prospects) who could deliver the cookies to you.

If you went to your father, who was absorbed in the Sunday afternoon football game, your request fell on deaf ears (poor opportunity). If you approached your older brother, you were apt to run into more disappointment since, out of sheer sibling rivalry, he would choose not to grant your request. If, however, you approached your mom (favorable prospect who could derive personal satisfaction, i.e., benefit from meeting your request, since she baked the cookies), you would likely meet with success providing that you met the following conditions:

• you did not ask right before dinner (timing)

• you were not greedy

Naturally, your petition emphasized how much you needed those cookies to the one person who would feel the most fulfilled in having met your request (appeal). Having successfully obtained your cookies, you came again and again to that generous donor (resources) for additional cookies.

What's true in cookie economics is true in all organized fundraising programs: First, identify your organization's needs; second, translate these needs into financial goals; third, determine your prospects; fourth, approach potential donors being mindful of the timing and immediacy of your appeal; and fifth, package your request in ways that match the donor's needs, style, and level of giving.

There are many activities from which to choose when drafting a fundraising plan. In selecting the *right* activity, begin by determining your center's financial needs. Then, balance your fundraising goal against the financial and human resources you have available to commit to the task of raising money.

Effective fundraising takes planning and time, not only from the director, but also from paid staff and volunteers. Finally, whatever activity you choose, whether it be an annual fundraiser or a gala special event, be certain that it is consonant with the goals and values of your center and is acceptable to the community.

Below are several effective approaches for large-scale fundraising.

Annual fund drives. Annual fund drives are the bread and butter of professional fundraisers. These drives solicit donors annually by letter to contribute funds for the continued operation of the organization. Annual fund drives work because they capitalize on the fact that donors already believe in their cause and will support the organization. It is a fundraising fact that if people give once they will usually give again. Annual fund drives are institutionalized and occur year after year, thereby expanding exponentially the number of donors and gifts that can be realized.

Capital campaigns are used to raise large amounts of money for capital improvements or program expansion. Capital campaigns selectively target donors who are capable of giving large contributions and have already demonstrated an interest in and willingness to donate to the organization. Capital campaigns are one-time events and focus 80% of available time on 10% of the potential donors who are most capable of giving 90% of the money needed.

Before you can reasonably expect a corporation to make a contribution to your center, you must first demonstrate your organization's viability and the community needs which you serve.

Special events are particularly attractive to for profit centers since they focus the community's attention on the organization and expand its community image.

Generally, special events such as house and garden tours, auctions, dinners, lecture series, etc. require an outlay of cash to produce the event and are time and labor intensive. Expenses to put on a special event can eat voraciously into the event's proceeds if not carefully monitored. Special events require a six to eight month lead time. Nevertheless, they can enhance an organization's image in the community and expand business presence.

Corporate philanthropy. Before you knock on corporate doors, remember that corporate giving is not just altruism. Corporations give because they realize tax benefits or see potential to expand their markets, e.g., McDonald's sponsorship of the Special Olympics. When making an appeal to corporate donors, consider how you will provide donor recognition. Before you can reasonably expect a corporation to make a contribution to your center, you must first demonstrate your organization's viability and the community needs which you serve.

Finally, have clearly stated goals, long-range plans, experienced leadership, a competent staff, an involved and resourceful board, and a fiscally sound budget in place before corporate solicitation begins. Corporations expect their investments to pay off both in terms of donor recognition and community needs fulfilled.

Before outlining your center's fundraising strategy, define the organization's mission and programs, identify funding goals, allocate available financial and human resources, select an approach, plan well, start early, and think positively.

Ask and ye shall receive.

*Patricia Scallan Berl is Division Vice President of the mid-Atlantic operations for Bright Horizons Family Solutions (www.brighthorizons.com) the world's leading provider of employer-sponsored child care, back-up care, early education, and work/life solutions, operating more than 600 child care and early education centers across the U.S., in Europe, and Canada. Patricia is a frequent contributor to **Exchange**. In addition to writing, she has a passion for Springer Spaniels and orchids.*

People Giving to People: Executing an Annual Giving Campaign

by Patricia Berl

Increasingly, child care centers are seeking ways to expand financial resources beyond parent tuition. Toward this end, fundraising strategies are taking on a greater significance in enhancing the economic survival of non profit centers.

While in the past fundraising was synonymous with flea markets, car washes, and door-to-door candy sales, today it requires a highly disciplined and managed process. Its success lies in:

- a thorough understanding of the center's goals and objectives;

- knowledge of the potential benefactors;

- rigorous planning and follow up.

Most child care directors recognize the need for fundraising. Yet, they are reluctant to initiate fund development programs, lacking experience as well as understanding of well established professional techniques for executing a successful campaign.

Gearing Up

Before you embark on a fundraising program, consider the first axiom of fundraising: *people give to people*. Since 1985, individuals have been contributing 90% of all private philanthropic dollars in the United States. Corporations and foundations give less than 10% of the total charitable giving. Clearly, the major source of philanthropy is the individual contributor. The fundraising challenge to directors is to tap the individual giver.

An effective fundraising campaign cannot be undertaken solely by the director. It must have the full understanding and support of the board of directors and the knowledgeable commitment of dedicated volunteers. The quality of this commitment among participants will define the scope of the fundraising campaign that can be realistically executed.

Annual Giving Campaigns

Fund drives known as *annual giving campaigns* are the most effective way to raise significant and supplemental operating funds for schools and centers. Because these campaigns directly target the current and potential families in your center, there is a strong incentive for donors to give. Furthermore, the inherent recurring nature of the annual giving campaign format reinforces the donor's connection with the center over time.

For the past seven years, I have conducted annual giving campaigns at two centers, raising an aggregate of over $150,000. In the course of conducting these campaigns, I have identified eight essential points for managing a successful fund drive. These are:

- Know why you are raising the money.

- Set a financial goal.

- Target the message.

- Tailor the appeal.

- Draft the letter.

- Cultivate donor response.

- Implement donor response.

- Evaluate the campaign.

Know Why You Are Raising the Money

Before you initiate an annual giving campaign, stop and consider why you wish to raise the money. To answer this question, begin by defining what your center is: how it communicates its needs, goals, and objectives to the community. In fundraising circles, this exercise of introspection is a *case statement*. It includes the following: your statement of purpose, list of current goals and objectives, history, statement of current needs and future needs, financial resources, list of previous donors, and an analysis of the market. In preparing the case statement, define your center in concise terms that will help gain consensus among the board of directors.

Next, consider how your center fits into the broader community — its market. Unfortunately, the *do good mentality* of most non profits is not sufficient justification for donors to give to your cause. Successful fundraising depends upon fundamental marketing principles.

Barry Nicholson, consultant to the Funding Center in Washington, DC,

sees it as the process of understanding and responding to the exchange relationship between the community and the non profit organization. According to Nicholson:

"Centers usually emerge in response to perceived needs in the environment. But the environment is constantly changing; and, therefore, non profits must remain sensitive to these changes or market requirements. Non profits must recognize that they are something more than do good entities, that they do not live in a vacuum. Market sensitivity requires that organizations continually look at their role in the community."

Summing up Nicholson, environments tend to dictate what people need, and this in turn dictates what organizations do. With an awareness of marketing principles, child care centers can examine their mission in light of the real (versus perceived) needs of the community.

Set a Financial Goal

Having identified your mission and needs, set a financial goal. Think realistically but think big, at least 50% more than you expect to raise. It is helpful to suggest a contribution amount sought from the donor. Left on their own, donors will frequently underestimate the amount of contribution needed. By specifying the size of the donation needed, chances are increased that the financial target will be attained.

Emphasizing 100% participation is also important, although personalized follow-ups are most effective when focused upon specific donors who have the greatest potential for giving

significant contributions. In fundraising, as well as in business, the 80/20 Paretto rule applies — 80% of the funds you receive will come from 20% or fewer of the donors solicited.

Concrete objectives stated with clearly understood price tags — for example, "the addition of a $3,000 piece of climbing equipment to improve the playscape for the two year olds" or "the creation of a continuing education fund for staff to pursue graduate education" — are appeals that attract donors. These goals have a visible and more lasting effect on your program and services.

Generally, avoid appeals aimed at improving administrative support. Computers in the office, while necessary, do not generate the same degree of interest as computers in the classroom.

Finally, determine the length of the campaign. Generally, six to eight weeks is a good rule of thumb since most responses will be received within 10 to 14 days of the appeal. Fund drives that extend beyond three months rarely justify the investment in time.

Target the Message

Identify potential donors and target the funding appeal to specific populations that share a mutuality of interest with your organization. Obviously, those who benefit most directly from your services — the families of the children in your center — are the primary donor base. But parents of current students are just one group within the universe of donors to whom you appeal.

Parents of former students who once benefited from your center, parents of children yet to come, and grandparents of presently enrolled students expand the potential donor base.

Secondarily, community service groups, vendors, and contractors who perform service for your center can also be considered as donor prospects. All have a stake in seeing that your center remains a viable and contributing organization in the community.

Tailor the Appeal

Tailoring a fundraising appeal can be one of the most challenging and creative aspects of the development process. It involves matching the donor's interests with the needs of your organization. Because people give to people and not to causes, the more you know about the donor's personal history, values, education, interests, and investment in your community, the greater your success at appealing to the mutuality of interests between your center and the prospective donors.

Each appeal should be designed around the profile and interests of the donor. Appeals to parents of current students can stress the urgency of receiving money now to enrich a specific program that directly benefits their children.

Appeals to parents of former students can remind the donor of the important start their child received from your school, and the value in supporting the center in its mission to others. Parents of younger sisters and brothers who will attend the center in the future can be approached from the perspective

that future viability depends upon the availability of the resources now.

When approaching the grandparents of children in your center as prospective donors, two considerations should be given: (1) gain the parents' permission before soliciting grandparents for contributions and (2) send some form of communication such as a newsletter or program brochure to the grandparents before mailing the appeal letter. Providing these guidelines are followed, grandparents can become a substantial donor group.

Finally, businesses, contractors, and all others who routinely provide services to the center can be approached from the perspective of the value your center adds to the community. When soliciting these groups, consider the length of time of the relationship, playing on the strength and continuity of that relationship.

Draft the Letter

The solicitation letter is the most direct way to reach donors. It consists of three parts: the letter; donor response card; and a return, school addressed, stamped envelope. Inserting a fact sheet, newsletter, or brochure of the school is also helpful to donors who are not currently parents in the center.

The length of the letter should be limited to a page and a half, single spaced, with a large signature block. The addition of the names of your board of directors in reduced type in the upper left hand margin contributes to a professional look.

In constructing the letter, do not exceed eight paragraphs. For the

opening, identify your center, its goals, and student population. You also may include a few sentences of brief history about your center. In the following paragraph, define your needs and announce the fund drive. State the financial requirements needed to achieve your goals. Emphasize the urgency of the need, the necessity of the annual giving campaign, and budget constraints.

Next, restate the financial goal of the campaign, specify the amount of individual contribution needed, and stress everyone's participation. Explain the donor response card, time frame for making the response, and any follow up planned.

In the closing paragraphs, reaffirm your need and reiterate the importance of the campaign's success. Express gratitude for the donor's consideration and participation.

Cultivate Donors

Many annual giving campaigns include a preappeal telephone contact with targeted donors to introduce the program and to entice special interest. Other campaigns send out solicitation letters, then follow up with a call to answer questions about the campaign, thereby encouraging each donor's careful consideration of appropriate levels of giving.

Social events such as receptions, dinners, and home-school events can provide a forum for introducing the annual campaign. Peer solicitation from parents to parents is most effective, as their common interests are integrated with the challenges and benefits of the campaign drive.

Implement Donor Response

The donor response card will help you track your donor and follow up pledge contributions. It will also provide you with the information necessary to update your mailing lists for subsequent fund drives. The response card includes donor name, status (parent of current child enrolled at the center, grandparent, friend of organization, board member, etc.), address, and contribution amount or pledge amount with date specified when pledge will be made. This card accompanies the donor's contribution, serves as the record, and becomes the future base for next year's donor list.

Respond to donors with a prewritten thank you note that contains a blank for filling in the contribution amount.

Add a written word of thanks at the end and personally sign all acknowledgments. A carboned letter is useful. The top copy is sent to the parent and the carbon is your record.

Evaluate the Campaign

Be sure to correct your donor lists against information provided from the return donor response card. Analyze your campaign results and establish next year's goals on the basis of your experience. If donors give once, they will give again, so continually follow up.

Remember, people give to people: believe in your organization and, above all, believe in yourself. Ask confidently for what you want, do not settle for less, and begin now!

Carefully executed, your annual fund campaign effort will not only generate ongoing financial support but will, additionally, and of equal importance, enhance your center's presence in the community.

Patricia Scallan Berl is Division Vice President of the mid-Atlantic operations for Bright Horizons Family Solutions (www.brighthorizons.com) the world's leading provider of employer-sponsored child care, back-up care, early education, and work/life solutions, operating more than 600 child care and early education centers across the U.S., in Europe, and Canada. Patricia is a frequent contributor to **Exchange**. *In addition to writing, she has a passion for Springer Spaniels and orchids.*

Step by Step to a Successful Annual Giving Telephone Campaign

by Jane Ewing and Susan Morris

Fundraising is a part of life in any non profit organization. A telephone campaign allows you the opportunity to personalize it. Ideally, you would be able to talk to each constituent face to face, but that isn't realistic with many potential donors and limited numbers of volunteers. The solution is a personal phone call to people that we know and that know us. At The Little School, we have had successful phone campaigns for nine years now, resulting in close to $200,000 in donations. With careful planning, telephone campaigns can be a source of much needed funds for any organization.

Step #1 — Rallying Board Support

Make sure that your board of trustees understands their responsibility to make annual giving successful. It is first and foremost the responsibility of the board to ensure the financial stability of the organization. The development committee needs to present information about the campaign to the board, well in advance of when the campaign is expected to start. If you have never done one before, you will need several months of preparation/explanation time. Often, there is resistance from board members who don't understand that this is part of their responsibility. They need to acknowledge the responsibility and then become enthusiastic about it. Information about annual giving campaign responsibilities should be given to prospective board members during the recruitment process.

Board members also need to know that they have a responsibility to contribute themselves. We don't tell our board members how much to give, but we do tell them that we expect everybody to give something. You can't expect your constituency to participate if your own board does not participate.

Step #2 — Preparing Your Constituency

If your organization has never had a formal organized annual giving campaign, in any form whatsoever, it would be realistic from the time that the board decides to have one, until you begin the campaign, to give yourself at least six months for low key explanations to your constituency. Information could be in your newsletter or in a preliminary letter that goes out over the signature of the president of the board. Tell people why — annual giving campaigns are needed because tuition or fees do not cover the cost of providing the services you offer. You are trying to keep these costs as low as possible but the time has come for an organized campaign. Let people know that you would appreciate all comments and questions. Let people know that the campaign is coming.

When people enroll in your program, inform them that fundraising is part of the life of the institution. We don't tell people a fixed amount or percentage to give, but we tell them that we do have an annual fundraising campaign and they will be asked to contribute. When a family enrolls, we request from them all of the information that is pertinent to their child, but we also want to know who they work for and any other demographic information that would give us a picture of what their capacity is as a donor. All of this is kept in the confidential files, accessible only to the development committee for the purposes of extracting pertinent information.

It is important to know who people work for, particularly when it comes to employees of a company like Boeing, where a gift matching program exists. For a list of com-panies who offer gift matching programs, consult the Develop-ment Officers Association or a large non profit organization.

One of the disappointments is that the vast majority of companies will not support educational programs below the secondary level. A few years ago, Boeing would not match gifts made by elementary level families; now they do. Get your constituency to be more and more aware of what their employer is willing to do.

Step #3 — Setting Your Sights

You need to establish a very specific monetary goal for budgeting purposes. Establish a realistic goal — one that you can and will achieve. The sense of accomplishment, success, and pleasure in achieving your goal is very important to all involved. Establish

your goals far in advance of beginning the campaign. Inform all prospective donors of the amount.

To figure the goal, look at the recent history of fundraising at your organization — note that, hopefully, the amount of funds raised has been steadily increasing over the years, look at the number of families enrolled in the school (or members or constituents of the organization), consider your current tuition or fees and how they might affect fundraising. The first year we had an established goal, it was roughly the equivalent of a 10% increase over the previous year's actual donations. Work with the finance committee in setting a realistic goal.

Step #4 — Maintaining Your Files

The development committee should keep its own complete files on all current families, all alumni families, all current and previous donors, and friends of the school who have been donors, or anyone who could have some interest in or connection to the school.

At the time of the annual giving appeal, go through these files and segment or divide them into relevant categories, such as their current association with the school. We also break the donors down into giving categories — donors who have given anywhere from nothing (if they are new families) up to $100, then $100 and over.

Review all of this information on an ongoing basis — keeping phone numbers and addresses up to date and noting separations, divorces, re-

marriages, births, deaths, and changes in employment status. If someone has had a big promotion or is now unemployed, you need to know that sort of thing.

A complete donor history is also included. It's very useful to see that somebody started out as a new family giving $25, increasing steadily until now, after being with the school for five years, they are giving $250. This information helps you know what kind of gift to ask for.

Step #5 — Getting the Timing Right

We find that fall is the best time of year to do annual giving, after school has been in session six to eight weeks. Try not to conduct a campaign close to Christmas or right after the first of the year. For tax purposes, there may be advantages to completing the campaign before the end of the year. In some cases involving the matching funds, you may not want donors to actually make their payment before year end if timing affects how the gift is matched.

Step #6 — Establishing a Time Frame

It is impossible to contact everybody in one or two nights. Spread the campaign out over a period of several weeks so people who are unavailable on specific nights of the week can be reached. Do not call after 9:00 p.m. or on a Friday night. If there is something going on, like the election last year, don't call on that night. If a big sports program is being televised, you can weigh whether or not they would be more annoyed at being interrupted or more likely to be at home. Think about the logistics of the timing.

Step #7 —
Making the Appeal:
The Letter

The appeal really matters! At least two weeks before the phone-a-thon, send a short personal letter to all of the people who will be contacted. It should go out over the signature of the chairperson of the development committee and the president of the board of trustees. It should be a combination of emotional appeal and factual information. Explain briefly that annual giving supports the annual operating budget, it covers a variety of different programs at the school, and we need to do fundraising because we attempt to keep tuition as low as possible. Let your constituency know that the phone calls will be coming; give them the dates and even the times so they know when you will be calling. Communicate in a positive, very upbeat way without the faintest whiff of an apology.

Send out the mailing so that it looks like first class mail but is really bulk mail. To do this, you need to use fairly decent stationery and get bulk mail stamps from the post office, instead of using an imprint. People are more inclined to read mail if it doesn't look like junk mail. DO NOT put a pledge return envelope in this mailing. You might elicit donations that are a smaller amount than what you would get from making a personal phone call. Sending out this pre-liminary mailing reduces the amount of time you need to

spend making your pitch on the telephone.

Step #8 —
Making the Appeal:
The Call

Look for donated office space so that you have access to many telephones and perhaps many separate offices. Privacy allows for more personal conversations and less awkwardness while callers are warming up.

Let all of your volunteers know well in advance what your dates are so that they can make commitments on their own calendars. Send reminders at least four to seven days before their night to call and include specific driving directions. Provide a light supper during the training.

We train our board members and other volunteers early in the first evening they work. Begin by acknowledging the importance of the volunteers to the campaign and that everyone is nervous and finds it difficult to ask for donations, but they will be effective after training and practice. We show a video on how to make solicitation phone calls.

Guidelines are very specific: be enthusiastic, supportive, and con-vincing. Ask the prospective donor for a specific amount. We give very clear guidelines of how to go about this. If somebody has been giving $25 a year for the last five years, try to move them up, either increase it by 10% or move up to a round number. This year, because it was the 30th anniversary of the school, we asked people to give $30.

Be creative but realistic! If somebody has been giving $25 a year, it would not be realistic to ask them for $500 unless you have very specific information about their financial circum-stances having changed. If a family has been giving generously but is no longer in the program and they appear reluctant to give, the appeal might be that we are asking all supporters of the school to continue to be supporters and would they con-sider giving a token gift. The language is very specific. Always ask WOULD you consider giving a gift of a certain amount. Let the person think about it briefly.

Inexperienced callers should call people who are in the modest gift giving range. Experienced callers should call major givers. If possible, have the same person call the same group year after year. There is a real advantage to this because a relation-ship is established. People who currently have children in the program are very effective in calling new families and other currently enrolled families because they have something in common. It is especially successful to have someone who was a new parent last year call people who are new parents this year.

Step #9 —
Documenting the
Response

When we make our phone calls, each solicitor has a loose leaf notebook with the printout — one sheet per person — of donor information. They record directly on the printout the results of their phone call — the person wasn't home, the person was home and declined to make a gift, the person was home and agreed to make a pledge of a specific amount or agreed to make a pledge of an unspecified amount. All of this needs to be noted, dated, and initialed.

Phone solicitors have a choice of three different form letters that they fill out after each phone call, depending on the results:

- One letter is a thank you for your pledge — the specific amount is filled in.

- The second one is a thank you for your pledge of an unspecified amount.

- The third one is a thank you for giving me the time to talk to you: I understand you don't wish to make a pledge; we hope that we can count on your support. Although this third letter is rarely productive, it is a gracious thing to do.

The volunteer notes on the donor's record the results of the phone call and fills out the form letter, personalized with the donor's name and a very brief personal note at the bottom. A pledge envelope accompanies this confirmation letter. The letters go out the next day by first class mail. It is very, very important to have an immediate follow up of the telephone call.

We have become much more skillful in capitalizing on matching gift potential, which has had a tremendous positive effect on our goal. We've been very successful in increasing the percentage of participation of the current families and in renewing donors who hadn't been giving in recent years. We have been able to go back to people who

had given consistently but who hadn't been actively giving in the last couple of years and make an appeal to them to simply elicit a modest gift which brings them back into active giving. Effectiveness comes from getting your files in order — knowing who these people are, why they were giving in the first place, and why they stopped — and tailoring your appeal in a way that makes sense.

Step #10 — Following Through

Toward the end of the calendar year, we put a reminder in our newsletter: "For those people for whom it's important to make their pledges before the end of the calendar year for tax purposes, this is a reminder."

We tell people when they make their pledge that they have until June 30th, which is the end of our fiscal year, in order for their pledge to count for that year's budget. Some people will tell us specifically they will make their pledge in February, etc. or will ask for a specific reminder.

To people who have not made their payment by the end of April, we send out a personalized reminder: "We are coming to the end of our fiscal year and the end of our school year. Our records indicate that you made a pledge of $75. This is just a reminder. We hope we can still count on you. If you have already sent in your pledge, please let us know so that we can make sure our records are accurate and up to date." This elicits the vast majority of pledges that have not been paid up until that point.

Before December 31st, we mail a letter to all of those people who received the initial appeal letter whom we were not able to reach by phone: "We are sorry we could not reach you. We hope that we can still count on you. We're at 70% of our goal and 70% of our participation." Give them a little update. DO include a pledge envelope. If these people do not respond to this letter, we usually don't contact them again.

The acknowledgment of pledges is very important. Our goal is to have an acknowledgment in the mail the same day each gift is received. We have preprinted acknowledgment cards that need to be filled in with the donor's name, the gift amount, and the date. When donations are received, the name and the amount are recorded in our donor receipts book and on their donor record file. We make a photocopy of every check as another form of back-up information about who the donors are and as a resource for updating addresses and phone numbers. All volunteers are thanked in writing.

When we print our annual report, the names of ALL donors are included unless somebody requests anonymity. It is essential to make sure that you include everybody who should be included in the annual report and that their names are listed in the way in which they wish to be acknowledged.

To conclude, the annual giving phone campaign is a way to keep your constituency giving. A personal phone call assures them that every contribution is valuable and appreciated. Be grateful for $5 gifts and for $500 gifts! Annual campaigns put you in the business of receiving gifts and acknowledging gifts, in the way you would acknowledge a birthday present. You want to be gracious and efficient about how you do it. This is important! If people are giving you their money, they want to give it to somebody who will manage it efficiently and gracefully.

Jane Ewing, at the time this article was written, was director of development at The Little School and a board member of Northwest Development Officers Association.

Susan Morris was a member of the board of trustees of The Little School.

Long Range Planning

*"While day-to-day survival sometimes feels like
a major accomplishment, you really shouldn't
pat yourself on the back until you are able to be working
on where the organization will be
two or three years into the future."*

How to Prepare a Business Plan

by Keith Stephens

> *"Cheshire-Puss," said Alice, "would you tell me, please, which way I ought to go from here?"*
>
> *"That depends a good deal on where you want to get to," said the Cat.*
>
> *"I don't much care where . . ." said Alice.*
>
> *"Then it doesn't matter which way you go," said the Cat.*
>
> *". . . so long as I get somewhere," Alice added as an explanation.*
>
> *"Oh, you're sure to do that," said the Cat, "if you only walk long enough."*
>
> — Lewis Carroll, ***Alice's Adventures in Wonderland***

Whether you are running General Electric or ABC Child Care Center, you will not succeed for long operating like Alice in Wonderland. Every business needs to know where it wants to go, and how it plans to get there.

For most child care operations, if there are any plans at all, they only exist in the head of the owner or the director. I am a firm believer in taking time to formally think through the directions for your child care business, and then committing the results to writing in the form of a business plan.

Having a business plan in place provides you with a starting point, a set of directions to guide your actions and decisions along the way, and a target to work towards. Having a specific goal is what drives most of us to accomplishment.

In addition, having thought through your business, set priorities, and documented your thinking, you will have a convenient vehicle for communicating with the people — staff, business advisors, bankers, etc. — who will help you accomplish your goals.

There is no set formula for writing a business plan. No matter how it is formatted, however, it should provide answers to five key questions:

Where are we?
What threats and opportunities do we face?
Where are we going?
How do we plan to get there?
What do the numbers say?

Where Are We?

Just like when you use a road map, before you can determine how to get to where you want to go, you have to start by identifying where you are. The description of your current status should address the following points:

- **What business are we in?** What is the service we are selling? (Is it child care, education, family support?) Who are our customers? (Spell out as specifically as you can a profile of your current customers in terms of where they live, how much they earn, where they work, and what they want for their children.)

- **What is our philosophy?** Not only is it important to spell out your philosophy for other people to understand but it also helps each of us to go through the process of making a clear statement about what we are trying to accomplish: what our attitudes are about the needs of children, about the process of education, about the needs of parents, and about our role in terms of the families and communities we serve.

- **What is our track record?** Where are we coming from? How did we get started? How successful have we been to date? What major changes have we made along the way? In putting together your historical data, it can be very helpful to use charts and graphs to depict your progress visually.

- **Where are we now?** This should be a snapshot of the status of your business: assets, locations, enrollments, organizational structure, key personnel, main competitors, and current financial position.

What Threats and Opportunities Do We Face?

Answering the first question will cause you to take a hard look within your organization. This second question will force you to look outside, at forces and trends that may impact your program's future.

- **What threats do we face?** What factors could interfere with the development of our program? Is our lease about to expire? Are any new centers opening up within our service area? Is the availability of qualified staff becoming a problem? Are the demographics of the neighborhoods we serve changing? Are

parents being attracted to centers with different philosophies or lower fee scales? Are pending changes in licensing requirements going to increase our cost of doing business?

- **What opportunities are there?** Is there new residential growth taking place that will increase the demand for child care? Are local employers exploring child care options for their employees? Is the developer of the community's new business park interested in having a child care center as an amenity for the development? Could we build a new structure that is a better facility, yet more economical? Are there nearby neighborhoods or communities where the demand for child care is going unmet? Are any national chains interested in buying our business?

- **How do we rate with the competition?** You may find it helpful to analyze your relative competitive position by completing the chart entitled *Competitive Position*. In the left hand column, "Bases of Competition," list the characteristics that customers use to choose a child care center. These might include location, service, staff, program, reputation, facilities, and pricing, among others. In the second column, assign a relative weight to each characteristic on a scale of 1 to 5 (5 being the most important, 1 being the least). Now, list your major competitors across the top, beginning with your organization. For each characteristic, rate each competitor — including yourself — relative to each other with a rating of +1, 0, or -1. For example, if one competitor is relatively strong in terms of *location*, you would place a

rating of +1 in the upper part of the box for *location*. If another competitor is average in terms of its pricing, you would place a rating of 0 in the upper corner of the *pricing* box.

Determine a score for each characteristic by multiplying the individual rating by the weight for each characteristic and writing that score in the lower corner of the box. For example, if an organization was rated +1 for location, and you have assigned a weight of 5 to location, the resulting score would be +5. Now, sum up all the scores for each organization to arrive at total score. Finally, rank each of the competitors in terms of their total scores.

Where Are We Going?

This is the focal point of your business plan. After reviewing the current status of your business, set goals for your organization.

There are many ways to express the goals of your organization:

- **Customer objectives.** You may set specific goals for generating new customers, or for reducing customer turnover. Alternatively, you may decide to shift your customer base ("We will increase the share of families enrolled in the center with incomes above $35,000 to 50%").

- **Staff development objectives.** You should take a look at what objectives you need to achieve in terms of recruiting and training staff. For example, such goals might include, "Each staff member will attend one seminar or class on child development each month," or "A gymnastics person will be added to staff by September 1."

- **Program enhancements**. This encompasses any plans to upgrade the operation of your program — such as adding a new playground, remodeling the interior of your center, or equipping your center with a new computer program.

- **Market share**. You should take a look at where you are going to be in the market. For example, if you are in a major city, one of your goals might be to increase your share of the market from 1% to 2% in order to solidify your business base in that community.

- **Growth rate**. Your goals for growth may be expressed in terms of *units* ("We will add two new centers a year for the next five years"); *enrollments* ("We will increase the number of children enrolled by 100%" or "We will increase the utilization rate of our center to 90%"); or *stability* ("We will maintain the utilization level of our current center").

- **Income objectives**, articulated in terms of *gross revenues* ("We will increase revenues at the rate of 20% per year for the next five years") or *profits* (We will increase center profits by 15% per year"). Since the revenue you collect is a function of the number of customers, the programs, and the rate charged, you may want to establish goals for each of these items ("We will increase the number of children served to 160 by September 30," and "We will add an after-school program serving 25 children by September 1," and "Our rate will be increased 5% on July 1").

- **Business ratios**. These can become useful as another means of measuring your progress. For example, you might state as your goals "reducing accounts receivable to less than one week's tuition" or "keeping my investment in property down to 50% of my total investment in the business." Expense ratios can be particularly helpful in the month-to-month management of your business. For example, such a goal might be "maintaining supply expenses at 5% of total program cost."

- **Personal objectives**. If you are the owner of the business, you need to be thinking about how the business fits into your own plans. Do you plan to run the center until your children are old enough to take it over? Are you grooming someone else to run the center for you when you are ready to retire? Or are you planning to build up a sound business and then sell it to a national chain? None of these will just happen. You need to recognize these personal issues in setting goals as well.

How Do We Plan to Get There?

Having written your goals is a major accomplishment. But it is not enough. You need to translate these goals into results by developing and implementing specific *strategies* or *action plans* for making them happen.

If your goals call for considerable expansion, you will need to develop strategies for securing financing, for locating suitable sites, for designing appropriate buildings, and for accelerating your marketing efforts. If your goals call for working more closely with employers, you will need to develop strategies for identifying and making inroads with employers likely to be interested in child care as a benefit.

People. No matter what your goals are, however, one area you will certainly need to look at in developing your action plans is people. Having the right people on board at the right time is crucial to the success of nearly anything you want to accomplish.

You need to look at your goals and ask: "Will we need to add people to accomplish what we plan to do?" "Will the types of people we need be readily available?" "What kind of training will be necessary to prepare people for what they will be doing?"

Structure. An organizational chart is a necessary part of analyzing your people requirements. Not only does it depict for you how your organization fits together, it also helps you identify key people you will need to bring in and when, or who will need to be upgraded by when, and when their training will need to start if they are going to be groomed from within.

In the business plan you may include more than one organizational chart — one for how your structure looks today and one for how it will look a few years down the line if you are to accomplish your goals.

Critical elements. A final step in analyzing your goals is an examination of elements critical to your success — things that absolutely have to be in place in order for you to accomplish your goals. Your business plan should include a listing of the three to five most critical elements. For example, if your intention is to locate new centers on fringes of development, then a critical element for your success will be infill — continued economic growth in communities you will be serving.

What Do the Numbers Say?

After you have defined your goals and strategies, it is time to assign numerical values to these plans. It is important to convert the plans to cash because cash is what drives the machine. However, it is important to recognize also that the numbers are only one part of the business plan — really the last part. Your budgets and projections are just a numerical statement of goals. If you do everything up front well, the writing of the budget will come easy. All you are doing is taking the thought process you went through and assigning numbers to what you plan to do.

A standard business plan will forecast financial statistics for three to five years. These statistics typically include:

- **Annual income and expense statements**. Forecast the revenues and expenses that are likely to be generated as a result of the goals you have established. Don't forget to assign a cost to training and promotional activities that will be required to implement your goals.

- **Cash flow projections**. These projections are important to do in tandem with your annual budgets because they give a running view of the ebb and flow of income and expenses. They can help you identify points in time when your plans will result in cash surpluses and cash deficiencies. In doing these projections, it is helpful to separate

out the cost of doing special projects (such as a major staff training effort or a one shot marketing campaign).

- **Balance sheets**. A balance sheet allows you to take a snapshot of what the business is worth at any point in time. It is a numerical assessment of how much the business owns (how much its assets are worth), how much it owes (how much its liabilities are), and what its net worth is (the difference between its assets and liabilities).

By projecting balance sheets on an annual basis, you can see the strength of the business and how it is changing from one year to the next — you don't really see that if you look only at your income and expense statements or at cash flow projections. They allow you to see when your cash balances are large so you can use this cash to do something else.

- **A statement of assumptions**. In making cost projections, you have to make certain assumptions. For example, you will have to make estimates about interest rates, food costs, and insurance costs. These assumptions will need to be spelled out in your business plan so that someone reading the plan can interpret your numbers.

A final caution: Developing a business plan is not a simple process. After you develop your goals and work out the numbers, you may find that you will end up losing money. You may have to go through the entire process several times in order to develop goals that are in line with your resources.

Q & A About Doing a Business Plan

Does every center really need to do a business plan? Without a doubt, every center can benefit from developing their own business plan. This is true whether you operate a chain of six centers or a single center for 40 children, whether you are seeking outside financing for a major expansion effort or you are content to remain at your current size. Every business needs to think through in a formal way where it is going and how it plans to get there. Without such a plan, your business will drift from year to year in no particular direction.

How far in advance should you forecast? The standard for business plans is three to five years. That is a reasonable time period for most larger centers. A smaller center not looking to expand can probably do just as well with a one or two year plan. In any case, the farther into the future your plans and projections are made, the less reliable they will be. Therefore, while your projections for the coming year can be, and should be, quite specific, there is no point in pinning activities down dollar for dollar or month by month for distant years. For example, your cash flow projections could be done on a monthly basis for the first year, on a quarterly basis for the second year, and on an annual basis after that.

How often should the plan be updated? Every year. Very seldom will what you write in your plan today be what you actually implement when you get there. Inevitably, many changes will occur. But annual updates are not too burdensome. Once you have done all the hard work developing the initial plan, tinkering with it to reflect changes should not be too difficult. This is particularly true if you perform this work on a computer. If major changes occur, however, you may have to update it more than once a year. If you start veering off course significantly, you may find that your business plan is not at all reflective of reality — in which case you may need to chuck it and start all over again.

Would you do a plan differently if you were using it as a tool for raising money outside? No! Your basic business plan should be developed just as thoughtfully if you are going to use it to raise money outside or if it will only be used internally. If you do a good job on your business plan, you should only need to add two or three pages to have a package to deliver to outsiders. For example, if you are presenting the plan to your banker, you would probably want to include an initial statement of the kind of money you are looking for and how you plan to use it. If you are looking for investors, you would have more of a sales presentation at the front of your plan, and you might include some analysis of what their return would be.

Even if you do not plan to send your plan outside, you should still package your final product well. The better job you do on the packaging, the more important the document (and the thought processes behind it) becomes. If you have a handwritten, two-page plan with one 13-column scratch pad, this product is probably not something that you would treat as significant for very long.

Your business plan needs to be a working document that you review, access for information, and monitor your progress against on a regular basis. I'm a firm believer in putting it into a good enough format that it takes on some significance to the writer and to other people who should use it.

Who should be involved in developing the plan? You will probably need an accountant to help you with the income projections. If you have any other business advisors, you should show them your plans to see if they make sense. In a small organization, board members who are involved in running a center need to be part and parcel in developing the plan.

It is also very important to involve employees. They can be particularly helpful in the evaluation of opportunities and threats — and in coming up with recommendations about what should be done.

Once the plan is completed, you should distribute it widely. My personal preference is to share all the information, even the financial information, with all officers and staff members. Your people are going to make the thing come about and they need to know what is expected and where the organization is going.

One reason to share information is that if the prospects are good, staff members already think they are better, and if prospects are bad, then they think they are good. It is a great asset for the people to know what the facts are, for them to know where the business is going, and what the opportunities are for them.

How should the final plan be formatted? The manner in which you commit your plans to print should first and foremost make sense to you. You can simply follow the format that was described above, with sections on the history and status of the organization, threats and opportunities, future plans, and financial projections. Or you can organize the information as a series of goal statements, with background information and action plans spelled out for each one.

However, no matter how the plan is organized, its first page should be your mission statement. While you will not be able to develop this until all other parts of the plan are completed, this statement should be up front as a capsule summary of what is to follow. The mission statement should briefly state: who we are (your markets), what we provide (your services), where we operate (your service area), where we are heading (your goals), and why we are going to be successful (your competitive advantage).

How pessimistic or optimistic should you be with your financial projections? When you initially do your cash flow projections, you should strive to be as objective as possible. Try to be realistic in estimating revenues and expenses. Then, since none of us project the future with 100% accuracy, go back and say, "What if the revenues we project are not as great?" or "What if the projects that we want to undertake cost more than we expected?" In other words, go back and take a very conservative look at the cash flow.

Your business plan should include both of these projections — the realistic and conservative one. Chances are, you will end up somewhere in that range.

Keith Stephens, a CPA, is the former president of Palo Alto Preschools, once the country's largest privately owned child care chain, and past president of the National Association for Child Care Management.

Guidelines for Selling Your Child Care Business

by Keith Stephens

My partner and I recently sold our child care business. Fortunately, we prepared for the process and got some good advice along the way. As a result, we were able to strike a deal that gave us an excellent return on all the money, time, and ideas we had invested in our business.

In retrospect, I can see that had we not been so well prepared and well informed, we could easily have thrown away a substantial share of our investment. So when **Exchange** invited me to share my insights from this experience, I jumped at the chance. I am eager to share with those of you who may be thinking about selling your child care businesses, either today or in ten years, some pointers I learned along the way.

The time to prepare for the sale of your business is now. In order to secure a satisfactory sale price, you need to do your homework. How you organize and manage your business today determines its salability tomorrow.

Have a sound record keeping system in place.

When it comes time to sell, potential buyers will be interested in not only what your bank balance is today but also how your business has performed over time. If you want to get a good price, you have to be able to make the case that you have a growing business with a solid track record. Without sound records, you have no case.

Keep financial information in standard formats.

In the sale of your business you need to communicate serious financial information to potential buyers. You need to present your information in a format that can be quickly understood by the recipient. Most buyers will not have the time, or the desire, to learn how to interpret information presented in a new or unusual way.

Keep the components of a financing package on file.

At Palo Alto Preschools, because of our ongoing need for capital for expansion, we always had a package of information about our business on file to present to bankers, mortgage brokers, and venture capitalists. Having the components of this package on file enabled us to respond quickly to unexpected needs and opportunities. Information you may want to start accumulating in your files will include:

- Overview on the status and trends of the child care industry;

- Current structure of your organization;

- Profiles of your key management personnel;

- Key strengths and unique features of your business;

- Detailed financial information;

- Enrollment records; and

- Summaries of mortgages and leases.

Build a management team.

Many child care businesses have prospered due to the toil and talent of the owners. However, even if these businesses are extremely successful, potential buyers may be scared away, fearing that the business will fall apart once the original owners leave.

The development of a management team in a closely held business cannot be left to the last minute. It is a slow, sometimes painful, process. First, you must adjust to the idea that you do not need to do it all. You must be willing to let others make some of the decisions. Second, you need to identify people with management talent. Finally, you need to bring them along slowly but steadily by giving them increasing amounts of responsibility.

Develop relationships with potential buyers.

In looking back, I find one factor about our sale to be especially interesting. All the companies that in the end were seriously negotiating with us were companies with whom we had a long-term relationship. All our other efforts to attract buyers produced nothing.

I cannot stress enough the importance of being visible in the industry. Building relationships now will pay off when the time comes to sell your business. If potential buyers already

know who you are, who your people are, what your strengths are, and where your business is heading, you stand a much better chance of attracting their interest. Otherwise, you are just one of many faces in the crowd vying for their attention.

Know Where You Stand

Before you start actively promoting the sale of your business, it is vital to determine what you hope to accomplish. Once you start negotiating, you can easily lose control of the process if you aren't clear in your own mind as to what constitutes favorable terms and conditions.

Set a value on your business.

Once we decided to sell Palo Alto Preschools, we sat down and worked out a sale price that we believed accurately reflected the net worth of our business. This was not a value that we plucked out of thin air, but one that we arrived at through a set of standard calculations for determining the value of a business. It was a price that would provide us with a favorable return on our investment, but also one that we could reasonably defend.

In dealing with potential buyers, we gave out this price right away. Serious buyers, of course, ended up generating their own numbers, based on their own calculations. But having our numbers on the table gave us a position to negotiate from, rather than forcing us to respond defensively to their numbers and their method of calculation.

In setting your sale price, you've got to be reasonable. You should expect a reasonable return on your investment, not a windfall. If your expectations are

too high, you will be engaging in a futile effort.

Determine how you will respond to various offers.

In addition to determining what your business is worth, it is also important to decide in advance what position you will take on various terms and conditions a potential buyer may propose. For example, the buyer may agree to your price, but recommend that payment be made over a period of years. Or the buyer may propose implementing the transfer of ownership by swapping stock in their company for stock in your company. To intelligently respond to alternatives such as these, you will need to consider your per-sonal cash needs as well as to investigate the tax implications of each of these alternatives, both for the buyer and yourself.

During negotiations, the nature of your involvement after the sale will undoubtedly become an issue. From the outset, you should have a position that covers under what conditions, if any, you will continue working for the business after the sale, either as a long-term employee or as a short-term consultant.

Prepare for the Process

The process of selling your business can be a draining experience, both physically and emotionally. If you are not fully prepared, your bargaining position may erode as your energy and emotions wear down.

Make an irrevocable decision to sell.

If you enter into the sale process only partially committed to doing a deal, you will not be as aggressive nor as effective a negotiator as you should be. You must be committed to following through until a deal is done or you will find too many excuses to back out, or equivocate, when the going gets tough.

Decide how much to inform staff and parents.

Once you have made the decision to sell, you need to decide when and how to inform the staff and parents. Some would argue that you should tell them as little as possible until the deed is done. The argument here is that if staff and parents know the center is on the blocks, they will become apprehensive and start abandoning ship.

We decided to take this approach with parents and did not officially inform them until after the sale was completed. Inevitably, of course, parents started finding out via the rumor mill. However, there were no serious repercussions.

With the staff, we chose to be completely open from early on. Shortly after we started receiving serious offers, we held a meeting of all the center directors to discuss what was taking place. We told them who we were negotiating with and how we thought things would change for them under each of these companies. We tried to stress the career opportunities they would have in each case.

We decided to be up front about all this because we figured that, with all the visitors going through taking pictures and asking questions, the staff would soon put two and two together, but would come up with the worst possible interpretations. Staff members

accepted the news surprisingly well, and in the end no one quit over this issue.

Set up your business to run without you.

Don't underestimate the demands that will be placed on you from the day you decide to sell your business. Much of your time will be consumed with preparing reports, meeting with your accountant and your lawyer, meeting with potential buyers, giving tours of the center, and tracking down endless pieces of information. In order not to frustrate potential buyers, you will need to drop whatever you are doing and find answers to their many questions.

Meanwhile, your business needs to keep operating in top form. If your business falls apart while you are preoccupied with making a deal, you may lose the deal and your business, too.

Therefore, you need to delegate, in an orderly fashion, the day-to-day operation of your business during this period. If you are a small child care operation owned by a husband and wife, possibly one spouse could take over the operation of the business and one the sale negotiations. In a larger operation, you will need to entrust operations to your management team.

Be prepared for the extreme emotions of the process.

One day you will be sky high about the prospect of receiving a high return on your investment, and the next you will be depressed because you are giving away your baby. One day you will be as proud as can be showing your excellent facility off to a prospec-

tive buyer, and the next you will be down in the dumps when they call back and say they're not interested in what you consider to be your centers' strengths, or that your centers aren't big enough, or they cost too much to operate.

You've got to be prepared for this emotional roller coaster. If you've cared enough about your business to make it a successful venture, inevitably you will have a difficult time letting go, and a difficult time accepting negative assessments of your business.

This is all very natural — there's nothing wrong with you if you experience these emotions. But you can't let these emotions preclude you from conducting the negotiations effectively.

One of the hardest issues to deal with will be when potential buyers start proposing changes they will make. For example, they might observe that they will have to bring in a new director to replace someone you have worked closely with for many years, someone you care about deeply. Or they may propose tearing out some walls to make the classrooms bigger, or doing away with the infant component, or closing your favorite center.

Your reaction to such proposals may well be one of anger — "They're going to tear apart in months what it has taken years to build up!" But you have to keep in mind that once you sell your business the new owners will inevitably want to put their stamp on it, to make changes to fit their goals, their style, their mode of operations. If you cannot accept such changes, you should not be selling your business.

Negotiate Openly and Knowledgeably

Now it's time to get serious. In actively seeking to sell your business, you need to find the most likely candidates, to give them a clear picture of your business, and to maintain your energy until the deal is done.

Hire a broker and a lawyer experienced in the sale of businesses.

You will want the best possible players on your team. The lawyer who has been handling your real estate deals and writing your contracts may not be capable of representing you properly in negotiating the sale of your business. You need a lawyer who is experienced in handling mergers and acquisitions, who is knowledgeable about the legal and tax questions you will encounter, and who is familiar with the up and down emotions of the acquisition process.

Next you need to find a good broker. You may be tempted to try to save some money by selling it yourself. But selling a business is a complicated process. You need to turn it over to someone who is trained to do it right. You also need someone on your team whose only interest is in keeping the deal moving. You will want a business broker, not a real estate broker. Selling a business is vastly different than selling a piece of property.

Aggressively approach potential buyers.

Sit down with your broker and draw up a list of any and all parties who may be interested in buying your business. This list will include child care chains known to be operating in or interested in your community, as well as any individuals and organizations that have expressed an interest in educational ventures in recent years.

Organizations looking to jump into the child care business in a big way may also be worth pursuing. These will, of course, be harder to locate; but contacts you have established through state and national organizations may help give you some leads.

Be open.

Don't be afraid to give people information. You're not going to make a deal unless you give the buyer a complete picture of what you are selling. A natural tendency is not to give away your company secrets. But in this industry there aren't that many secrets — it's really a matter of who works the hardest.

In selling Palo Alto Preschools, we gave out detailed information to all interested parties. In one case, a company looking to expand in the child care business came back to us over and over again with requests for more information. In all, we devoted over 100 hours to educating them about our company. And we never heard from them again. I felt that we had been taken advantage of. But this was a risk that we decided we needed to take. If we hadn't been completely open with everyone, we wouldn't have maintained the interest of the three potential buyers.

Be honest.

Don't try to fudge the facts. Companies that are in the business of acquiring other companies have better accountants, better lawyers, and better business people at their disposal. There is no advantage in trying to make your numbers look better than they really are because they are going to uncover this. And once they do, the deal is off. All you are doing is raising a red flag to mistrust all the information you are supplying.

Be persistent.

Even in the smoothest of sales, it's going to take a long time from start to finish. In our case, it took seven intense months. There will be many times when you get frustrated, angry, or discouraged. There may be times when you feel like bagging the whole deal, or settling for a lesser deal just to get it over with.

However, if you have invested 10 to 20 years of your life building up your business, you don't want to throw this away because you can't hang in there to the finish. Your mental toughness in the final weeks of negotiating will pay dividends that you will appreciate the rest of your life.

Keith Stephens, a CPA, is the former president of Palo Alto Preschools, once the country's largest privately owned child care chain, and past president of the National Association for Child Care Management.

Valuing Your Child Care Business

by Dave Linsmeier with Dick Richards and Ed Routzon

Owning and operating a successful child care company takes a lot of time, talent, and hard work. Most owners have invested their heart and soul into their business not to mention cold hard cash. They understand the business of child care but often don't know the value of the business they have built. Business owners can usually benefit from knowing the value of their company. Even non-profit child care organizations, which do not have owners but a Board of Directors, may, from time to time, need to value their organization.

Reasons for Valuing Your Business

Here are some of the events that may trigger the need to value a business:

- Gifting the company to a family member

- Borrowing money from a bank

- Strategic planning

- Finding investors

- Buying out a partner

- Selling the business

Types of Valuations

There are many different values you could assign to a company. The purpose for the valuation can help determine which valuation method you would use.

Book Value

The book value of a business is the value shown on the company's balance sheet as the Owner's Equity or Net Worth. The balance sheet lists the assets, liabilities, and equity of an organization. The Owner's Equity is equal to the value of the company's assets less the liabilities. Typical assets are cash on hand and in the bank, accounts receivable which are the amounts parents and government agencies owe you, purchases of equipment that have a useful life of more than one year, vehicles, and buildings. The amount of the equipment, vehicles, and buildings showing on the balance sheet would be the original purchase price of those assets less the amount that has been depreciated to date. The original purchase price less depreciation is called the book value of the assets. Your accountant will maintain a depreciation schedule which doubles as an inventory list. This can be presented to a potential buyer.

Liabilities are equal to the amount of money the company owes to others. Typical liabilities are accounts payable which are items purchased on credit, payroll taxes withheld from employees' paychecks that have not yet been paid, bank loans, leases, and mortgages.

The Book Value of the company equals the book value of the assets minus the liabilities.

Balance Sheet Account Balance		Current Assets
$ 58,000		
Accumulated Depreciation	−	46,000
Asset Book Value	=	12,000
Liabilities	−	6,000
Company Book Value	=	$ 6,000

The Book Value is the easiest valuation method to calculate. However, this method does not reflect the earnings potential of a company. It will often calculate a low value. An owner may want to use this method for tax purposes such as gifting stock to family members. However, the owner must be prepared to defend this method of valuation to the IRS.

Liquidation Value

The Liquidation Value of the business is the amount of cash you would have remaining in the business after all the assets were sold and the liabilities were paid. The book value of the assets is usually different than the sales price of the assets.

Balance Sheet Account		Current Balance
Proceeds from Sale of Assets		$ 30,000
Liabilities	−	6,000
Liquidation Value	=	$ 24,000

A bank or financial institution that is considering loaning money to a company, whether it is a for-profit or a nonprofit organization, often considers the Liquidation Value when deciding whether to make a loan to the company. The bank wants to know what they will receive if they sell the assets of the company should it default on a loan, rather than what they will receive if they go through the lengthy

process of selling the business. This method also does not reflect the earnings potential of a business.

Fair Market Value

The Fair Market Value is the amount that you would receive if the company were sold. This is also called the sale price.

The Fair Market Value is not as easy to determine. This method takes into consideration the market value of the assets less the liabilities and includes the earnings potential of the business. This method is used when selling the company, when finding investors, when buying out a partner, or for strategic planning.

Fair Market Valuation Formulas

Some industries use formulas to estimate the value of a company. These formulas are used as a guideline for valuing a *typical* company in that industry.

Formula based on Gross Revenue

This formula calculates the value as a percent of gross annual revenue. The formula is total annual revenue times a percent such as 20%.

Income Category		Annual Amount
Tuition		$ 413,000
Registration Fees	+	2,000
Government Subsidy Payments	+	134,000
Fundraising Income	+	6,000
Child and Adult Care Food Program Reimbursements	+	11,000
Total Revenue	=	$ 566,000
20% of Total Revenue	x	20%
Estimated Business Value	=	$ 113,200

Dick Richards, child care broker and seller's advocate from St. Louis, Missouri, who has been selling child care centers for almost 20 years, "does not believe that a buyer or a seller can rely on the Gross Revenue as a method of valuing a child care business. A buyer cannot place a value on a business without taking expenses into consideration."

Formula based on Earnings Before Interest, Taxes, Depreciation and Amortization (EBITDA)

Another formula calculates the value by multiplying the annual net revenue before deducting interest, income tax, depreciation, and amortization expenses times a factor to be determined on a center-by-center basis. This factor will vary depending upon the economy, financial health of the organization, demographics of the area, potential for growth, competition, etc.

Category		Annual Amount
Total Revenue		$ 566,000
Variable Expenses	−	480,000
Fixed Expenses	−	55,000
Interest Expense	−	2,000
Depreciation and Amortization Expense	−	1,000
Income Taxes	−	8,000
Net Revenue	=	$ 20,000
Interest Expense	+	2,000
Depreciation and Amortization Expense	+	1,000
Income Taxes	+	8,000
EBITDA		$ 31,000
Factor of 3	x	3
Estimated Business Value	=	$ 93,000

If the owners are drawing a salary and receiving perks and other compensation that are above what is normally paid to operate the business, you should also add the extra compensation amounts back to EBITDA then multiply the factor to calculate the Estimated Business Value.

The Corporate Valuation

The formulas used in the previous section are an estimate of the value of a company. There are other things to include in a good valuation. It may be worth the expense to hire an appraiser who is a seller's advocate and is familiar with the child care industry, to perform a detailed valuation. This valuation can help justify the value of your company to the IRS, banks, or potential buyers.

A good evaluator should review your financial reports for the last three to five years. The evaluator should look at the child care demand in the area currently and projected for the future. The evaluator should understand the neighborhood you are located in and where the children in your center live and the parents work. The evaluator should evaluate the potential for growth taking into consideration where new housing developments are. If the purpose of the valuation is for the sale of the business, confidentiality needs to be considered when information is provided to a buyer. The valuation should consider your enrollment, rates, strengths, and weaknesses compared to the competition. The evaluator should look at the condition of your facilities and equipment. It may be worthwhile to also hire a building inspector to do a thorough inspection of the facility.

Any information available on sales of other child care businesses in the area is extremely helpful. June Kiehnau, a business opportunities broker in Wisconsin for 23 years who has specialized in the sale of child care businesses for the last four years says that, "it is very difficult to estimate the sale price of a child care business because sales are usually private and there are no comparisons." A broker, familiar with the child care industry, can provide the knowledge gained from previous sales that he or she has been involved in to help determine the sale price of your business.

Valuing Assets Included in the Sale

Most owners include other assets in the sale. These assets may include classroom equipment, office equipment, playground equipment, vehicles, and the building. The equipment and vehicles do not add much, if anything, to the sale price of the business. However, the value of the building can be a significant portion of the sale price.

Ed Routzong, a partner in Bailey-Routzong & Associates, LLC of Houston, Texas, who has been a child care center owner and a broker for 27 years, says that the real estate can have two values. The first value is based on the land and building without the business. This value is derived from the current appraised value of the land and building only without the on-going business.

The second approach to real estate valuation typically producing the greatest value, results from applying a capitalization rate "Cap Rate" to the annual rent or mortgage the business

can sustain given its current financial success. I would recommend hiring a commercial real estate appraiser/broker, with child care valuation experience, to help you determine the value of the real estate.

Using a Team of Experts

Dick Richards recommends using a team of people to assist with the sale of your business.

An Accountant can help organize your financial data and help you consider the tax consequences from the sale of your business.

An Attorney can be used to draft and review the documents involved in the sale and to close the transaction.

A Broker can assist with the valuation and sale of the business. Brokers can be used to assist with the business decisions, identify potential buyers, and to do the negotiations.

A Real Estate Appraiser can help determine the value of the real estate.

Even if you hire the experts, you are the one who knows your business the best. You know why you have decided to sell the business and what you would like to realize from it. The experts can give you good advice but you should be making the decisions based on your best interests. Remember, pricing too high can cost you the sale. When pricing too low, you may leave money on the table.

Resources

Lipman, F. D. (1996). *How Much Is Your Business Worth?* Rocklin, CA: Prima Publishing.

Tips for Selling Your Business

■ When selling a business it is paramount to keep the transaction confidential. Parents and staff can become overly concerned if they find out the company is for sale. Staff morale can suffer and you could lose enrollments and staff should they find out about the sale before the transaction is finalized. This can significantly lower the sale price or scare away a potential buyer. A responsible broker will have potential buyers sign a confidentiality agreement before they even reveal the seller's name or location.

■ A successful child care business that has a well-established reputation with parents and the community can ask a higher price.

■ If the child care facility is leased, the lease agreement should allow for the transfer of the lease to a new owner. If the owner is considering selling the company at any time, this should be taken into consideration at the time of the original lease negotiation. Otherwise, the new owner may have a difficult time negotiating a new lease with the landlord under the same terms and conditions. The remaining term of the lease will have a direct impact on the value of the business. The shorter the term of the lease the lower the value.

■ Just as in the sale of a house, location makes a big difference in the value of a child care business. Facilities located near a neighborhood with lots of small children or a major employer can fetch a premium price.

■ Keeping well-organized, accurate, and timely financial reports gives the buyer information to make a good decision. Purchasers can be scared away from a sale if they are not sure the information you are providing is accurate.

■ You can become emotionally attached to the children, parents, and the company you have built. You have struggled to make the business a success. Due to these reasons, you need to be careful that you are not putting a higher value on the company than the market will bear. Having too high of a sales price will prevent the sale from happening.

■ Staff salaries and benefits can be close to 50% of the total cost of providing child care. If staff salaries and benefits are high compared to other child care businesses in the area, a buyer may be reluctant to pay as much knowing that they will have higher costs than the competition, unless the seller provides lower ratios and a superior curriculum.

■ A child care company with multiple locations may be willing to buy a business for a higher price because they will experience cost savings. Costs such as advertising that is already being done by the company may not need to be increased with a new location.

■ Keeping your building, vehicles, and equipment in good condition can add value to the business.

■ The timing of the sale can make a big difference in the price. If enrollments are temporarily low but are anticipated to increase, it might be advisable to wait until enrollments increase to sell the business.

■ The sales process is a lengthy process. You should be planning it well in advance. Trying to sell the company quickly can result in a substantially lower price.

Dave Linsmeier is the executive director of Mary Linsmeier Schools, Inc., a non-profit organization founded in 1964 that operates 21 preschools and child care centers in Wisconsin. Dave teaches the Financial Management and Planning in Early Childhood Programs at the University of Wisconsin–Milwaukee that is one of the courses offered as part of the Administrators' Credential for Early Childhood Professionals. He is also president and owner of Child Care Business Solutions, Inc., a training and consulting company.